# Creative Greenfoot

Build engaging interactive applications, games, and simulations using Java and Greenfoot

**Michael Haungs**

[PACKT] PUBLISHING
open source
community experience distilled

BIRMINGHAM - MUMBAI

# Creative Greenfoot

First published: April 2015

Production reference: 1230415

Published by Packt Publishing Ltd.
Livery Place
35 Livery Street
Birmingham B3 2PB, UK.

ISBN 978-1-78398-038-3

www.packtpub.com

# Credits

**Author**

Michael Haungs

**Reviewers**

Thomas Cooper

Keenan Gebze

Foaad Khosmood

Kevin Rowan

**Commissioning Editor**

Sam Wood

**Acquisition Editor**

Sam Wood

**Content Development Editor**

Arvind Koul

**Technical Editor**

Parag Topre

**Copy Editor**

Sarang Chari

**Project Coordinator**

Nikhil Nair

**Proofreaders**

Safis Editing

Paul Hindle

Linda Morris

**Indexer**

Hemangini Bari

**Graphics**

Sheetal Aute

**Production Coordinator**

Melwyn D'sa

**Cover Work**

Melwyn D'sa

# About the Author

**Michael Haungs** is a professor at California Polytechnic State University, San Luis Obispo, where he teaches and conducts research in game design, game development, web application development, and distributed systems. He received his bachelor's degree in science in industrial engineering and operations research from UC Berkeley, his master's degree in science in computer science from Clemson University, and his PhD from UC Davis. He is the author of PolyXpress (`http://mhaungs.github.io/PolyXpress`)—a system that allows the writing and sharing of location-based stories. Haungs is actively involved in curriculum development and undergraduate education. Through industry sponsorship, he has led several K-12 outreach programs to inform and inspire both students and teachers about opportunities in computer science. Haungs is also a co-director of the liberal arts and engineering studies (LAES) program. LAES is a new, multidisciplinary degree offered jointly by the College of Liberal Arts and the College of Engineering at Cal Poly and represents a unique focus on graduating creative engineers.

I would like to thank the staff at Packt Publishing for their patience and consultation throughout the book-writing process, especially the technical reviewers, including Foaad Khosmood, Kevin Rowan, Keenan Gebze, and Thomas Cooper, for their sage advice and candid feedback. They greatly helped me improve this book.

# About the Reviewers

**Thomas Cooper** is the technology department chair at The Walker School in Marietta, Georgia. The Walker School is a private pre-K-12 school that excels in science, technology, and the arts. Thomas has been teaching for over 20 years and has taught courses in science, technology, and the humanities at both secondary and college levels. He has given talks on technology integration and collaborative learning for Google, National Geographic, and The College Board and has helped develop training and curricular programs for many schools and districts. He currently teaches a game and simulation programming course using the Greenfoot platform.

**Keenan Gebze**, born in Jakarta, Indonesia, on December 6 1993, has been interested in computers and programming since the time he was in middle school. He is not much of an expert but has been an eager enthusiast of the Java programming language after learning Greenfoot. He is currently pursuing a major in geography at the University of Indonesia.

Keenan is the winner of the first Greenfoot CodePoint 2008 contest (category under-16), which is held on the Greenfoot site, with his game *SonarWay* (http://www.greenfoot.org/scenarios/347) that earned him a Nintendo Wii. Sonarway is one of the games that he's really proud of in Greenfoot.

**Foaad Khosmood** is the Forbes professor of computer engineering at California Polytechnic State University where he teaches courses on artificial intelligence and interactive entertainment. Professor Khosmood is the president of the nonprofit organization Global Game Jam, Inc. He has given numerous talks on games and game jams at conferences such as Game Developers Conference (GDC) and ACM SIGGRAPH. He has also helped organize three academic workshops on game jams. He holds a PhD in computer science from the University of California Santa Cruz (2011).You can reach him at http://foaad.net.

**Kevin Rowan** has been teaching high school computer science for 38 years in Winnipeg, Manitoba, Canada. During that time, he worked with a variety of technologies (from keypunch cards to desktop computers and LEGO robots) and programming languages (from Fortran and Cobol, through Pascal and Visual Basic, to Java). For the past 6 years, he has been teaching Java programming using Greenfoot.

Kevin has been actively involved in the promotion of computer science education in Manitoba, serving on two different provincial curriculum design committees. He is currently serving on the executive of the Manitoba chapter of Computer Science Teachers Association (CSTA).

# www.PacktPub.com

## Support files, eBooks, discount offers, and more

For support files and downloads related to your book, please visit www.PacktPub.com.

Did you know that Packt offers eBook versions of every book published, with PDF and ePub files available? You can upgrade to the eBook version at www.PacktPub.com and as a print book customer, you are entitled to a discount on the eBook copy. Get in touch with us at service@packtpub.com for more details.

At www.PacktPub.com, you can also read a collection of free technical articles, sign up for a range of free newsletters and receive exclusive discounts and offers on Packt books and eBooks.

https://www2.packtpub.com/books/subscription/packtlib

Do you need instant solutions to your IT questions? PacktLib is Packt's online digital book library. Here, you can search, access, and read Packt's entire library of books.

## Why subscribe?

- Fully searchable across every book published by Packt
- Copy and paste, print, and bookmark content
- On demand and accessible via a web browser

## Free access for Packt account holders

If you have an account with Packt at www.PacktPub.com, you can use this to access PacktLib today and view 9 entirely free books. Simply use your login credentials for immediate access.

*I dedicate this book to my family – three beautiful princesses (Clara, Ella, and Chandler) and one lovely and talented queen (Bethany Fisher). The four of you are an endless source of pride and joy!*

# Table of Contents

# Preface

This book is designed to help you learn how to program games and other interactive applications quickly using a learn-by-doing approach. Unlike other texts, which start with a detailed description of all aspects of a language or development platform, we will only cover exactly what is needed for the task at hand. As you progress through the book, your programming skill and ability will grow as you learn topics such as animation, collision detection, artificial intelligence, and game design. Project-based learning is a proven approach and becoming prominent in primary, secondary, and higher education. It enhances the learning process and improves knowledge retention.

The topics presented in this book closely follow the ones I cover in my game design class. Through years of teaching this material, I have found that a project-based learning approach can quickly get students successfully programming and creating interesting games and applications. I hope that you too will be amazed with how much you can accomplish in a short amount of time.

We will code our games in Java. Java is one of the most popular and powerful programming languages in the world and is widely used in the finance industry, gaming companies, and research institutions. We will be doing our programming in Greenfoot (www.greenfoot.org)—an interactive Java development environment. This environment allows both novice and experienced programmers to quickly create visually appealing applications. It provides a safe environment for experimentation and allows you to share your work on a variety of platforms.

To get the most out of this book, you should:

- Open Greenfoot and code as you are reading the book

- Experiment with the code you have after completing a chapter

- Know that some details not covered in a chapter will be addressed in an upcoming chapter

- Be proud of your accomplishments and share them with friends, family, and the Greenfoot community

Learning is not a passive activity. Dig into each chapter and experiment, add your own unique twists, and then code something uniquely your own. I can't wait to see what you can do.

# What this book covers

*Chapter 1, Let's Dive Right in...,* takes you through a complete tutorial for creating a simple game complete with an introduction screen, game over screen, a score, mouse input, and sound. This tutorial serves the purpose of introducing you to Greenfoot basics, Java basics, and good programming practices.

*Chapter 2, Animation,* discusses how to perform animation in Greenfoot. Animation requires appropriate and well-timed image swapping as well as realistic movement around the screen. After reading the given topic and seeing an example, you will apply learned animation techniques to the game you created in *Chapter 1, Let's Dive Right in....*

*Chapter 3, Collision Detection,* discusses why collision detection is necessary for most simulations and games. You will learn how to use Greenfoot's built-in collision detection mechanisms and then learn more accurate methods to do collision detection. You will use both border-based and hidden-sprite methods of collision detection to create a zombie invasion simulation.

*Chapter 4, Projectiles,* talks about how actors in creative Greenfoot often have movement that can best be described as *being launched*. A soccer ball, bullet, laser, light ray, baseball, and firework are examples of this type of object. You will learn how to implement this type of propelled movement. You will also learn how gravity, if present, affects it by working through the implementation of a comprehensive platform game.

*Chapter 5, Interactive Application Design and Theory,* discusses creating engaging and immersive experiences in Greenfoot, which is far more involved than compiling a collection of programming effects into one application. In this chapter, you will learn how to engage your user by understanding the relationship between user choice and outcome, conditioning the user, and including the right level of complexity into your work. You will be shown a proven iterative development process that helps you put the theory into practice.

*Chapter 6, Scrolling and Mapped Worlds*, discusses how to create worlds that are much more extensive than the ones that can fit into the confines of a single screen. At the beginning of the chapter, you will code a scrolling exploration game and by the end of the chapter you will expand it into a large mapped game.

*Chapter 7, Artificial Intelligence*, talks about how AI, despite being a deep and complex topic, has some simple techniques you can learn to give the illusion of having intelligent, autonomous actors in your worlds. First, you will learn how to effectively use random behaviors. Next, you will implement simple heuristics to simulate intelligent behavior. Last, you will learn the A* search algorithm to allow game actors to intelligently bypass obstacles when moving between two locations on the screen.

*Chapter 8, User Interfaces*, discusses adding an interface to your Greenfoot scenarios. In this chapter, you will learn how to communicate with your user through buttons, labels, menus, and a heads-up display.

*Chapter 9, Gamepads in Greenfoot*, discusses the capabilities of a gamepad device and then teaches you how to set up Greenfoot to work with it. You will then add gamepad support to the game we created in *Chapter 1, Let's Dive Right in…*, and *Chapter 2, Animation*.

*Chapter 10, What to Dive into Next…*, gives you an opportunity to reflect on the skills you learned during the course of this book. I then go on to suggest projects you should attempt in order to continue your journey as a programmer and interactive application author.

# What you need for this book

For this book, you will need to download Greenfoot from `http://www.greenfoot.org/door` and install it on your computer. Greenfoot is free and works on Windows, Mac, and Linux. The Greenfoot website provides easy-to-follow installation instructions. After installation, you should work through the six simple tutorials found on `http://www.greenfoot.org/doc`. These tutorials can be completed in less than two hours and will give you all you need to know to get the most from this book.

# Who this book is for

If you are ready to explore the world of creative programming, then you will appreciate the methods, tips, and processes described in this book. Appropriate for Java programmers of all levels (novice to expert), it methodically guides you through topics crucial to building engaging interactive applications. You will learn how to build games, simulations, and animations through guided programming exercises.

# Conventions

In this book, you will find a number of styles of text that distinguish between different kinds of information. Here are some examples of these styles, and an explanation of their meaning.

Code words in text, database table names, folder names, filenames, file extensions, pathnames, dummy URLs, user input, and Twitter handles are shown as follows: "As you can see, we made some really simple changes to the Enemy class."

A block of code is set as follows:

```
private void increaseLevel() {
    int score = scoreBoard.getValue();

    if( score > nextLevel ) {
      enemySpawnRate += 2;
      enemySpeed++;
      nextLevel += 100;
    }
}
```

When we wish to draw your attention to a particular part of a code block, the relevant lines or items are set in bold:

```
public void act() {
    if( Greenfoot.mouseClicked(this) ) {
      AvoiderWorld world = new AvoiderWorld(pad);
      Greenfoot.setWorld(world);
    }
}
```

**New terms** and **important words** are shown in bold. Words that you see on the screen, in menus or dialog boxes for example, appear in the text like this: "Hit the **Ok** button in the **New class** pop-up window, and then, in the main scenario window, hit the **Compile** button."

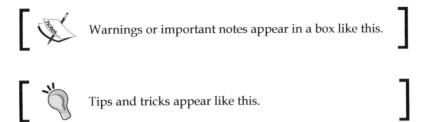

Warnings or important notes appear in a box like this.

Tips and tricks appear like this.

# Reader feedback

Feedback from our readers is always welcome. Let us know what you think about this book—what you liked or may have disliked. Reader feedback is important for us to develop titles that you really get the most out of.

To send us general feedback, simply send an e-mail to feedback@packtpub.com, and mention the book title via the subject of your message.

If there is a topic that you have expertise in and you are interested in either writing or contributing to a book, see our author guide on www.packtpub.com/authors.

# Customer support

Now that you are the proud owner of a Packt book, we have a number of things to help you to get the most from your purchase.

# Downloading the example code

You can download the example code files for all Packt books you have purchased from your account at http://www.packtpub.com. If you purchased this book elsewhere, you can visit http://www.packtpub.com/support and register to have the files e-mailed directly to you.

# Downloading the color images of this book

We also provide you a PDF file that has color images of the screenshots/diagrams used in this book. The color images will help you better understand the changes in the output. You can download this file from: http://www.packtpub.com/sites/default/files/downloads/B00626_ColorImages.pdf

# Errata

Although we have taken every care to ensure the accuracy of our content, mistakes do happen. If you find a mistake in one of our books—maybe a mistake in the text or the code—we would be grateful if you would report this to us. By doing so, you can save other readers from frustration and help us improve subsequent versions of this book. If you find any errata, please report them by visiting http://www.packtpub. com/submit-errata, selecting your book, clicking on the **errata submission form** link, and entering the details of your errata. Once your errata are verified, your submission will be accepted and the errata will be uploaded on our website, or added to any list of existing errata, under the Errata section of that title. Any existing errata can be viewed by selecting your title from http://www.packtpub.com/support.

# Piracy

Piracy of copyright material on the Internet is an ongoing problem across all media. At Packt, we take the protection of our copyright and licenses very seriously. If you come across any illegal copies of our works, in any form, on the Internet, please provide us with the location address or website name immediately so that we can pursue a remedy.

Please contact us at copyright@packtpub.com with a link to the suspected pirated material.

We appreciate your help in protecting our authors, and our ability to bring you valuable content.

# Questions

You can contact us at questions@packtpub.com if you are having a problem with any aspect of the book, and we will do our best to address it.

# 1

# Let's Dive Right in...

*"It does not matter how slowly you go as long as you do not stop."*
—*Confucius*

In this chapter, you will build a simple game where the player controls a character using the mouse to try to avoid oncoming enemies. As the game progresses, the enemies become harder to avoid. This game contains many of the basic elements needed to create interactive Greenfoot applications. Specifically, in this chapter, you will learn how to:

- Create introduction and game-over screens
- Display a user score
- Use the mouse to control the movement of an actor
- Play background music
- Dynamically spawn enemies and remove them when appropriate
- Create game levels

Throughout this chapter, we'll learn basic programming concepts and gain familiarity with the Greenfoot development environment. As you proceed, think about the concepts presented and how you would use them in your own projects. If you are new to Java, or it's been a while since you've programmed in Java, be sure to take the time to look up things that may be confusing to you. Java is a well-established programming language, and there are endless online resources you can consult. Similarly, this book assumes a minimal understanding of Greenfoot. Be sure to look at the simple tutorials and documentation at www.greenfoot.org when needed. *Experiment with the code and try new things – you'll be glad you did*. In other words, follow the advice of Confucius, quoted in the first line of this chapter.

Many of the chapters in this book are independent; however, most are dependent on this chapter. This chapter provides the framework to create Greenfoot applications that we will continue to use, and refer to, in later chapters.

# The Avoider Game tutorial

This tutorial is heavily based on *AS3 Avoider Game Tutorial* by Michael James Williams (`http://gamedev.michaeljameswilliams.com/as3-avoider-game-tutorial-base/`). In that tutorial, you build a game that creates smiley-faced enemies that rain down from the top of the screen. The goal for the player is to avoid these enemies. The longer you avoid them, the higher your score. We will build the same game in Greenfoot, instead of Flash and ActionScript. As with Michael James Williams' tutorial, we will start small and slowly layer on functionality. We will pause frequently to consider best practices and good programming practice. Enjoy these learning opportunities!

We will first build the basic components of the Avoider game, including the initial scenario, the game environment, the enemies, and the hero. Then, we will layer on additional functionality, such as scoring, introduction and game-over screens, and the notion of levels.

As mentioned in the preface, we'll assume you have downloaded Greenfoot and have it installed. If you still haven't, do so now. Go to `www.greenfoot.org` for easy-to-follow instructions on downloading and installing Greenfoot. While you are there, make sure you are minimally familiar with all the tutorials provided on `http://www.greenfoot.org/doc`.

# Basic game elements

All games have an environment in which the game takes place and objects interact. In Greenfoot, the environment is represented by the `World` class, and objects that interact in the environment are represented by the `Actor` class. In this section of the chapter, we will create a world, add enemies to the world, and add a hero that will be controlled by the player.

# Creating a scenario

Start Greenfoot and create a new scenario by clicking on **Scenario** in Greenfoot's Menu bar and then clicking on **New…**. You will see the window shown in *Figure 1*. Type `AvoiderGame` as the name of the file, and then hit the **Create** button.

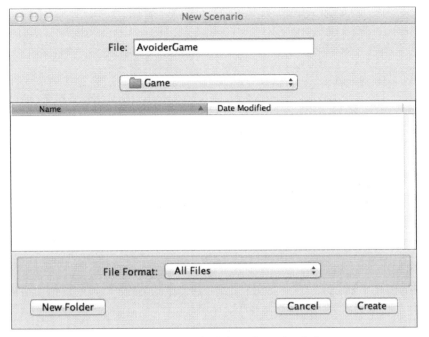

Figure 1: Here's Greenfoot's New Scenario window

# Creating our world

Next, we need to create a world for our game. We do this by right-clicking
(or ctrl-clicking on Mac) on the **World** class in the scenario window (see *Figure 2*)
and choosing **New subclass...** in the pop-up menu that appears.

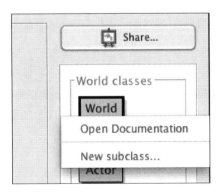

Figure 2: This is about right-clicking on the World class in order to subclass it

In the **New class** pop-up window, name the class AvoiderWorld, select the **backgrounds** image category, and then select the space1.jpg library image as the new class image. Once this is done, the pop-up window should resemble *Figure 3*.

 Once you associate an image with a new World class or Actor class, that image will be copied to the images directory in your Greenfoot project. We will count on this in later chapters.

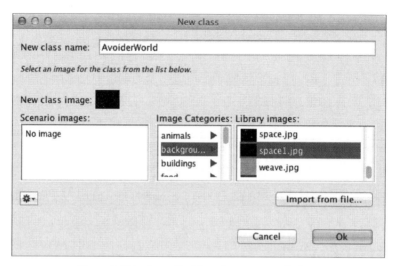

Figure 3: This shows the New class pop-up window

Hit the **Ok** button in the **New class** pop-up window, and then, in the main scenario window, hit the **Compile** button. You should now have a scenario that looks like that shown in *Figure 4*.

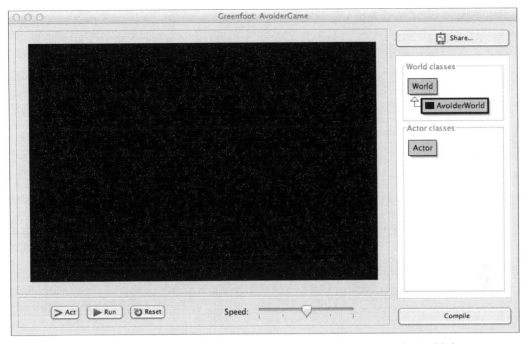

Figure 4: This shows our AvoiderGame scenario after compiling the AvoiderWorld class

We now have our own world, named `AvoiderWorld`, which we will soon populate with actors.

Later in this chapter, we will add two subclasses of `World` to our game—one for our introduction screen and one for our game-over screen. Those instructions will be abbreviated. Be sure to refer back to this section if you need detailed instructions on subclassing the `World` class.

# Creating our hero

Let's create the character our players will control when they play our game. Greenfoot makes this really easy. We will just follow the same steps we used to create the `World` class earlier. Start by right-clicking on the `Actor` class in the scenario window (see *Figure 5*) and choose the **New subclass...** menu item.

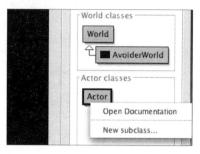

Figure 5: This shows right-clicking on the Actor class in order to subclass it

In the **New class** pop-up window, name the class `Avatar` and select `symbols->skull.png` as the new class image. In the main scenario window, hit the **Compile** button.

Now, to create an enemy, you perform the same steps you just did for the hero, except choose `symbols->Smiley1.png` as the image and `Enemy` as the class name. Again, hit the **Compile** button when this is done.

You should now have a scenario that looks like the one shown in *Figure 6*.

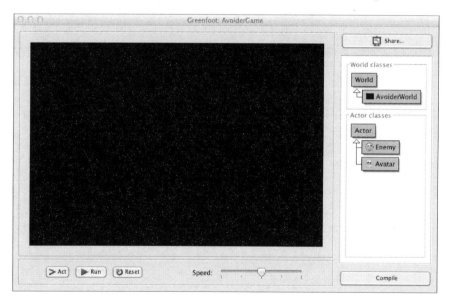

Figure 6: This shows the Avoider Game scenario after creating the world and adding two actors

# What have we just done?

Greenfoot views a scenario as World that contains Actor. The main responsibilities of World is to add and remove each Actor from the screen and to periodically call the act() method of each Actor. It is the responsibility of each Actor to implement their act() method to describe their actions. Greenfoot provides you with the code that implements general World and Actor behavior. (You right-clicked on those implementations previously.) As a game programmer, you must code specific behaviors for World and Actor. You do this by subclassing the provided World and Actor classes to create new classes and writing code in them. You have already done the subclassing, and now it is time to add the code.

Look at http://www.greenfoot.org/files/javadoc/ to learn more about the World and Actor classes.

Oracle provides an excellent overview of object-oriented programming concepts at http://docs.oracle.com/javase/tutorial/java/concepts/. If you are serious about learning Java and writing good Greenfoot scenarios, you should read that material.

# Adding our hero

Last, we need to add our hero to the game. To do this, right-click on the Avatar class, select new Avatar() from the pop-up menu, drag the picture of the skull that appears collocated with your mouse pointer to the center of the screen and then click the left mouse button. Now, right-click anywhere on the black space background (do not right-click on the skull) and choose **Save the world** in the pop-up menu that appears.

Doing this will permanently add our hero to the game. If you hit the **Reset** button on Greenfoot's scenario window, you should still see the skull you placed in the middle of the screen.

# Using the mouse as a game controller

Let's add some code to the Avatar class that will allow us to control its movement using the mouse. Double-click on Avatar to pull up the code editor (You can also right-click on the class and select **Open editor**).

You will see a code-editing window appear that looks as shown in *Figure 7*.

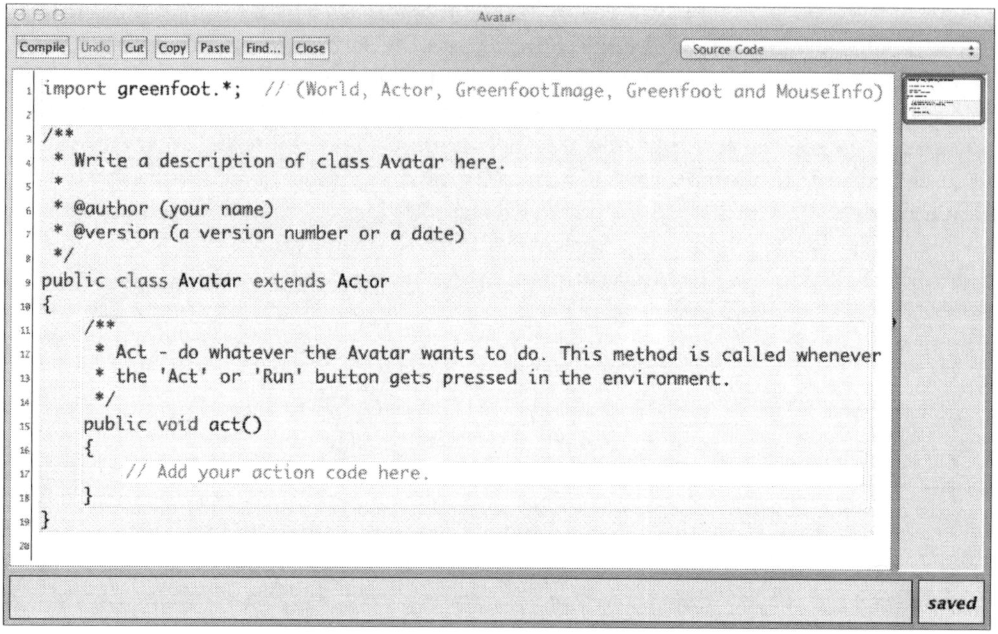

Figure 7: This is the code for our Avatar class

You can see the `act()` method we discussed earlier. Because there is no code in it, `Avatar` will not move or display any other behavior when we run our scenario. What we would like, is to have `Avatar` follow the mouse. Wouldn't it be nice if there was a `followMouse()` method we could use? *Let's pretend there is!* Inside the `act()` method, type `followMouse();`. Your `act()` method should look like *Figure 8*.

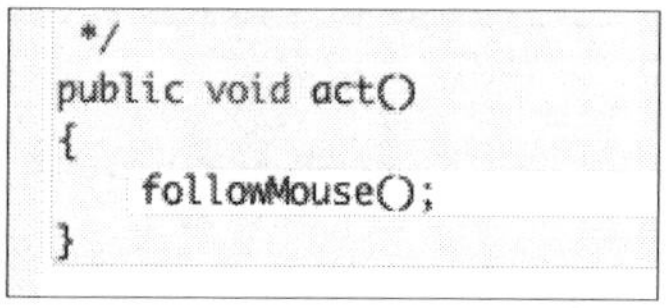

```
    */
    public void act()
    {
        followMouse();
    }
```

Figure 8: This shows the act() method with the followMouse() function added

Just for fun, let's compile this and see what happens. What do you think will happen? Click the **Compile** button to find out. Did you see something like what is shown in *Figure 9*?

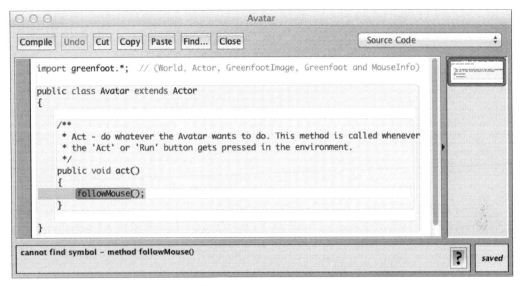

Figure 9: This is about viewing a compilation error in Greenfoot

If you look at the bottom of the window in *Figure 9*, you'll see that Greenfoot has provided us with a useful error message and has even highlighted the code that has the problem. As we know, we were pretending that the method `followMouse()` existed. Of course, it does not. We will, however, write it soon. Throughout the course of this manual (and during any Java coding), you are going to make errors. Sometimes, you'll make a "typo" and at other times, you'll use a symbol that doesn't exist (just as we did earlier). There are other common errors you will make as well.

**Help! I just made a programming error!**

Don't panic! There are a number of things you can do to remedy the situation. I will list some here. First and foremost, the process you use to code can greatly aid you in debugging code (finding errors). The process you should follow is called *Incremental Development*. Simply follow these steps:

- Code a couple of lines of code. *(Really!! Don't code any more!)*
- Save and compile.
- Run and test your code. *(Really!! Try it out!)*
- Repeat.

Now, if you get an error, *it has to be due to the last 2-5 lines of code* you just wrote. You know exactly where to look. Compare this to writing 30 lines of code and then testing them out. You will have compounding bugs that are hard to find. Here are some other debugging tips:

- Very carefully read the error message you get. While they can be cryptic, they really do point you to the location of the bug (sometimes even giving line numbers).
- Sometimes, you get multiple, long error messages. Don't worry. Just go to the top and read and deal with only the first one. Often, by fixing the first one, many others will be taken care of too.
- If you just can't find it, have someone else read your code. It's amazing how fast someone else can spot your error.
- Print some information out. You can use `System.out.println()` to print out variables and check that the code you are looking at is actually running.
- Learn how to use a debugger. This is a very useful tool, but beyond the scope of this book. Learn what a debugger is and use it. *Greenfoot has a nice, built-in debugger you can use.*

In the extremely rare case that there is an error in the Greenfoot program, report it by following the instructions found at `http://www.greenfoot.org/support`.

## Creating the followMouse function

Ok, let's get back to our hero. We last left our hero (the `Avatar` class) with an error, because there was actually no `followMouse()` method. Let's fix that. Add the method shown in the following code after the `act()` method in the `Avatar` class:

```
private void followMouse() {
  MouseInfo mi = Greenfoot.getMouseInfo();
  if( mi != null ) {
```

```
        setLocation(mi.getX(), mi.getY());
    }
}
```

We now have an implementation of `followMouse()`. Save the file, compile the
Greenfoot scenario, and try the code out. The picture of the skull should follow your
mouse. If something went wrong, look closely at the debugging window (shown
in Figure 9) to see the clues Java is giving you about your error. Did you mistype
something? Verify that the code in your `Avatar` class looks exactly like the code in
Figure 10. *Follow the debugging tips provided earlier.*

```
public class Avatar extends Actor
{
    /**
     * Act - do whatever the Avatar wants to do. This method is called whenever
     * the 'Act' or 'Run' button gets pressed in the environment.
     */
    public void act()
    {
        followMouse();
    }

    private void followMouse() {
        MouseInfo mi = Greenfoot.getMouseInfo();
        // Check for null in case the mouse is off the screen
        if( mi != null ) {
            setLocation(mi.getX(), mi.getY());
        }
    }
}
```

Figure 10: This shows the Avatar class with completed followMouse() method

Hey, wait! How did I come up with the code for the `followMouse()` method?
Was I born with that information? No, I actually just looked over the Greenfoot
documentation (http://www.greenfoot.org/files/javadoc/) and saw there
was a class named `MouseInfo`. I clicked on that and read about all of its methods.

Go read the Greenfoot documentation now. It's actually pretty
short. There are only seven classes and each only has around 20,
or fewer, methods.

## Breaking down the code

Let's break down this code. First, we get access to an object that represents mouse data via `Greenfoot.getMouseInfo()`. We then use that object to get the location of the mouse, via `getX()` and `getY()`, and then set the *x* and *y* locations of our hero using `setLocation(x,y)`. How did I know to use `setLocation()`? Again, it is in the Greenfoot documentation for the `Actor` class. It is a method that Greenfoot provides for all actors. Last, we had to include the `if(mi != null)` part because if you accidentally move the mouse outside the Greenfoot window, there will be no mouse information, so trying to access it will cause an error (check out the comment in the code in *Figure 10, line 22*).

Since the `followMouse()` method is called in the `act()` method, our hero will continually be moved to the location of the mouse.

When typing a method in Greenfoot, you can hit *Ctrl* + space bar and Greenfoot will display a list of potential methods you may have been trying to write. Select a method from the list and Greenfoot will autocomplete the method for you, including space holders for method parameters.

# Adding enemies

We're going to add enemies to our game in two steps. First, we need to write the code for the `Enemy` class, and then we will add code to our world, `AvoiderWorld`, to create a never-ending army of enemies. Both steps are surprisingly simple.

## Enemy code

Double-click on the `Enemy` class and change its `act()` method to look like the following code snippet:

```
public void act() {
    setLocation(getX(), getY() + 1);
}
```

Remember using `setLocation()` earlier in the `Avatar` class? We use it again here to move an enemy down one pixel every time the `act()` method is called. In Greenfoot, the upper-left corner of the screen is the coordinate (0,0). The *x* coordinate increases as you move to the right and the *y* coordinate increases as you move down. That is why we set the *x* location of the enemy to be its current *x* coordinate value (we are not moving to the left or the right) and its *y* location to be its current *y* coordinate plus one (we are moving down one pixel.)

Save your Enemy class, and then compile your scenario. Run the scenario, right-click on the Enemy class, and choose new Enemy() in the pop-up menu. Add this enemy to the screen and watch it move down.

## Creating an army

Now that we have completed our Enemy class, we can use it to create an army. To do this, we are going to add code to the act() method in our AvoiderWorld class. Open the editor for AvoiderWorld by double-clicking on it, or right-clicking on it and selecting **Open editor** in the pop-up menu. If you look around the code for AvoiderWorld, you'll notice that Greenfoot does not automatically create an act() method for you. No problem, we'll just add it. Put the following code in AvoiderWorld:

```
public void act() {
    // Randomly add enemies to the world
    if( Greenfoot.getRandomNumber(1000) < 20 ) {
        Enemy e = new Enemy();
        addObject(e, Greenfoot.getRandomNumber(getWidth()-20)+10, -30);
    }
}
```

The act() method starts by checking whether a randomly generated number between 0 and 1000, including 0 but not 1000, was less than 20. In the long run, this code will run 2 percent of the times the act() method is called. Is this enough? Well, the act() method is typically called 50 times per second (ranges from 1 to 100, depending on the position of the speed slider bar), so 2 percent of 50 is 1. Therefore, on average one enemy will be created per second. This feels about right for the starting level of our game.

Inside the if statement, we create an enemy and place it at a specific location in the world using the method addObject(). The addObject() method takes three parameters: the object to add, the *x* coordinate of the object, and the *y* coordinate of the object. The *y* coordinate is constant and chosen so that the newly created enemy starts off at the top of the screen and will appear as it slowly moves down. The *x* coordinate is trickier. It is dynamically generated so that the enemy could appear on any valid *x* coordinate on the screen. The following is the code we are talking about:

```
Greenfoot.getRandomNumber( (getWidth() - 20) + 10, -30);
```

*Figure 11* demonstrates the range of *x* coordinate values that are generated. In this figure, the rectangles represent the possible set of values for the *x* coordinate for the given code. This method of generating ranges of values for screen coordinates is common in Greenfoot.

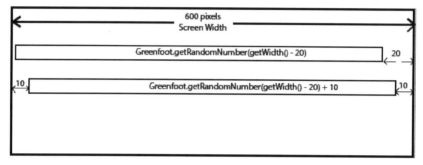

Figure 11: This is the range of x coordinate values generated by the code

Compile and run the scenario; you should see a continuous stream of enemy hordes moving down the screen.

## Unbounding the world

After running the scenario, you'll notice that the enemies end up piling up at the bottom of the screen. In Greenfoot, you can create worlds that are bounded (where actors are not allowed to go past the screen borders) and unbounded (where actors are allow to exit the screen.) By default, Greenfoot creates bounded worlds. However, changing the world to unbounded is extremely easy. Double-click on `AvoiderWorld` to open the code editor. Take this line of code:

```
super(600, 400, 1);
```

Change the preceding code to the following line of code:

```
super(600, 400, 1, false);
```

Looking at the Greenfoot documentation for the `World` class, we notice there are two constructors (see `http://www.greenfoot.org/files/javadoc/greenfoot/World.html` for detailed information on these constructors): one that takes three parameters and another that takes four. The constructor with four parameters has the same parameters as the one that takes three, plus one additional `boolean` parameter that indicates whether the world is bounded or not. Our code change added the fourth Boolean parameter and set it to `false` (no bounds in the world.)

Now, compile and run the scenario. The enemies fall off the bottom of the screen as required.

Where do all those enemies go? We'll deal with that next.

# Memory management

In Greenfoot applications, you'll create hundreds and thousands of actors. When we are done with an actor, such as when it is killed or goes off screen, we would like to remove that object and not have it consume any more system resources. Java manages memory resources via a method called **garbage collection**. With this method, Java tries to automatically determine whether you no longer need an actor, and if you don't, it deletes that actor and frees up all resources associated with it. In Greenfoot, you can let Java know you are done with the actor by removing it from World using the removeObject() method. This is what we want to do to an Enemy actor, after we have successfully avoided it and it has moved off the screen.

The most convenient place to remove an Enemy, after it has gone off the screen, is within the Enemy class itself. Add the following code as the last line of code inside the act() method in the Enemy class:

```
checkRemove();
```

Now, we need to add the checkRemove() method. Put the definition of this method below the act() method. Here is the definition:

```
private void checkRemove() {
  World w = getWorld();
  if( getY() > w.getHeight() + 30 ) {
    w.removeObject(this);
  }
}
```

The code for your `Enemy` class should look like that shown in *Figure 12*.

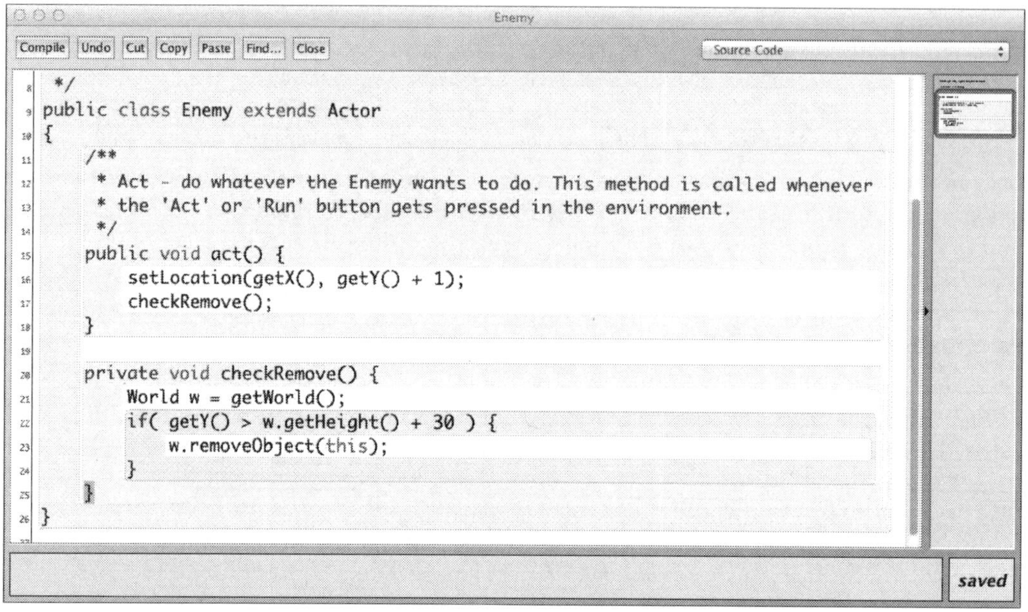

```
*/
public class Enemy extends Actor
{
    /**
     * Act - do whatever the Enemy wants to do. This method is called whenever
     * the 'Act' or 'Run' button gets pressed in the environment.
     */
    public void act() {
        setLocation(getX(), getY() + 1);
        checkRemove();
    }

    private void checkRemove() {
        World w = getWorld();
        if( getY() > w.getHeight() + 30 ) {
            w.removeObject(this);
        }
    }
}
```

Figure 12: This shows the adding of code to remove the enemy if it goes off the bottom of the screen

Now, compile and run the scenario. The enemies fall of the bottom of the screen, as before, but you can feel good knowing that they are soon removed from the world and the garbage is collected.

# Your assignment

Learning is not passive, and you really need to engage in the process. Before moving on to the next section of this chapter, you should:

1.  Make sure your version of our Avoider Game works, click on **Scenario** in Greenfoot's main application menu, and then choose **Save as...** to create an experimental copy of Avoider Game. Let's name this experimental copy `AvoiderGameIExperimentation`.

2.  Play around with your experimental copy. Change the spawn rates of the enemies. Change how fast the enemies descend.

3.  Add `turn(5);` to the `act()` method of the Enemy class. Compile and run. What's going on? Try different values instead of `5` as the input parameter to `turn()`.

If things get too crazy, delete your experimental copy and make a new copy to play with from our original Avoider Game. There's no harm done, nor any foul.

> Throughout this book, take this approach of experimenting with the code. Much learning will happen during the playing. The very act of thinking about how to change the code provides your brain with a new way to process and understand it. Making mistakes in a controlled environment will better prepare you to handle mistakes later on. You will start to become familiar with Greenfoot's error messages.

## Next...

Great work until now! We have built the basics of our game and will next add some things, such as an introduction screen, game-over screen, and a score, to make it look and feel more like a game.

# Making it a game

In this section, we will add a game-over screen, an introduction screen, and some background music. But, before we do all that, we need to know when our hero touches one of the enemies. This will be our cue to end the game. The act of determining when two actors touch is called **collision detection**. Collision detection is used to tell whether a bullet hit an enemy, whether the player landed on a platform after jumping, or to tell whether a falling leaf landed on a surface. We will discuss this important topic next and spend considerable time on it in the upcoming chapters.

# Detecting collisions

Greenfoot provides several `Actor` methods you can use to determine whether you are touching another `Actor`. These methods, in no particular order, are: `getIntersectingObjects()`, `getNeighbors()`, `getObjectsAtOffset()`, `getObjectsInRange()`, `getOneIntersectingObject()`, and `getOneObjectAtOffset()`. They all provide slightly different ways of determining collision. For our game, we are going to use `getOneIntersectingObject()`. The prototype of this method is as follows:

```
protected Actor getOneIntersectingObject(java.lang.Class cls)
```

This method takes one parameter, which is the class of the objects you want to check for collision. This method defines collision in terms of **bounding boxes**; a bounding box is the minimal rectangle that can surround all pixels in the graphic. This method is efficient and fast, but not the most accurate. In *Figure 12*, we can see a picture of a skull and a picture of a smiley face. Even though the pixels of the two pictures are not overlapping, we can see that their bounding boxes are overlapping; therefore, `getOneIntersectingObject()` would report that these two actors are touching. In *Chapter 3, Collision Detection*, we will explore more advanced methods of collision detection.

Figure 13: This shows the bounding boxes of two actors

Armed with this new information, we are going to add collision detection to our `Avatar` class. We will remove our hero from the game if it touches one of the enemies. (Later in this chapter, we will display a game-over screen after removing our hero.) Double-click on the `Avatar` class to bring up its editing window. Change its `act()` method to this:

```
public void act() {
  followMouse();
  checkForCollisions();
}
```

Then, add this `checkForCollisions()` method's definition under the `act()` method:

```
private void checkForCollisions() {
  Actor enemy = getOneIntersectingObject(Enemy.class);
  if( enemy != null ) {
    getWorld().removeObject(this);
    Greenfoot.stop();
  }
}
```

The `Avatar` class should look like the code shown in Figure 14.

```
import greenfoot.*;   // (World, Actor, GreenfootImage, Greenfoot and MouseInfo)

public class Avatar extends Actor {

    public void act() {
        followMouse();
        checkForCollisions();
    }

    private void checkForCollisions() {
        Actor enemy = getOneIntersectingObject(Enemy.class);
        if( enemy != null ) {  // If not empty, we hit an Enemy
            getWorld().removeObject(this);
            Greenfoot.stop();  // For now, pause the World
        }
    }

    private void followMouse() {
        MouseInfo mi = Greenfoot.getMouseInfo();
        // Check for null in case the mouse is off the screen
        if( mi != null ) {
            setLocation(mi.getX(), mi.getY());
        }
    }
}
```

Figure 14: The Avatar class with collision detection added.

Let's examine exactly what's going on in the `checkForCollisions()` method. The first thing we do is call `getOneIntersectionObject()` and save its return value in the variable `enemy`. This variable will be `null` if this object is not touching any enemies, in which case, the expression in the `if` statement will evaluate to `false`, and we will not execute the statements inside. Otherwise, we are touching an object of the type `Enemy` and do execute the contents of the `if` statement.

There are only two lines of code in the `if` statement. In the first line, we use the method `getWorld()`, implemented in the `Actor` class, to get a reference to the instance of the `World` we are in. Instead of saving the reference in a variable, we immediately invoke the `World` method `removeObject()` supplying the keyword `this` as the argument to remove our hero. Lastly, we use the `stop()` method in the `Greenfoot` utility class to pause our game.

Now, compile and run the scenario. Enemies should stream down from the top of the screen and exit out at the bottom. You should be able to control the hero, an instance of the Avatar class, by moving your mouse. If our hero touches one of the enemies, the game should stop.

## Adding a game-over screen

First, you need to draw an entire game-over screen in your favorite graphic design/drawing program, such as GIMP, CorelDRAW, Inkscape, Greenfoot's built-in graphic editor, or even Windows Paint. I used Adobe Illustrator to create the screen shown in *Figure 15*.

Figure 15: My AvoiderGame game-over screen; try designing your own.

Whatever you use to draw your image, make sure you can save it in either PNG or JPG format. Its size should be 600 x 400 (the same size as your world). Save this image in the images folder in your AvoiderGame scenario.

Using the same steps that you used to create AvoiderWorld (*The Avoider Game tutorial* section), create another world; call it AvoiderGameOverWorld and associate the image you created earlier with it. In the **World classes** area of your scenario, you should see what is shown in *Figure 16*.

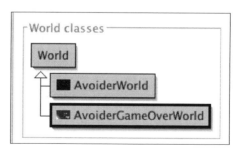

Figure 16: The World classes section after adding AvoiderGameOverWorld

# Switching scenes

Now, we want to display the game-over screen if our hero touches an enemy. To do this, we need to perform the following three steps:

1. Detect when we collide with an enemy and then tell (by calling a method) our world, `AvoiderWorld`, that the game is over.

2. In our `AvoiderWorld` class, we need to implement the game-over method that the `Avatar` will use to signal the end of days.

3. In our game-over method, set the world to be `AvoiderGameOverWorld`, instead of `AvoiderWorld`.

Let's start with step 1. Previously, in the *Detecting collisions* subsection of this section, you wrote code to remove the hero from the game if it touches one of the enemies. This code was contained in the method `checkForCollisions()`. To implement step 1, we need to change that method to the following method:

```
private void checkForCollisions() {
   Actor enemy = getOneIntersectingObject(Enemy.class);
   if( enemy != null ) {
     AvoiderWorld world = (AvoiderWorld) getWorld();
     world.endGame();
   }
}
```

The only difference is the code inside the `if` statement. I hope it makes sense that we are now asking the world to end the game, as opposed to removing the hero object. The part that could be confusing is the substitution of `AvoiderWorld` for `World` and the addition of the `(AvoiderWorld)` part. The problem, is that we are going to implement `endGame()` in `AvoiderWorld`, not `World`. So, we need some way of specifying that the return value of `getWorld()` will be treated as `AvoiderWorld` and not just plain old ordinary `World`. In Java terms, this is called **casting**.

Now, let's look at steps 2 and 3. Here's the code you need to add to `AvoiderWorld`.

```
public void endGame() {
    AvoiderGameOverWorld go = new AvoiderGameOverWorld();
    Greenfoot.setWorld(go);
}
```

Figure 17: This shows the endGame() method added to AvoiderWorld

We have changed, and added, a minimal amount of code, but if you have followed along carefully, you should be able to save, compile, and run the code. See the game-over screen when our hero touches an enemy? (If not, go back and retrace your steps. Something you typed in is wrong.)

**The three Ps: Plan, Plan, and Plan**

Coding is complicated stuff. When you have a problem to solve, you don't just want to sit down and start hacking away at the computer until you bang out a solution. You want to sit down with a stylus and ePad (used to be pen and paper in my day) and plan. I gave you a small example when I wrote out the three steps needed to display the game-over screen. One of the best methods to help you design a solution is a **top-down design** (also know as divide and conquer).

In the top-down design, you start thinking of a solution to a problem at a very high level and then repeatedly break down this solution into subsolutions until the subsolutions are small and manageable

## Adding a "play again" button

The game-over screen is great and all, but we don't want to just stare at it all day. OK, so let's make it so that you can restart the game by clicking on the game-over screen. AvoiderGameOverWorld needs to keep checking whether the mouse has been clicked and then set the world back to AvoiderWorld, so that we can play the game again. Looking at the Greenfoot documentation, we can see the mouseClicked() function. Let's use that method in the act() method of AvoiderGameOverWorld, along with the change world code. Add the following code to AvoiderGameOverWorld:

```
public void act() {
  // Restart the game if the user clicks the mouse anywhere
  if( Greenfoot.mouseClicked(this) ) {
    AvoiderWorld world = new AvoiderWorld();
    Greenfoot.setWorld(world);
  }
}
```

This code should look very familiar to you. The code inside the if statement is nearly identical to the code we added to the endGame() method in the AvoiderWorld class, except this time we are creating and switching to AvoiderWorld.

The new part is to check to see whether the user clicked the mouse anywhere on the screen. The `Greenfoot.mouseClicked()` method returns true if the user just clicked on the object supplied in its parameter. We supplied the `this` variable, which represents the whole instance of the `AvoiderGameOverWorld` world.

Compile and run. Great job! Our game is coming along nicely!

## Adding an introduction screen

Adding an introduction screen is really easy, and we just need to perform many of the same steps we did in creating a game-over screen. First, we need to create an introduction screen image in whatever graphics editor program you want. The one I created is shown in *Figure 18*.

Figure 18: The image of the introduction screen for our game.

Make sure the image is either in PNG or JPG format and has a pixel size of 600 x 400. Save this image in the `images` folder in your `AvoiderGame` scenario.

Create a new world (by subclassing `World`), call it `AvoiderGameIntroScreen`, and associate the image you just created with it. When you are done with this, the **World classes** area of your scenario should look like the screenshot shown in *Figure 19*.

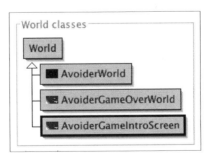

Figure 19: These are all the worlds you created in your AvoiderGame

## Setting the initial screen

We obviously want our new introduction screen to display first when the player first starts the game. To select `AvoiderGameIntroScreen` world as our starting `World`, we need to right-click on it in the **World classes** area and select the `new AvoiderGameIntroScreen()` menu option in the pop-up window that appears (see *Figure 20*).

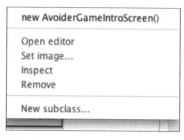

Figure 20: This is about selecting our starting world

Let's make sure everything is hooked up correctly. Compile and run your Greenfoot application. You should start with the introduction screen you just created, but can't do much else. We'll fix that now.

## Adding a "play" button

We are going to repeat exactly the same steps we did in implementing the restarting of the game from the game-over screen.

Add the following code to `AvoiderGameIntroScreen`:

```
public void act() {
  // Start the game if the user clicks the mouse anywhere
  if ( Greenfoot.mouseClicked(this) ) {
    AvoiderWorld world = new AvoiderWorld();
    Greenfoot.setWorld(world);
  }
}
```

This code should look very familiar to you. This is exactly the same code we added to the `AvoiderGameOverWorld` class.

Compile and run. Have some fun. See how long you can last!

So far so good, but it is definitely missing some key gaming elements.

# Adding background music

In this part of the tutorial, you need to search the Web for a song (.mp3) you would like to play during the game.

**Acquiring music**

Whenever you are adding assets (music or graphics) to your game, make sure you do so legally. There are many sites on the Internet that offer free use of the music or pictures provided. Never use proprietary music, and always cite the sources from which you acquired assets. I got the music I added to the game from newgrounds.com, and I gave credit to the author in my code.

We only want the music to play when we start playing the game, not during the introduction or game-over screens. Therefore, we'll start the music when we display AvoiderWorld and turn it off before we display AvoiderGameOverWorld. We only want to start the music once, so we don't want to add the code to play the music in the act() method—imagine the noise from doing that! What we need is a method that is only called once at the creation of the object. That's what the **constructors** of a class provide. (If you need to review what a class and an object are, see the information box in the *What have we just done?* section)

**What is a constructor?**

In programming in Java (and other object-oriented languages), we write code in classes. A **class** describes the methods and attributes of objects we want to create in our program. You can think of a class as a blueprint for building objects. For example, our Enemy class describes the behavior and attributes of every enemy object that appears in our Avoider Game. Each *class* has a *constructor* that performs all initialization needed for each object created. You can identify the constructor of a class easily. Constructors have exactly the same name as the class they are in and have no return type. As a quick test, find the constructor in our AvoiderWorld class. Found it?

We call the constructor every time we create a new object. In Greenfoot, right-click on the Enemy class and you'll see that the top-menu choice is new Enemy(). The Enemy() part is the constructor. The new keyword creates the new object and the Enemy() initializes that new object. Got it?

The following are some good resources you should read to learn more about constructor functions:

http://docs.oracle.com/javase/tutorial/java/javaOO/constructors.html

http://java.about.com/od/workingwithobjects/a/constructor.htm

# Writing the music code

Now that we know where to put the code (everyone say `constructor`), we need to know what code to write. Greenfoot provides a class for playing and managing music called `GreenfootSound`. This class makes playing music really easy. Before I show you the code to put in the constructor, you should take a look at the documentation for `GreenfootSound` and see if you can figure out what to write.

 No, really! Go read the documentation! Trying to do it on your own will really help you.

Here's the code you need to add to the constructor of `AvoiderWorld`.

```
public AvoiderWorld()
{
    // Create a new world with 600x400 cells with a cell size of 1x1 pixels.
    super(600, 400, 1, false);

    // Initialize the music
    bkgMusic = new GreenfootSound("sounds/UFO_T-Balt.mp3");
    // Music Credit:  http://www.newgrounds.com/audio/listen/504436 by T-balt
    bkgMusic.playLoop(); // Play the music

    prepare();
}
```

Figure 21: Here's the constructor for AvoiderWorld

# Analyzing the music code

Let's look at every line of code in the `AvoiderWorld` constructor. First, you have the call to the superclass's constructor, which is needed, as described earlier, to properly initialize your game world. Next, we have this line:

```
bkgMusic = new GreenfootSound("sounds/UFO_T-Balt.mp3");
```

This creates a new `GreenfootSound` object and saves a reference to it in the `bkgMusic` variable. You need to change the preceding code, so that instead of `sounds/UFO_T-Balt.mp3`, you use a string that gives the name of the music file you downloaded to play (you need to save the music in your `sounds` folder in your Greenfoot project's folder). We also need to declare the `bkgMusic` variable we are using in the constructor. To do that, you need to add a variable declaration at the top of your class, as shown in *Figure 22*. By declaring the variable at the top of your class, it will be accessible to all the methods in your class. This will be important when we add code to stop playing the music.

```
1   import greenfoot.*;   // (World, Actor, GreenfootImage,
2
3   public class AvoiderWorld extends World
4   {
5       private GreenfootSound bkgMusic;
6
7       public AvoiderWorld()
8       {
9           // Create a new world with 600x400 cells with
10          super(600, 400, 1, false);
11
```

Figure 22: This shows the variable declaration for bkgMusic in the AvoiderWorld class

The next line of code we have to discuss is this one:

```
bkgMusic.playLoop();
```

This line starts playing the music and will start it over once it finishes. If we would have only done `bkgMusic.play()`, then the song would have played through only once.

The last line in the constructor is a very important one, and it was added automatically by Greenfoot. Remember when, back in the *Adding our hero* section of this chapter, I instructed you to place an instance of the `Avatar` class (our hero) in the center of the **screen**, right-click, and choose the menu option **Save the World**? When you did this, Greenfoot created this `prepare()` method. If you look at the contents of this method, you will see that it contains the code to create an `Avatar` object and add it to the **screen**. Then, it added the call to use `prepare()` in the constructor. If you choose the menu option **Save the World** again, this `prepare()` method will be updated.

OK, save, compile, and run. Did it work? If not, go back and find the typo.

## Stop the music

If you ran your code, you had music during the game, but it did not turn off when you died and went to the game-over screen. We have to explicitly turn off the music before displaying `AvoiderGameOverWorld`. This is super easy! All we need to do is add the following line of code at the beginning of the `endGame()` method you added to `AvoiderWorld` earlier:

```
bkgMusic.stop();
```

Now, save, compile, and run. It should all work according to plan.

**Private, Protected, and Public**

The Java keywords `private`, `protected`, and `public` modify how a variable, method, or class is accessed in Java. Good programming practice dictates that you make all of your class instance variables `private` and require access to that variable to only occur through methods. For methods, you want to make ones you only access within the `private` class; otherwise, make it `public`. The keyword `protected` is used to a method available to subclasses of the class but not to external classes. For more information, refer to the following links:

- `http://docs.oracle.com/javase/tutorial/java/javaOO/accesscontrol.html`
- `http://www.tutorialspoint.com/java/java_access_modifiers.htm`

# Your assignment

Perform the following actions before continuing:

- Once the game-over screen is displayed, play music. Are you going to make it peppy music to lift the spirits of your player or sad and morose to really rub it in? Make sure you turn it off before switching to `AvoiderWorld`.

- Our enemy's movements are pretty vanilla. Can you spice it up? Some ideas are to have the enemy characters have variable speed, drift left or right, or enter from the top or bottom. What will you come up with?

Remember to create a backup copy of `AvoiderGame` before trying these challenges.

# Next...

Almost done! We have built the basics of our game and will next add some things to make it challenging.

# Enhancing playability

In the final section of this chapter, we will add code to increase the game's playability. First, we will add a score. Next, we need to increase the challenge of the game over time. As the player gets better at the game, we want to ramp up the challenge; we will add a leveling system to do this.

# Game scoring

Our game is evolving; however, we need a way to judge how well we are doing in the game. There are many ways to judge game performance, for example, levels completed, time, progression, and so on—but the most common method is to assign the player a score. We are going to add a scoring system to the game that rewards players for the number of enemies they avoid.

## Adding the Counter class

Keeping a count of things and displaying that count is so common in games that Greenfoot provides you with a **Counter** class. To get access to this class, you need to import it into your scenario. To do this, select **Edit** in Greenfoot's main menu, and then select the **Import Class...** submenu choice. You will see a window, like the one shown in *Figure 23*. Make sure the **Counter** box is selected on the left-hand side and then click on the **Import** button.

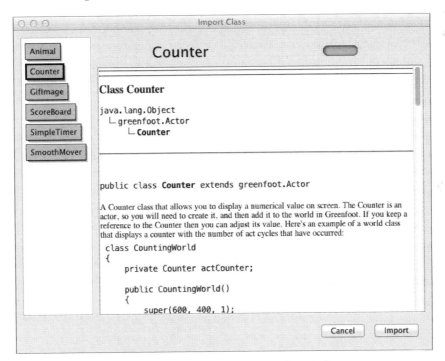

Figure 23: Here's Greenfoot's Import Class window

This will add the `Counter` class to your list of **Actor classes** available for use in our game as shown in *Figure 24*.

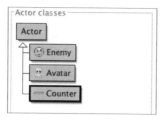

Figure 24: The Actor classes section of your scenario window now includes the Counter class

We want the score to appear immediately in the game. In tutorial 4 (`http://www.greenfoot.org/doc/tut-4`) on the Greenfoot site, you were introduced to "Saving the World" to have the `World` class automatically place `Actor` in your world. I'm going to describe how to place `Actor` in your world manually; specifically, you are going to add an instance of the `Counter` class to your `AvoiderWorld` world.

We discussed that Greenfoot already added the call to the `prepare()` method in your `AvoiderWorld()` constructor. Locate the definition of this method in the `AvoiderWorld` class. Change this method to look like the following code:

```
private void prepare() {
    Avatar avatar = new Avatar();
    addObject(avatar, 287, 232);
    scoreBoard = new Counter("Score: ");
    addObject(scoreBoard, 70, 20);
}
```

The first two lines of this method were already present. The last two lines put a score display on our game screen. The `scoreBoard = new Counter("Score: ");` code creates a new Counter object with a label `Score:` and stores a reference to it in the `scoreBoard` variable (we haven't declared this variable yet, but will soon.) The next line of code adds our `Counter` to the upper-left corner of our game screen.

Lastly, we need to declare the `scoreBoard` variable at the top of our class. Add `private Counter scoreBoard;` above the constructor, as shown in *Figure 25*.

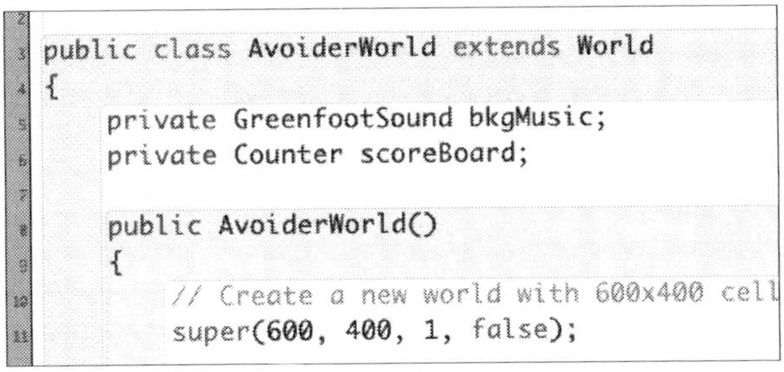

```
public class AvoiderWorld extends World
{
    private GreenfootSound bkgMusic;
    private Counter scoreBoard;

    public AvoiderWorld()
    {
        // Create a new world with 600x400 cell
        super(600, 400, 1, false);
```

Figure 25: The declaration of the scoreBoard variable in the class AvoiderWorld.

Compile, run, and test your scenario.

# Increasing the score over time

We need to do just one more thing. We need to call `setValue()` on our `scoreBoard` variable to increase our score over time. One place we could do this is where we create the enemies in `AvoiderWorld`. The thinking, is that you get some points for every enemy created, because you will ultimately have to avoid it. Here's how you should change the `act()` method in `AvoiderWorld`:

```
public void act() {
  // Randomly add enemies to the world
  if( Greenfoot.getRandomNumber(1000) < 20) {
    Enemy e = new Enemy();
    addObject( e, Greenfoot.getRandomNumber(getWidth()-20)+10, -30);
    // Give us some points for facing yet another enemy
    scoreBoard.setValue(scoreBoard.getValue() + 1);
  }
}
```

The only thing I changed was adding the comment about points and adding the call to `setValue()` on `scoreBoard`. This line of code retrieves the current score using `getValue()`, adds 1 to it, and then sets the new value using `setValue()`. The typical usage of the `Counter` class is also provided in a comment at the top of the `Counter` class. Check it out!

Compile your `AvoiderGame` scenario and try it out. Are you getting an increased score?

# Adding levels

Our game isn't very challenging at this point. One thing we could do, is make the game become more challenging over time. To do this, we are going to add the notion of levels to Avoider Game. We are going to increase the challenge of the game by periodically increasing the rate at which enemies spawn and the speed at which they travel.

## Increasing spawn rates and enemy speed

In `AvoiderWorld`, add two variables, `enemySpawnRate` and `enemySpeed`, and give them initial values; we will use these two variables to increase difficulty. The top of your `AvoiderWorld` class should look like *Figure 26*.

```
public class AvoiderWorld extends World
{
    private GreenfootSound bkgMusic;
    private Counter scoreBoard;
    private int enemySpawnRate = 20;
    private int enemySpeed = 1;
```

Figure 26: This shows the variables in AvoiderWorld

## Increasing difficulty based on the score

Next, we need to add a method that increases the difficulty of the game based on the player's score. To do this, we need to add the following method to `AvoiderWorld`:

```
private void increaseLevel() {
  int score = scoreBoard.getValue();

  if( score > nextLevel ) {
    enemySpawnRate += 2;
    enemySpeed++;
    nextLevel += 100;
  }
}
```

We introduced a new variable, nextLevel, in increaseLevel(), and we need to add its declaration at the top of the AvoiderWorld class. Here is the declaration you need to add next to the variable declarations of enemySpawnRate and enemySpeed:

```
private int nextLevel = 100;
```

As evident from the code in increaseLevel(), we increase both enemySpawnRate and enemySpeed as the player's score increases. The last thing we need to do is use the enemySpawnRate and enemySpeed variables in the creation of enemies and call increaseLevel() from the act() method in AvoiderWorld. Here is the new act() method:

```
public void act() {
    // Randomly add enemies to the world
    if( Greenfoot.getRandomNumber(1000) < enemySpawnRate) {
        Enemy e = new Enemy();
        e.setSpeed(enemySpeed);
        addObject( e, Greenfoot.getRandomNumber(getWidth()-20)+10, -30);
        // Give us some points for facing yet another enemy
        scoreBoard.setValue(scoreBoard.getValue() + 1);
    }
    increaseLevel();
}
```

## Implementing enemy speed increases

I'd love to yell *compile and run!* at this point, but there is one last detail. In the act() method, we use the line e.setSpeed(enemySpeed); to change the speed of the enemy; however, we never have implemented that method in the Enemy class. In addition, we need to change the Enemy class a bit to use the newly set speed.

*Figure 27* gives the complete code for the `Enemy` class.

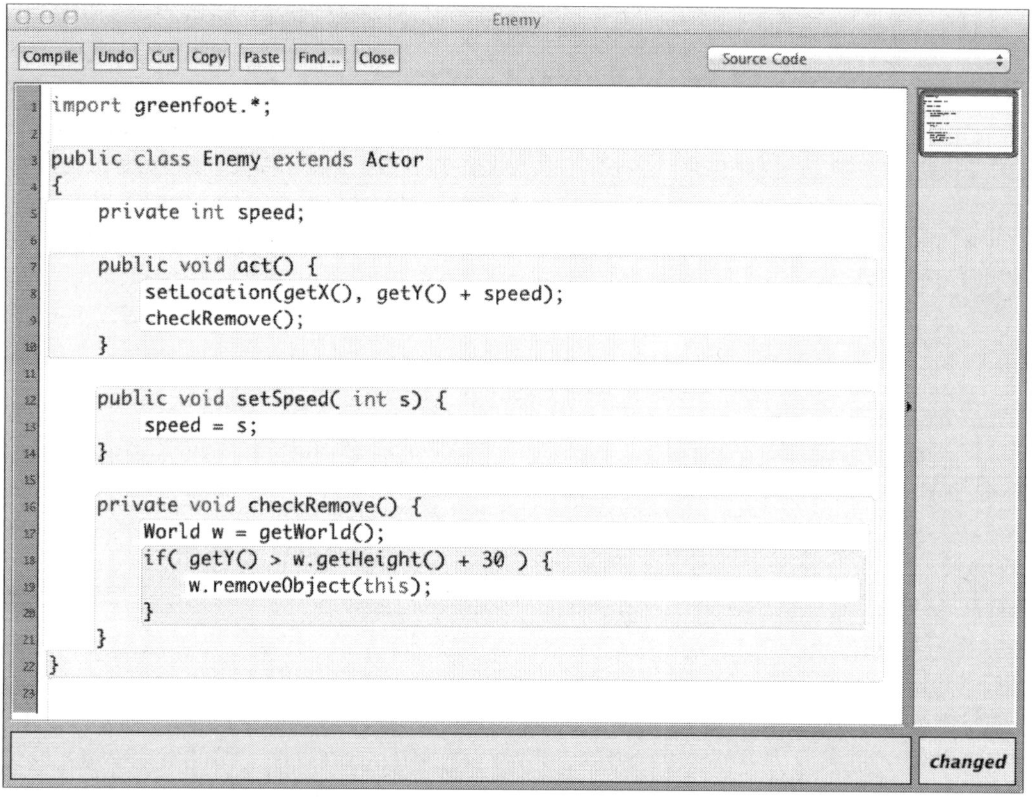

```
import greenfoot.*;

public class Enemy extends Actor
{
    private int speed;

    public void act() {
        setLocation(getX(), getY() + speed);
        checkRemove();
    }

    public void setSpeed( int s) {
        speed = s;
    }

    private void checkRemove() {
        World w = getWorld();
        if( getY() > w.getHeight() + 30 ) {
            w.removeObject(this);
        }
    }
}
```

Figure 27: This shows the finished Enemy class

As you can see, we made some really simple changes to the `Enemy` class. We added the `setSpeed()` method, which simply accepts an integer parameter and uses that value to set the `speed` variable that has been declared at the top of the class. In the `act()` method, we use the value of the `speed` variable in the `setLocation()` call; we continually add `speed` to the current *y* coordinate.

*Compile and run and enjoy your new game!*

# Your assignment

Since this is the end of the Avoider Game instruction. I'm going to give you a few challenge assignments. Good luck! Try to implement the following:

- Once the player's score is above 600, add a new enemy that spawns in addition to the enemies we have now. The new enemy should visually be very distinct from our existing enemies. If you are feeling up to it, have the new enemy move differently from the existing enemies too.

- Periodically, spawn a power-up that gives our hero a special ability. For example, the power-up could make our hero temporarily invincible, allow our hero to kill three enemies, or shrink the size of the avatar making it easier to avoid enemies.

- Display the player's final score on the game-over screen.

These challenges will definitely take some time and you should not feel compelled to try them. I just wanted to give those who are really interested a way to continue working on the Avoider Game. You will not need to have completed these challenges to move on to the next chapter.

## Next...

Congratulations! You did it! Have fun. Play your new game.

# Summary

This chapter demonstrated how to make a fun and engaging game. We have mouse control, a hero, enemies, a score, and introduction and game-over screens.

As this book assumes you have some experience working in Greenfoot, this chapter also served the purpose of refreshing your memory of how to program in Greenfoot.

In the upcoming chapters, we'll look at advanced programming concepts in Greenfoot that will allow you to create fun, innovative, and engaging applications. These chapters will assume that you have mastered the material in this one.

# 2
# Animation

*"Study without desire spoils the memory, and it retains nothing that it takes in."*

*– Leonardo da Vinci*

It is fairly simple to move actors around in Greenfoot scenarios by handling keyboard or mouse events and using `setLocation()` appropriately. However, we can do better. By animating our actors further, we can breath life into them. We can give our players/users the illusion of a vibrant, living world.

In essence, programming animation is the art of illusion. By adding small movements or image changes at the right time, we beguile our users into believing our creations are more than just static pixels on a screen. In this chapter, you will learn the following techniques for animating Greenfoot actors:

- Image swapping and movement
- Timing and synchronization
- Easing

Greenfoot is a wonderful platform for creating interactive and engaging applications that you can share on the Internet or use as a desktop application. It is your desire to create these types of applications that brought you here, and, according to Leonardo da Vinci, it is that desire that will help you retain the information in this book indefinitely.

# Revisiting Avoider Game

In this chapter, we are going to continue to work on Avoider Game, which we created in *Chapter 1, Let's Dive Right in…*. If you skipped that chapter, or just prefer to start off with a fresh copy, you can download the code for this game from this book's product page on the Packt Publishing website at http://www.packtpub.com/support. Any concepts I gloss over in this chapter were most likely covered in detail in the previous chapter; be sure to refer to that chapter as needed. Now, open the AvoiderGame scenario in Greenfoot and read on.

# Image swapping and movement

Image swapping is the age-old technique for animating. Perhaps as a child, you drew a stick figure in the corner of a pad of paper and slightly changed it on every succeeding page. When you rapidly flipped through the pages, your stick figure came to life. *Figure 2* shows my attempt at this type of animation.

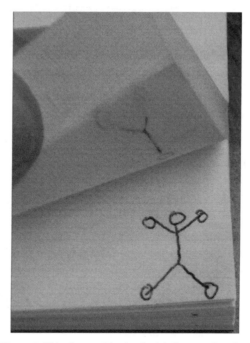

Figure 1: This shows old-school stick figure animation

In Greenfoot, we are going to animate actors by rapidly switching between images and achieve the same effect as the paper animation shown in *Figure 1*. We will learn how to use Greenfoot's setImage() method to do this.

# Using setImage()

When we create a new Actor in Greenfoot by subclassing from the Actor class, or one of our subclasses of Actor, Greenfoot prompts us to enter in the name of our new class and to select an image for it. Greenfoot also allows us to dynamically set the image of our Actor objects while the scenario is running, using the method setImage() provided by Greenfoot's Actor class. The following is an excerpt from Greenfoot's documentation:

```
public void setImage(java.lang.String filename)
throws java.lang.IllegalArgumentException

Set an image for this actor from an image file. The file may be in
jpeg, gif or png format. The file should be located in the project
directory.

Parameters:
filename - The name of the image file.
```

As you can see, setImage() allows us to set an image of an actor by specifying the path to any JPEG, GIF, or PNG file. By default, Greenfoot looks in the images folder contained in your Greenfoot project. You should place all images you are going to use in your scenario in this folder.

Let's use this method to animate the enemies in Avoider Game.

# Making enemies less happy

The enemies in Avoider Game are just too happy. Let's animate them to get sad and disappointed, as they realize that our hero is going to avoid them.

## Finding assets

The first thing we need to do, is to find a set of appropriate smiley images that we can switch to for our Enemy actor in our scenario. Often, you'll need to create your own image assets using Greenfoot's built-in image editor, or tools such as GIMP or Adobe Illustrator, or you could download images from the Internet; there are plenty of free images available. Luckily, the default installation of Greenfoot already contains all the images we need. On OSX, the images are in the following folder:

```
/Applications/Greenfoot 2.3.0/Greenfoot.app/Contents /Resources/Java/
greenfoot/imagelib/symbols
```

On Windows, the images are in the following folder:

```
C:/Program Files/Greenfoot/lib/greenfoot/imagelib/symbols
```

For your convenience, I have made all the smiley images available in this book's file repository on the Packt Publishing website at `https://www.packtpub.com/sites/default/files/downloads/0383OS_ColoredImages.pdf`.

You'll need to place the files `smiley1.png`, `smiley3.png`, `smiley4.png`, and `smiley5.png` into the `images` folder in your `AvoiderGame` directory. After doing this, your images folder should contain the files shown in *Figure 2*.

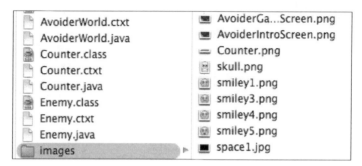

Figure 2: These are the contents of the images folder in your AvoiderGame project.

Now that we have our images available to us, we can start coding.

 Notice that once you set an actor's image to one provided by Greenfoot at creation time, such as `skull.png` in *Figure 2*, Greenfoot automatically places the image in your `images` folder. So, instead of copying the smiley images from their location on the disk, you could have created a new actor and then set the image of this actor to be each of the smiley faces in turn. Then, you could just delete this new actor. You will see that your images folder will look like that shown in *Figure 2*.

## Calling setImage() based on Actor location

Double-click on the `Enemy` actor in the **Actor classes** section of Greenfoot's main scenario window to begin editing the `Enemy` code. We practice good functional decomposition and simply add a call to `changeDispositon()` in the `act()` method of `Enemy`; we will write that method soon. Your `act()` method should now look like this:

```
public void act() {
  setLocation(getX(), getY() + speed);
  changeDisposition();
  checkRemove();
}
```

Now, we will implement the `changeDisposition()` method. In this method, we want to change the disposition of the enemies, as they slowly realize they will not get the hero. Let's presume our enemies remain optimistic until they reach the middle of the screen. After that, we will slowly have them succumb to despair.

In the implementation of `changeDisposition()`, we are going to use an instance variable to keep track of what image we need to display next. You need to add this variable *declaration* and *initialization* right below the declaration of the speed instance variable (at the top of the class outside of any method):

```
private int timeToChange = 1;
```

With that in place, we can now view the implementation of `changeDisposition()`. The following is our code:

```
private void changeDisposition() {
    int ypos = getY();
    int worldHeight = getWorld().getHeight();
    int marker1 = (int) (worldHeight * 0.5);
    int marker2 = (int) (worldHeight * 0.75);
    int marker3 = (int) (worldHeight * 0.90);
    if ( timeToChange == 1 && ypos > marker1) {
        setImage("smiley4.png");
        timeToChange++;
    }
    else if ( timeToChange == 2 && ypos > marker2) {
        setImage("smiley3.png");
        timeToChange++;
    }
    else if ( timeToChange == 3 && ypos > marker3) {
        setImage("smiley5.png");
        timeToChange++;
    }
}
```

The logic behind this code is simple. We want to pick specific locations in the downward motion of the enemy to change the image. One complication is that the enemy's speed can be changed through the `setSpeed()` method. We use this method in the `AvoiderWorld` class to increase the speed of the enemy, so as to increase the difficulty of the game. So, we cannot simply change the image of the enemy with code such as `if ( ypos == 300)` because the actor might never have a *y* position of exactly `300`. For example, if the enemy's speed was 7, then it would have the following *y* positions as it went down: 7, 14, 21, ..., 294, 301, 308, and so on.

As we can see, the enemy never has a *y* position of exactly 300. You might next want to try code such as `if( ypos > 300 )`; however, this is suboptimal, as this will cause the image to *continually be set for every y position it has over 300*. Therefore, we should take the approach demonstrated in `changeDisposition()` and use `timeToChange` to control a one-time, sequential image change.

Now that we understand the logic behind `changeDisposition()`, let's go over it line by line. The first thing we do is create variables to hold the positions where we want to change the image of the enemy. These positions are based on the height of the scenario; `marker1` is at 50 percent of this height, `marker2` is at 75 percent of this height, and `marker3` is at a position slightly before the enemy exits off the bottom of the screen. The `if` statements test for two conditions before changing the image of the actor. It checks to see whether to use `timeToChange` to that specific image and whether the actor has passed a given *y* position.

In the previous code, there are lines that convert a decimal number (of type `double`) into a whole number (of type `int`), such as this one:

```
int marker1 = (int) (worldHeight * 0.5)
```

For more information on converting one variable into another (also called casting), refer to the following link:

```
http://docs.oracle.com/javase/specs/jls/se7/html/jls-
5.html
```

Compile your Greenfoot scenario and play the game. See if you can get a score greater than 250! *Full disclosure: after writing that last sentence I played the game four times in a row and got the following scores: 52, 33, 28, 254. Woot! 254!*

**Functional decomposition**

Functional decomposition is closely related to the top-down design, a process of repeatedly redefining the problem in terms of smaller, less complex subproblems. When you are writing code for a specific action or functionality in your program, try to think of smaller methods you could write that you could compose to solve the larger issue.

Typically, you would like to write methods that contain less than 40 lines of code and which only implement one well-defined task. I actually prefer to go much smaller when possible. You'll find code is easier to write, debug, and modify if you follow this practice. In this book, I use functional decomposition. You'll notice that the `act()` methods throughout the book mainly contain a sequence of calls to other methods.

# Using setLocation()

The method `setImage()` is by far the most useful Greenfoot method for animating actors; however, moving an actor in certain ways can also produce interesting effects. We already use `setLocation()` to move both the enemies and our hero; let's use it now to animate the background star field to make it seem like we are flying through space.

# Creating a star field

Our star field is going to provide various sized stars moving in the background at various speeds, to produce the effect of moving through space at high speed. Creating a star field is very simple and we have already written very similar code. Imagine that our enemies had the image of a small speck of light, instead of a smiley face and we had many more of them. Voila! You have a star field.

## A blank slate

If we are going to create our own dynamic star field, then we no longer need the current background image associated with `AvoiderWorld`. However, if we change this class to have no image associated with it, then we will get a white background—not a very good representation of outer space.

The solution is to create a new pure black, 600 x 400 pixel image and then select that as the background image for the `AvoiderWorld` class. Start up your favorite image editor or use Greenfoot's built-in editor, create a big black rectangle, save it as a PNG file in your **Avoider** project's `images` folder, and then set `AvoiderWorld` to use this new image as the background.

## The Star class

For our stars, we are going to do something a little different. Instead of setting the image of the star to a file containing a graphic, we are going to dynamically draw the image. This will be easy to do since a speck of light is not very complicated.

To create our star actor, right-click on the `Actor` class in the **Actor classes** section and choose **New subclass...**. In the **New class** window that pops up, enter `Star` as **New class name** and choose **No image** as **New class image**.

Remember, we went over how to create new actors in *Chapter 1*, *Let's Dive Right in…*.

Open up a code editor window for your new Star class and add the following constructor to it:

```
public Star() {
    GreenfootImage img = new GreenfootImage(10,10);
    img.setColor(Color.white);
    img.fillOval(0,0,10,10);
    setImage(img);
}
```

This constructor dynamically creates an image to use for the image of our Star class. First, we create a new image that has a width of 10 pixels and a height of 10 pixels. Next, we set the color to use for any drawing we do in this image. We gain access to the Color class (see the information box below to learn more about it) by adding the following import statement at the top of our class file:

```
import java.awt.Color;
```

After setting the color, we draw an oval using the fillOval() method. The first two parameters of fillOval() specify the offset of the upper-left corner of the shape we are drawing from the offset of the upper-left corner of our image. *Figure 3* displays this mapping. The next two parameters of fillOval() specify the width and height of the bounding box containing our oval. Since our width and height are the same, fillOval() will draw a circle. Finally, we set the image of our actor to be the new image we just created.

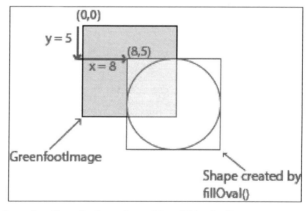

Figure 3: This shows the effect of using values of 8 and 5 for the first two parameters of fillOval()

**Working with color**

In the Star() constructor, we do an operation that involves color. There are several different ways to represent color on computers (and basically anything with a screen), and we are going to use an RGBA color model. If you are curious, you can read more about it at http://en.wikipedia. org/wiki/RGBA_color_space.

Luckily, we don't have to know much about the theory. Java provides a class – Color – that manages most of the complexity for us. To get this Color class into your code, you need to have an import statement at the top of the file. The import statement is import java.awt.Color;. If you don't add this to the code above, you'll get compile errors.

To learn more about this Color class, look at the official documentation at http://docs.oracle.com/javase/7/docs/api/java/awt/Color.html.

The next thing to do to our Star class, is fill in the act() method. We just need to slowly move this actor down the screen and then remove it once it has exited off the bottom of the screen. We use setLocation() to do the former and the checkRemove() method to do the latter. The following is the completed code for both act() and checkRemove():

```
public void act() {
   setLocation(getX(), getY()+1);
   checkRemove();
}

private void checkRemove() {
   World w = getWorld();
   if( getY() > w.getHeight() + 30 ) {
     w.removeObject(this);
   }
}
```

The checkRemove() method is exactly the same code as the one used in the Enemy class and explained in *Chapter 1, Let's Dive Right in…*. In fact, there are many similarities between the Star class and the Enemy class, so much so, that I think we should pre-emptively add the setSpeed() method the Enemy has to the Star class, as it is very likely we will need it later in our implementation of a moving star field. Add this method to the Star class:

```
public void setSpeed( int s) {
   speed = s;
}
```

Just as we did in the `Enemy` class, we need to add the instance variable `speed` at the top of the class. Here's the code for the variable declaration:

```
int speed = 1;
```

We should make one more change in the `act()` method to now use the `speed` variable to move `Star` objects. Change the `setLocation()` code in the `act()` method to this:

```
setLocation(getX(), getY() + speed);
```

The complete code for the `Star` class is shown in *Figure 4*.

```java
import greenfoot.*;  // (World, Actor, GreenfootImage, Greenfoot and MouseInfo)
import java.awt.Color;

public class Star extends Actor
{
    int speed = 1;

    public Star() {
        GreenfootImage img = new GreenfootImage(10,10);
        img.setColor(Color.white);
        img.fillOval(0,0,10,10);
        setImage(img);
    }

    public void act() {
        setLocation(getX(), getY()+speed);
        checkRemove();
    }

    public void setSpeed( int s) {
        speed = s;
    }

    private void checkRemove() {
        World w = getWorld();
        if( getY() > w.getHeight() + 30 ) {
            w.removeObject(this);
        }
    }
}
```

Figure 4: This shows the completed Star class implementation

This would be a great time to compile the scenario and make sure you do not have any spelling errors. We have not added any stars to our game, so you will not notice any difference in the game. Adding stars is what we are going to do next.

# Creating a moving field

We will generate our stars in the AvoiderWorld class. Open the editor window for this class and add a line of code to the act() method to call the method generateStars(), which we haven't written yet, but will soon. Your act() method should now look like this:

```
public void act() {
  generateEnemies();
  generateStars();
  increaseLevel();
}
```

The generateStars() method creates new stars in a way similar to how generateEnemies() creates new enemies. Here is the code for generateStars():

```
private void generateStars() {
  if( Greenfoot.getRandomNumber(1000) < 350) {
    Star s = new Star();
    addObject( s, Greenfoot.getRandomNumber(getWidth()-20)+10, -1);
  }
}
```

The if statement determines whether or not we want to create a star at this point in time. With a 35 percent probability, we will create a star, which ultimately creates a fairly dense star field. Inside the if statement, we create a new Star object and add it to the World. Add this code and compile and run the game, and see what you think. Do you like the stars? They're OK, but it looks a little more like it's raining golf balls. We can do better.

# Using parallax

Parallax is the effect that closer objects seem to be in different positions relative to farther objects based on the viewing angle. For example, if you have ever looked out of a car window and watched trees go by, you'll notice that the trees closer to you seem to move faster than the trees in the background. We can use this phenomenon to give the illusion of depth to our star field.

Let's change our generateStars() method to create two types of stars. Some will be near and some will be far. Nearer stars will move faster and be brighter than stars that are further away, but we will generate more stars that are far away. If you imagine our screen as a window out into space, we will have a wider view of objects that are far away, as opposed to close by. Therefore, we need more of them. *Figure 5* illustrates this point.

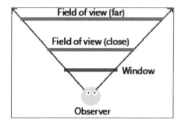

Figure 5: This demonstrates that you have a wider field of view for objects that are further away when looking through a window

Finally, we want to add some random variation in the stars, so that the resulting star field does not look too uniform. Here's our parallax-augmented generateStars() method:

```
private void generateStars() {
  if( Greenfoot.getRandomNumber(1000) < 350) {
    Star s = new Star();
    GreenfootImage image = s.getImage();
    if( Greenfoot.getRandomNumber(1000) < 300) {
      // this is a close bright star
      s.setSpeed(3);
      image.setTransparency(
      Greenfoot.getRandomNumber(25) + 225);
      image.scale(4,4);
    } else {
      // this is a further dim star
      s.setSpeed(2);
      image.setTransparency(
      Greenfoot.getRandomNumber(50) + 100);
      image.scale(2,2);
    }
    s.setImage(image);
    addObject( s, Greenfoot.getRandomNumber(
    getWidth()-20)+10, -1);
  }
}
```

We have added accessing the current image of the star, changing the image, and then setting it to be the new image for the star. The inner `if-else` statement handles the changes for nearby and faraway stars. With a 30 percent chance, the star will be a near one. Nearby stars are faster (`setSpeed()`), brighter (`setTransparency()`), and larger (`scale()`).

The `setTransparency()` method accepts one integer parameter that specifies how *see-through* the image is. You would enter in the value `255` for a completely opaque object and `0` for a completely transparent object. We make stars that are far away more transparent so that more of the black background will come through and make it less bright. The `scale()` method on `GreenfootImages` changes the size of the image, so that it fits into the bounding box defined by the first two parameters of this method. As we can see in the code, nearby stars are scaled to fit into a 4 x 4 pixel image and stars further away are scaled to fit into a 2 x 2 pixel image.

We are so close to finishing our star field. Compile and run the scenario and see what you think of it up to now.

The star field is looking great, but there are still two problems. First, when the game starts, the background is completely black, and then stars start to fall. To really keep the illusion that you are in space, we need the game to start in a field of stars. Second, the stars are being generated over the enemies, our hero, and the score counter; this really wrecks the illusion that they are far away. Let's fix this.

Solving the issue that the stars are in front of other actors on the screen is a one-liner. Here's the line of code you need to add to the constructor in `AvoiderWorld`:

```
setPaintOrder(Avatar.class, Enemy.class, Counter.class);
```

The `setPaintOrder()` method is defined in the `World` class that `AvoiderWorld` subclasses. This method allows you set the order of classes displayed on the screen. So, we list the `Avatar` class first (it will be at the top of everything), then the `Enemy` class, and last the `Counter` class. With this ordering, for example, our enemies will be displayed above the score. Any class not listed will be drawn behind all the ones listed; therefore, our stars will be behind all actors on the screen.

Drawing the initial field of stars is easy if we make a small change to the `generateStars()` method. Presently, our stars are hardcoded to start with a *y* coordinate of -1 because of this line:

```
addObject( s, Greenfoot.getRandomNumber(getWidth()-20)+10, -1);
```

If we change `generateStars()` to take one integer parameter that specifies the *y* value to draw the star at, then we can use this method to create the initial star field. Take the first line of `generateStars()`:

```
private void generateStars() {
```

Change it to this:

```
private void generateStars(int yLoc) {
```

Take the last line of the method:

```
addObject( s, Greenfoot.getRandomNumber(getWidth()-20)+10, -1);
```

Change it to this:

```
addObject( s, Greenfoot.getRandomNumber(getWidth()-20)+10, yLoc);
```

These two line changes allow us to specify any starting *y* value for our stars. Because of this change, we need to change the call to `generateStars()` in our `act()` method to the following line of code:

```
generateStars(-1);
```

If you compile and run the scenario, the only difference you should see is that the stars are now truly in the background. We still need to add one simple method definition and call to draw the initial star field. The method definition is as follows:

```
private void generateInitialStarField() {
  for( int i=0; i<getHeight(); i++ ) {
    generateStars(i);
  }
}
```

If the height of our game is four hundred, then this method calls `generateStars()` four hundred times. Each time, it supplies a different *y* value to draw stars on. We will fill up the screen with stars by adding this line to our constructor:

```
generateInitialStarField();
```

We have made a lot of changes to the `AvoiderWorld` class definition, making it increasingly likely that you may have put code in the wrong place. Here is the full listing of the `AvoiderWorld` class you can use to check your code against:

```
import greenfoot.*;

public class AvoiderWorld extends World {
  private GreenfootSound bkgMusic;
  private Counter scoreBoard;
```

```
private int enemySpawnRate = 20;
private int enemySpeed = 1;
private int nextLevel = 100;

public AvoiderWorld() {
  super(600, 400, 1, false);
  bkgMusic = new GreenfootSound("sounds/UFO_T-Balt.mp3")
  // Music Credit:
  //    http://www.newgrounds.com/audio/listen/504436 by T-balt
  bkgMusic.playLoop();
  setPaintOrder(Avatar.class, Enemy.class, Counter.class);
  prepare();
  generateInitialStarField();
}

public void act() {
  generateEnemies();
  generateStars(-1);
  increaseLevel();
}

private void generateEnemies() {
  if( Greenfoot.getRandomNumber(1000) < enemySpawnRate) {
    Enemy e = new Enemy();
    e.setSpeed(enemySpeed);
    addObject( e, Greenfoot.getRandomNumber(
    getWidth()-20)+10, -30);
    scoreBoard.setValue(scoreBoard.getValue() + 1);
  }
}

private void generateStars(int yLoc) {
  if( Greenfoot.getRandomNumber(1000) < 350) {
    Star s = new Star();
    GreenfootImage image = s.getImage();
    if( Greenfoot.getRandomNumber(1000) < 300) {
      // this is a close bright star
      s.setSpeed(3);
      image.setTransparency(
      Greenfoot.getRandomNumber(25) + 225);
      image.scale(4,4);
    } else {
      // this is a further dim star
      s.setSpeed(2);
```

```
            image.setTransparency(
            Greenfoot.getRandomNumber(50) + 100);
            image.scale(2,2);
        }
        s.setImage(image);
        addObject( s, Greenfoot.getRandomNumber(
        getWidth()-20)+10, yLoc);
    }
}

private void increaseLevel() {
    int score = scoreBoard.getValue();
    if( score > nextLevel ) {
        enemySpawnRate += 2;
        enemySpeed++;
        nextLevel += 100;
    }
}

public void endGame() {
    bkgMusic.stop();
    AvoiderGameOverWorld go = new AvoiderGameOverWorld();
    Greenfoot.setWorld(go);
}

private void prepare() {
    Avatar avatar = new Avatar();
    addObject(avatar, 287, 232);
    scoreBoard = new Counter("Score: ");
    addObject(scoreBoard, 70, 20);
}

private void generateInitialStarField() {
    int i = 0;
    for( i=0; i<getHeight(); i++ ) {
        generateStars(i);
    }
}
}
```

Compile and run your game. This is getting good. Your game should look like the screenshot shown in *Figure 6A*.

Figure 6A: This shows our game up to now

# Using GreenfootImage

Wait a minute. How did I know about Greenfoot's `GreenfootImage` class and the `setColor()` and `fillOval()` methods it contains? The answer is simply that I read the documentation. I learned that Greenfoot provides the class `GreenfootImage` to aid in the handling and manipulation of images. In general, Greenfoot provides a useful set of classes to help programmers create interactive applications. We learned about the `World` class and `Actor` class in *Chapter 1, Let's Dive Right in.... Figure 6B* displays all the classes Greenfoot provides.

| **Package greenfoot** | |
|---|---|
| **Class Summary** | |
| Actor | An Actor is an object that exists in the Greenfoot world. |
| Greenfoot | This utility class provides methods to control the simulation and interact with the system. |
| GreenfootImage | An image to be shown on screen. |
| GreenfootSound | Represents audio that can be played in Greenfoot. |
| MouseInfo | This class contains information about the current status of the mouse. |
| UserInfo | The UserInfo class can be used to store data permanently on a server, and to share this data between different users, when the scenario runs on the Greenfoot web site. |
| World | World is the world that Actors live in. |

Figure 6B: This shows the classes provided by Greenfoot to help you write applications. This screenshot is taken directly from Greenfoot's help documentation.

You can access Greenfoot's documentation by going to Greenfoot's website, as I suggested in *Chapter 1, Let's Dive Right in…*. If you are not online, you can access the documentation by selecting the **Help** menu option in Greenfoot's main menu and then selecting **Greenfoot Class Documentation** from the drop-down menu. This will bring up Greenfoot's class documentation in your default web browser.

 Greenfoot's class documentation is very short and concise. You should take 20–30 minutes to read about each class Greenfoot provides and each method contained in those classes. This will be a very good investment of your time.

# Timing and synchronization

Timing is very important in creating realistic animations in Greenfoot. Often, we have the need for an actor to do temporary animation in response to an event. We need a way to allow (or prevent) things for a certain amount of time. It is possible to wait for a specific amount of time using the `SimpleTimer` class provided by Greenfoot (you can import it into your scenario in the same way you imported the `Counter` class in *Chapter 1, Let's Dive Right in…*); however, waiting for a specific amount of time is rarely the right choice.

Why is that? Well, Greenfoot provides the player/user with the ability to slow down and speed up a scenario via the **Speed** slider that is located at the bottom of Greenfoot's main scenario window. If you waited for 2 seconds in your code and then the player sped the game up, the 2 seconds wait would last much longer in the game relative to the speed of everything else; the reverse effect would happen if the user slowed down the scenario. We want to use a method for "waiting" in Greenfoot that scales with the speed of the game.

We will look at three different ways to time events in Greenfoot: delay variables, random actions, and triggered events.

# Delay variables

Delay variables are very similar to the concept of a timer. However, instead of counting seconds (or milliseconds), we will count the number of calls to the `act()` method that have gone by. This will exactly scale with the **Speed** slider, as this slider controls the time between `act()` method calls. Next, we will take a look at an example of using a delay variable.

# Hurting the avatar

Our game is a little unforgiving. If you touch an enemy once, you die. Let's change the game, so that you take damage for every hit and it takes four hits to kill our hero. The first thing we need to do, is create an instance variable that is going to keep track of the health of our hero. Add this instance variable to the top of the Avatar class outside of any method:

```
private int health = 3;
```

Every time our hero touches an enemy, we are going to subtract one from this variable. When this variable is 0, we will end the game.

When our hero is hit by an enemy, we want to provide visual feedback to the player. We could do this with a health bar or life indicator at the top of the game; however, let's just animate our hero so that it *looks* injured. To do this, we need to create copies of the skull.png image that is used to represent an instance of the Avatar class and augment them to look damaged. You can make the changes using an image editor, such as GIMP, Adobe Illustrator, or others. *Figure 7* shows my versions of the damaged skull.png image. Make sure you name your skull images exactly the way I did. The first image skull.png is already in the images folder; the other three need to be named skull1.png, skull2.png, and skull3.png. The reason why it is so important to name them in this manner will become apparent soon.

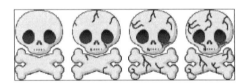

Figure 7: These are my four copies of skull.png showing increased damage.
They are named skull.png, skull1.png, skull2.png, and skull3.png, respectively.

Presently, our act() method in the Avatar class looks like the following code snippet:

```
public void act() {
  followMouse();
  checkForCollisions();
}
```

We are going to change the implementation of checkForCollisions() to handle our hero having life and looking damaged. It presently looks like the following code snippet:

```
private void checkForCollisions() {
  Actor enemy = getOneIntersectingObject(Enemy.class);
  if( enemy != null ) {
```

```
        getWorld().removeObject(this);
        Greenfoot.stop();
    }
}
```

We need to change it to this:

```
private void checkForCollisions() {
  Actor enemy = getOneIntersectingObject(Enemy.class);
  if( hitDelay == 0 && enemy != null ) {
    if( health == 0 ) {
      AvoiderWorld world = (AvoiderWorld) getWorld();
      world.endGame();
    }
    else {
      health--;
      setImage("skull" + ++nextImage + ".png"););
      hitDelay = 50;
    }
  }
  if( hitDelay > 0 ) hitDelay--;
}
```

As we can see, we added quite a bit of code. The first if statement checks the two conditions that need to be true before we take damage from an enemy: firstly, that enough time has passed since the last time we took damage from an enemy, and secondly, that we are presently touching an instance of the Enemy class. When the hero touches an enemy and takes damage, we want to give our hero a short time of invulnerability in order to move away, without continuing to take damage every time the act() method is called. If we didn't do this, the hero would take four hits before you could blink your eye. We use the hitDelay integer variable to count how long to wait. If we have been hit, we set hitDelay to 50, as shown in the else part of the inner if-else statement. The last if statement in the function continues to decrement hitDelay. When hitDelay gets to 0, we can be hit by an enemy and no longer decrement hitDelay.

**Java increment and decrement operators**

In the last bit of code, we used Java's increment (++) and decrement (--) operators quite a bit. They simply add one or subtract one, respectively, from the variable they are applied to. However, there is a bit of subtlety you need to be aware of in their use. Look at the following code:

```
int x = 0, y=0, z=0;
y = ++x;
z = x++;
```

Notice that the increment operator can be applied before (prefix) or after (postfix) the variable. After this code completes, x is 2, y is 1, and z is 1. You might be surprised that z is 1 and not 2. The reason is that the postfix increment operator will return the value of the variable before it is incremented. Refer to the following link for more information:

```
http://docs.oracle.com/javase/tutorial/java/
nutsandbolts/op1.html
```

In the inner `if-else` statement, we know we have been hit by an enemy. We check to see if our `health` is 0; if it is, we are dead, and the game ends as before. If we still have `health`, we decrement our `health`, change our image, and set `hitDelay`.

The way we change our image to the next, more damaged, image is based on how we named the files earlier. We build the name of the file by concatenating the `skull` string with an integer and then again with the `.png` string. This method provides us with a short and easy programmatic way of changing the image. The alternative would be to use a `switch` statement that calls `setImage()` with different file names based on the value of `health`. In our new version of `checkForCollisions()`, we used two new instance variables; we still need to declare and initialize those variables. Add these lines at the top of the class under the declaration of the `health` variable we added at the beginning of this section:

```
private int hitDelay = 0;
private int nextImage = 0;
```

Now, compile your scenario and verify that your hero takes four hits to die.

> The `hitDelay` variable is a good example of a delay variable. Throughout the rest of the book, we will use delay variables to time various activities. Make sure you understand how we use `hitDelay` before continuing.

# Random actions

Random actions are one of the most effective ways to approximate simple intelligence or natural phenomena. It repeats actions in a non-predictable way and adds both suspense and challenge to a game. We already randomly generate a flow of enemies our hero has to avoid. We will now use them to improve our star field animation.

## Blinking

The stars already look great and provide a real sense of movement in the game. We are going to enhance them by making them twinkle like real stars. To do this, we use the method `setTransparency()` to make the star completely *see-through* and use a delay variable to wait for a short period of time before making the star opaque again. We will use Greenfoot's random number generator to ensure that the stars twinkle infrequently. First, we add a method call, `checkTwinkle()`, to the `act()` method in the `Star` class:

```
public void act() {
  setLocation(getX(), getY()+speed);
  checkRemove();
  checkTwinkle();
}
```

We need to add the following delay variable and the variable to hold the current transparency of the object at the top of the class under the declaration of the `speed` variable:

```
int twinkleTime = 0;
int currentTransparency = 0;
```

The following is an implementation of `checkTwinkle()`:

```
private void checkTwinkle() {
  GreenfootImage img = getImage();
  if( twinkleTime > 0 ) {
    if( twinkleTime == 1) {
      img.setTransparency(currentTransparency);
    }
    twinkleTime--;
  } else {
    if( Greenfoot.getRandomNumber(10000) < 10) {
      twinkleTime = 10;
      currentTransparency = img.getTransparency();
      img.setTransparency(0);
```

```
        }
      }
   }
```

Let's look at the `else` part of the outer `if-else` statement. With a small random probability, we set `twinkleTime` (our delay variable) to `10`, save the current transparency of the star so that we can restore it later, and then set the transparency to `0`.

The `if` part of the initial `if-else` statement decrements `twinkleTime` if it is greater than `0` and restores the transparency of our star when `twinkleTime` equals `1`. Because `twinkleTime` is only set to `10`, the star will only be invisible for a very short period of time. This short flicker gives the illusion that the star twinkles.

Compile and run the scenario and see whether you can catch a star twinkling. If you have a hard time verifying this, change the frequency at which the twinkling occurs and try again.

# Triggered events

Triggering a change in an actor when a certain event occurs is another way to do animation. For example, you might have an enemy actor that will only chase you when you get within a certain range. You might also have an actor respond to keyboard events or location.

In this section, we are going to give our hero eyes. Obviously, our hero is very concerned with nearby enemies and definitely wants to keep an eye on them.

 Adding animated eyes to an actor is a fantastic way to give that actor personality. Eyes are very expressive and can easily portray excitement, sadness, or fear. Never hesitate to add animated eyes.

# Adding eyes

This might seem a bit weird, but we are going to create a separate `Eye` actor. We are going to do this for a couple of reasons. First, to get the eyes to look around is going to take a fair amount of code. We can encapsulate this code in the `Eye` class and keep our `Avatar` class more streamlined. Second, having the eyes as separate entities means we could add them to future actors and they would still work even if we changed the image of the `Avatar` class.

The alternative would be to create a skull image with eyes for every direction we would want to look. The fact that we have different images for our hero to show different levels of damage would further complicate matters. Therefore, we are going to create a separate `Eye` actor.

Create a new subclass of `Actor` called `Eye`. Do not associate an image with this `Actor` class. We will dynamically draw an image of an eye and redraw it appropriately when we need to look in a different direction. Here is the implementation of the `Eye` class:

```java
import greenfoot.*;
import java.awt.Color;
import java.util.List;

public class Eye extends Actor {

  public Eye() {
    drawEye(2,2);
  }

  public void act() {
    lookAtEnemies();
  }

  public void lookAtEnemies() {
    List<Enemy> eList = getObjectsInRange(120, Enemy.class);
    if( !eList.isEmpty() ) {
      Enemy e = eList.get(0);
      if( e.getX() < getX() ) {
        if( e.getY() < getY() ) {
          drawEye(1,1);
        } else {
          drawEye(1,3);
        }
      } else {
        if( e.getY() < getY() ) {
          drawEye(3,1);
        } else {
          drawEye(3,3);
        }
      }
    }
  }
}
```

```
private void drawEye(int dx, int dy) {
    GreenfootImage img = new GreenfootImage(10,10);
    img.setColor(Color.white);
    img.fillOval(0,0,10,10);
    img.setColor(Color.black);
    img.fillOval(dx,dy,6,6);
    setImage(img);
  }
}
```

The two main methods of this class are the `drawEye()` method and the `lookAtEnemies()` method. The `drawEye()` image uses the same methods to draw an eye that we used to draw the image of a star in the `Star` class. For an eye, we just need to draw one additional black circle to serve as the iris. The method `drawEye()` takes two integer parameters that provide the position of the iris in the eye. This offset portion of `fillOval()` was demonstrated in *Figure 3*. To summarize, the first `fillOval()` command draws the larger white part of the eye, and the second `fillOval()` command draws the small black iris at a given offset to simulate staring in a certain direction.

The `lookAtEnemies()` method finds all enemies within a given distance of the eye and uses `drawEye()` to stare at the first enemy it finds. Using `if` statements to compare the $x$ and $y$ position of the enemy with its own position, the eye classifies the enemy as being in one of four quadrants: upper-left, lower-left, upper-right, and lower-right. Using this information, `drawEye()` is called with the integer parameters `(1,1)`, `(1,3)`, `(3,1)`, and `(3,3)`, respectively. *Figure 8* demonstrates the correlation between the quadrant the enemy is in and the call to `drawEye()`.

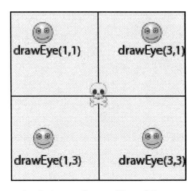

Figure 8: This shows the mapping between the position of the enemy and the call to drawEye()

In `lookAtEnemies()`, we used a new collision detection method called `getObjectsInRange()`. This method differs from `getOneIntersectingObject()` in two ways. First, instead of using the bounding box of the calling `Actor` class to determine whether a collision occurred, it draws a circle around the calling `Actor` class that has a radius of the size defined by the first parameter of `getObjectsInRange()`. This method returns all of the enemies found in that circle, instead of just one enemy. The enemies are returned in a Java `List` array. At the top of our `Eye` class, we need to include the code `import java.util.List;` to work with the `List` data type. We only have the ability to stare at one enemy at a time, so we choose to stare at the first enemy in this list using the method `get()` and passing it the integer value `0` to access it. Here's Greenfoot's documentation on `getObjectsInRange()`:

```
protected java.util.List getObjectsInRange(int radius, java.lang.Class
cls)
```

The preceding line of code returns all objects within range `radius` around this object. An object is within range if the distance between its center and this object's center is less than, or equal to, `radius`.

The parameters of the the `getObjectsInRange()` methods are described as follows:

- `radius`: This is the radius of the circle (in cells)
- `cls`: This is the class of objects to look for (passing `null` will find all objects)

## Giving our hero sight

Now that we have an `Actor` class called `Eye`, we just need to make a few modifications to the `Avatar` class in order to add eyes to our hero. We need to create two eyes, place them on our hero, and then we need to make sure the eyes stay in place every time our hero moves. We start by adding instance variables to the `Avatar` class:

```
private Eye leftEye;
private Eye rightEye;
```

We then create and place those eyes on the skull image by adding this method:

```
protected void addedToWorld(World w) {
  leftEye = new Eye();
  rightEye = new Eye();
  w.addObject(leftEye, getX()-10, getY()-8);
  w.addObject(rightEye, getX()+10, getY()-8);
}
```

Initially, you might think that we could create the eyes and add them in the constructor method for Avatar. Normally, this would be an excellent location for code that is run once at creation time. The problem is that before we can add the eyes to the world, an instance of the Avatar class needs to be in a world. If we look at the code in AvoiderWorld that adds our hero, we see this:

```
Avatar avatar = new Avatar();
addObject(avatar, 287, 232);
```

The creation of our hero is a two-step process. First, an instance of the Avatar class is created (the first line), and then we add this instance to the world (the second line). Notice that the constructor runs before that object is placed in a world, so we cannot access the instance of the world we are in via the method getWorld(). The developers of Greenfoot recognized that some actors will need to access the world they are in to complete their initialization, so they added the addedToWorld() method to the Actor class. The Actor class overrides this method when initialization requires world access, and it will be called by Greenfoot every time an actor is added to a world. We use this method in our Avatar class in order to place the eyes on our hero.

We have now created our eyes and added them to our hero. Now, we just need to ensure that the eyes stay with our hero whenever it moves. To do that, we add the following lines to our followMouse() function in the Avatar class:

```
leftEye.setLocation(getX()-10, getY()-8);
rightEye.setLocation(getX()+10, getY()-8);
```

The preceding code is added after the following line of code:

```
setLocation(mi.getX(), mi.getY());
```

Why do the 10s and 8s in the setLocation() call leftEye and rightEye? These are the values that correctly place the eyes in the sockets of our hero. I determined these values through trial and error. *Figure 9* presents the details.

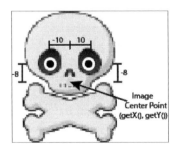

Figure 9: This shows how the location of the eyes was determined

It is now time to have some fun. Compile and run your game and enjoy the fruits of your labor. Your game should look like the screenshot shown in *Figure 10*.

Figure 10: Our game has animated enemies, a moving background star field (with twinkles), and a hero with eyes that visually changes when hit

# Easing

For our last major section of this chapter, we are going to look at using easing equations to move our actors around in interesting ways. Easing functions use easing equations to calculate position as a function of time. Just about every animation you've seen on the web, your mobile device, or in the movies uses easing at some point in time. We are going to add three new actors to our game that move according to three different easing functions: linear, exponential, and sinusoidal.

# Power-ups and power-downs

Power-ups are an excellent way to add new challenges and balance player skill. Power-ups provide players with momentary boosts in speed, power, health, or some other game-related skill. They often appear randomly and might not be in the most convenient location, so they require players to make fast, real-time decisions where they have to weigh the risk of moving to the power-up versus its beneficial effects.

Similarly, we can create randomly appearing game objects that negatively affect the player's ability to do well. I call these *power-downs*. They also require the player to make fast, real-time decisions, but now they are deciding between avoiding them and staying on their current trajectory and suffering the negative impact.

We are going to add two new actors to our game that will be power-downs and one new actor that will be a power-up. All three of them will use easing for movement. We will first introduce a new `Actor` class that will contain all the common code for easing and being a power item (power-up or power-down.) Our power-ups and power-downs will inherit from this class. It is good object-oriented programming practice to use inheritance and polymorphism to write concise, flexible, and maintainable code.

# Base class

Creating a well-thought-out base class for our power items will provide the means to easily create new power items and augment existing ones in the future. Before we talk about the code for our new class, we need to import a new Greenfoot-supplied class into our project, in the same way we imported the `Counter` class in *Chapter 1, Let's Dive Right in....* The class we are going to import is `SmoothMover`. We need this class as it more accurately tracks the position of `Actor`. Here's an excerpt from its documentation:

```
public abstract class SmoothMover extends greenfoot.Actor


A variation of an actor that maintains a precise location (using
doubles for the co-ordinates instead of ints). This allows small
precise movements (e.g. movements of 1 pixel or less) that do not lose
precision.
```

To import this class, click on **Edit** in Greenfoot's main menu and then click on **Import Class...** in the drop-down menu that appears. In the **Import Class** window that appears next, select `SmoothMover` on the left-hand side and then click on the **Import** button.

Now that we have `SmoothMover` in our project, we can create the `PowerItems` class. Right-click `SmoothMover` and choose **New subclass...**. You will not need to associate an image with this class, so choose **No Image** in the **Scenario Images** section in the **New class** window.

Let's take a look at the implementation of `PowerItems` (our new base class for power-ups and power-downs):

```
import greenfoot.*;

public abstract class PowerItems extends SmoothMover
{
  protected double targetX, targetY, expireTime;
  protected double origX, origY;
  protected double duration;
```

```
    protected int counter;

    public PowerItems( int tX, int tY, int eT ) {
      targetX = tX;
      targetY = tY;
      expireTime = eT;
      counter = 0;
      duration = expireTime;
    }

    protected void addedToWorld(World w) {
      origX = getX();
      origY = getY();
    }

    public void act() {
      easing();
      checkHitAvatar();
      checkExpire();
    }

    protected abstract double curveX(double f);

    protected abstract double curveY(double f);

    protected abstract void checkHitAvatar();

    protected void easing() {
      double fX = ++counter/duration;
      double fY = counter/duration;
      fX = curveX(fX);
      fY = curveY(fY);
      setLocation((targetX * fX) + (origX * (1-fX)),
      (targetY * fY) + (origY * (1-fY)));
    }

    private void checkExpire() {
      if( expireTime-- < 0 ) {
        World w = getWorld();
        if( w != null ) w.removeObject(this);
      }
    }
  }
}
```

We first need to discuss all the instance variables of this class. There are seven of them. Two of them are used to track the starting coordinates (origX and origY) and two of them are used to track the ending coordinates (targetX and targetY). The instance variable expireTime specifies how many calls of the act() method this actor should execute before removing itself. In other words, it specifies the lifespan of the actor. The duration instance variable simply saves the initial value of expireTime. The expireTime variable is continually decremented until it reaches a value of 0, but we need to know its original value for our easing equations. The counter variable records how many times this actor has moved. *Figure 11* shows these variables pictorially.

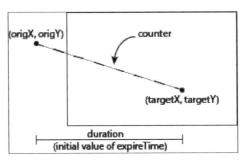

Figure 11: This shows the meaning of the instance variables in PowerItems graphically

The instance variables are initialized in the constructor except for origX and origY, which are initialized in the method addedToWorld() (the purpose of this method was discussed earlier in this chapter), so that we can set them to the current *x* and *y* location of the actor.

Because of our judicious use of functional decomposition, the act() method is straightforward to understand. First, it moves the actor by calling easing(). Next, checkHitAvatar() is called to see if it collided with our hero. This method is abstract, which means its implementation is left to subclasses of this class. This is done because each subclass will want to apply its own unique effect on our hero if they did collide. Last, it checks to see whether the act() method has been called expireTime times. If so, PowerItem has had its desired lifespan, and it's time to remove it. We will talk about the specific implementation of easing(), checkHitAvatar(), and checkExpire() next.

The easing() method is really the key method of this class. It contains a generic form of an easing equation that is flexible enough to allow us to define many different types of interesting movements. The method moves the actor some fraction of the way between the starting point and the endpoint. It starts by calculating the percentage of the distance we need to travel at this point in time between the origin value and the target value in the $x$ direction and a similar calculation for the $y$ direction and saves those values in the local variables fX and fY, respectively. Next, we use the curveX() and curveY() functions to manipulate these percentages, and then we use those percentages in a call to setLocation(). As with checkHitAvatar(), curveX() and curveY() are abstract, as their details depend on the classes that subclass from PowerItems. We'll discuss the abstract methods checkHitAvatar(), curveX(), and curveY(), as well as provide a detailed example in the next section.

Before that, let's look quickly at the last method in the act() method of PowerItems. The last method, checkExpire(), simply removes the actor when expireTime reaches 0.

**Abstract classes**

Abstract classes are an effective way to share code and instance variables between several related classes. In the abstract class, you implement as much code as you can without needing specific knowledge that would be contained in a child class (subclass). For us, the class PowerItems is an abstract class that contains the code common to all of our power-ups and power-downs. Visit http://docs.oracle.com/javase/tutorial/java/IandI/abstract.html for more information on abstract classes.

# Linear easing

The first power-down we are going to add to the game is one that temporarily stuns our hero if touched. Keeping with our game's motif, where good things (smiley faces) are bad, we will make our new power-down look like a cupcake. To create our new Actor, right-click PowerItems in the **Actor classes** section of Greenfoot's main scenario window, and select **New subclass...** from the menu that appears. Name the class Cupcake and choose the image of the muffin (it looks like a cupcake to me!) located in the **food** category.

Open up the Cupcake class in an editor window, and make it look like this:

```
import greenfoot.*;

public class Cupcake extends PowerItems
{
  public Cupcake( int tX, int tY, int eT) {
    super(tX, tY, eT);
  }

  protected double curveX(double f) {
    return f;
  }

  protected double curveY(double f) {
    return f;
  }

  protected void checkHitAvatar() {
    Avatar a = (Avatar) getOneIntersectingObject(Avatar.class);
    if( a != null ) {
      a.stun();
      getWorld().removeObject(this);
    }
  }
}
```

Because we are inheriting from the code from PowerItems, Cupcake is pretty short and concise. The constructor for this class merely passes its parameters to the constructor in PowerItems. Since PowerItems is an abstract class, we need to implement the abstract methods in PowerItems (curveX(), curveY(), and checkHitAvatar()) here.

The Cupcake class is going to be our example of *linear easing*. It will move in constant, linear steps from the starting position to the ending position. Because it is linear, our curveX() and curveY() methods are extremely simple. They don't change the input parameter at all.

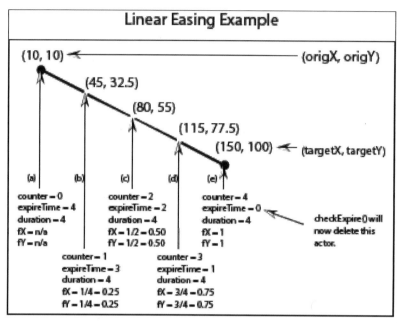

Figure 12: This is an example showing how instances of the Cupcake class move linearly across the screen

Let's look at the example shown in *Figure 12*. In this example, Cupcake was called with the target location **(150, 100)** and an expire time of 4 and was added to the world at the location **(10,10)**. Location **(a)** shows the initial values of the object. Locations **(b)**, **(c)**, **(d)**, and **(e)** show the values associated with the object after one, two, three, and four act() method calls, respectively. As we can see, this actor moves in a straight line. To better understand linear easing, let's discuss why the values are as shown at location **(b)**. After initialization (shown at location **(a)**), the functions in the act() method (inherited from PowerItems) are called. The easing() method sets counter to 1 and then sets fX and fY to 0.25, as shown in this code:

```
double fX = ++counter/duration; // counter is incremented to 1
double fy= counter/duration;   // counter remains 1
```

The `curveX()` and `curveY()` methods in `Cupcake` do not alter `fX` and `fY`. For the given values, the first parameter to `setLocation()` has a value of 45 *((150 * 0.25) + (10 * 0.75))* for its first parameter and 32.5 *((100*0.25) + (10 * 0.75))* for its second parameter.

After `easing()`, the next method called in the `act()` method is `checkHitAvatar()`. This method simply invokes the method `stun()` on an instance of `Avatar` (our hero) if it collides with it. The `stun()` method will be shown after all the power-ups and power-downs have been discussed. At this time, we will show all the changes needed to the `Avatar` class.

# Exponential easing

Now that we have discussed most of the theory behind power-ups and power-downs, we can quickly discuss the remaining ones. The next actor we are going to add is a power-up. It will heal our hero from some of the damage sustained. Given the motif of our game, this beneficial actor will have to look bad. We will make it a rock.

To create our new `Actor` class, right-click on `PowerItems` in the **Actor classes** section of Greenfoot's main scenario window and select **New subclass...** from the menu that appears. Name the class `Rock` and choose the image `rock.png` located in the **nature** category.

Open up the `Rock` class in an editor window and change it to this:

```
import greenfoot.*;

public class Rock extends PowerItems
{

  public Rock( int tX, int tY, int eT ) {
    super(tX, tY, eT);
  }

  protected double curveX(double f) {
    return f;
}

  protected double curveY(double f) {
    return f * f * f;
}

  protected void checkHitAvatar() {
```

```
Avatar a = (Avatar) getOneIntersectingObject(Avatar.class);
if( a != null ) {
  a.addHealth();
  getWorld().removeObject(this);
}
}
}
```

The two main differences between the Cupcake class and the Rock class are the implementation of curveY() and the fact that checkHitAvatar() calls addHealth() instead of stun(). We will describe addHealth() later, as mentioned earlier. The changes in curveY() give this actor a curved directory by cubing the value it is given. The effect of this is demonstrated in the example shown in *Figure 13*. Compare the changes in the *y* position for each location. The *y* value grows exponentially. First, it only moves 1.4 pixels (from location **(a)** to location **(b)**) and in the end, jumps approximately 52 pixels (from location **(d)** to location **(e)**).

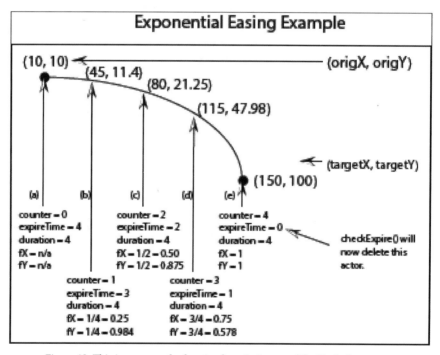

Figure 13: This is an example showing how instances of the Rock class move exponentially in the y direction across the screen

# Sinusoidal easing

The last power-down we are adding is `Clover`. It will slow our hero down for a short time and employ *sinusoidal easing*. To create this class, right-click on `PowerItems` in the **Actor classes** section of Greenfoot's main scenario window and select **New subclass...** from the menu that appears. Name the class `Clover` and choose the image of the `shamrock` located in the **nature** category. Open it in an editor window and change it to this:

```java
import greenfoot.*;
import java.lang.Math;

public class Clover extends PowerItems
{
  public Clover(int tX, int tY, int eT) {
    super(tX, tY, eT);
  }

  protected double curveX(double f) {
    return f;
  }

  protected double curveY(double f) {
    return Math.sin(4*f);
  }

  protected void checkHitAvatar() {
    Avatar a = (Avatar)
    getOneIntersectingObject(Avatar.class);
    if( a != null ) {
      a.lagControls();
      getWorld().removeObject(this);
    }
  }
}
```

Like the `Rock` class, the `Clover` class does something unique in its `curveY()` method. It imports Java's math library at the top of the class and uses `Math.sin()` in its implementation of `curveY()`. This makes the *y* motion oscillate like a sine wave.

In `Clover`, `checkHitAvatar()` calls `lagControls()` on the instance of the `Avatar` class it collided with, instead of `stun()` or `addHealth()`. In the next section, we will implement `stun()`, `addHealth()`, and `lagControls()` in the `Avatar` class.

# Changes to the Avatar class

To accommodate the effects of our new power items, the Avatar class needs to implement a few methods and change some existing ones. These methods are stun(), addHealth(), and lagControls().

 Here's an extra challenge before continuing ahead in the chapter. Try to implement these methods yourself. Think each one through and rough them out on paper. The worst case scenario for attempting this is that you learn a lot.

The implementations of stun() and lagControls() involves adding delay variables and using them to affect movement. In the Avatar class, all movement is handled in the followMouse() method. To stun our hero, we only need to disable the followMouse() method for a small period of time. Here is how we would change this method:

```
private void followMouse() {
  MouseInfo mi = Greenfoot.getMouseInfo();
  if( stunDelay < 0 ) {
    if( mi != null ) {
      setLocation(mi.getX(), mi.getY());
      leftEye.setLocation(getX()-10, getY()-8);
      rightEye.setLocation(getX()+10, getY()-8);
    }
  } else {
    stunDelay--;
  }
}
```

We also need to define the stunDelay instance variable at the top of the class:

```
private int stunDelay = -1;
```

This follows the pattern of usage for the instance variable hitDelay we added at the beginning of this chapter. It was our example of a delay variable. Now, we implement stun():

```
public void stun() {
  stunDelay = 50;
}
```

Every time stun() is invoked, the followMouse() method will not work for 50 cycles (calls of the act() method).

Implementing `lagControls()` is similar, except that we need to temporarily change the movement, instead of blocking it. Again, we need to change the `followMouse()` method:

```
private void followMouse() {
  MouseInfo mi = Greenfoot.getMouseInfo();
  if( stunDelay < 0 ) {
    if( mi != null ) {
      if( lagDelay > 0 ) {
        int stepX = (mi.getX() - getX())/40;
        int stepY = (mi.getY() - getY())/40;
        setLocation(stepX + getX(), stepY + getY());
        --lagDelay;
      } else {
        setLocation(mi.getX(), mi.getY());
      }
      leftEye.setLocation(getX()-10, getY()-8);
      rightEye.setLocation(getX()+10, getY()-8);
    }
  } else {
    stunDelay--;
  }
}
```

Let's first add the instance variable `lagDelay` and then talk about how it is used in `followMouse()`. Add this line at the top of the class under `stunDelay`:

```
private int lagDelay = -1;
```

While `lagDelay` is a value greater than 0, it will implement the laggy controls. In the inner `if-else` statement in the above method, the lag is implemented by only moving our hero one-fortieth of the way to the location of the mouse. This makes our hero slowly crawl towards the location of the mouse. The delay variable, `lagDelay`, is decremented until it is less than 0. How does it get above 0? It is set in the `lagControls()` method called by the `Clover` class. Here is the code for that method:

```
public void lagControls() {
  lagDelay = 150;
}
```

All we need to do now is implement the `addHealth()` method. Here is the code:

```
public void addHealth() {
  if( health < 3 ) {
    health++;
    if( --nextImage == 0 ) {
```

```
      setImage("skull.png");
    } else {
      setImage("skull" + nextImage + ".png");
    }
  }
}
```

This method simply undoes the damage that occurs when we hit an enemy. This
method does nothing if we are already at full health; otherwise, it increments the
`health` instance variable, decrements `nextImage`, so that it stays in sync with the
image we are displaying, and sets the image of the `Avatar` to the previous, less
damaged image. Pretty cool!

We made some substantial changes to the `Avatar` class. Here is its code in
its entirety:

```
import greenfoot.*;
public class Avatar extends Actor {
  private int health = 3;
  private int hitDelay = 0;
  private int stunDelay = -1;
  private int lagDelay = -1;
  private int nextImage = 0;
  private Eye leftEye;
  private Eye rightEye;

  protected void addedToWorld(World w) {
    leftEye = new Eye();
    rightEye = new Eye();
    w.addObject(leftEye, getX()-10, getY()-8);
    w.addObject(rightEye, getX()+10, getY()-8);
  }

  public void act() {
    followMouse();
    checkForCollisions();
  }

  public void addHealth() {
    if( health < 3 ) {
      health++;
      if( --nextImage == 0 ) {
        setImage("skull.png");
      } else {
```

```
      setImage("skull" + nextImage + ".png");
    }
  }
}

public void lagControls() {
  lagDelay = 150;
}

public void stun() {
  stunDelay = 50;
}

private void checkForCollisions() {
  Actor enemy = getOneIntersectingObject(Enemy.class);
  if( hitDelay == 0 && enemy != null ) {
    if( health == 0 ) {
      AvoiderWorld world = (AvoiderWorld) getWorld();
      world.endGame();
    }
    else {
      health--;
      setImage("skull" + ++nextImage + ".png");
      hitDelay = 50;
    }
  }
  if( hitDelay > 0 ) hitDelay--;
}

private void followMouse() {
  MouseInfo mi = Greenfoot.getMouseInfo();
  if( stunDelay < 0 ) {
    if( mi != null ) {
      if( lagDelay > 0 ) {
        int stepX = (mi.getX() - getX())/40;
        int stepY = (mi.getY() - getY())/40;
        setLocation(stepX + getX(), stepY + getY());
        --lagDelay;
      } else {
        setLocation(mi.getX(), mi.getY());
      }
      leftEye.setLocation(getX()-10, getY()-8);
      rightEye.setLocation(getX()+10, getY()-8);
    }
```

```
        } else {
          stunDelay--;
        }
      }
  }
```

We are so close to trying all this out. We just need to randomly create and add the power-ups and power-downs in the `AvoiderWorld` class.

## Changes to the AvoiderWorld class

We need to create three new instance variables at the top of the `AvoiderWorld` class to specify the probability we use to generate one of our new power items. Add these lines of code under the declaration and initialization of `nextLevel`:

```
private int cupcakeFrequency = 10;
private int cloverFrequency = 10;
private int rockFrequency = 1;
```

Initially, the creation of these items will not be very frequent, but we will change that by incrementing them in the `increaseLevel()` function. Here is the code:

```
private void increaseLevel() {
   int score = scoreBoard.getValue();

   if( score > nextLevel ) {
     enemySpawnRate += 3;
     enemySpeed++;
     cupcakeFrequency += 3;
     cloverFrequency += 3;
     rockFrequency += 2;
     nextLevel += 50;
   }
}
```

In the `act()` method, we call a function to generate enemies and another to generate stars. Following this pattern, add this line to the `act()` method:

```
generatePowerItems();
```

Because all of the power item classes inherits from `PowerItems`, we can use polymorphism to write some pretty concise code. Here is the implementation of `generatePowerItems()`:

```
private void generatePowerItems() {
    generatePowerItem(0, cupcakeFrequency); // new Cupcake
    generatePowerItem(1, cloverFrequency); // new Clover
    generatePowerItem(2, rockFrequency); // new Health
}
```

It's pretty nice that we can use one method to create our new power items—`generatePowerItem()`. This method takes an integer describing the type of power item we want to create and a frequency to generate those particular items. Here's the implementation:

```
private void generatePowerItem(int type, int freq) {
    if ( Greenfoot.getRandomNumber(1000) < freq ) {
        int targetX = Greenfoot.getRandomNumber(
        getWidth() -80) + 40;
        int targetY = Greenfoot.getRandomNumber(
        getHeight()/2) + 20;
        Actor a = createPowerItem(type, targetX, targetY, 100);
        if ( Greenfoot.getRandomNumber(100) < 50) {
            addObject(a, getWidth() + 20,
            Greenfoot.getRandomNumber(getHeight()/2) + 30);
        } else {
            addObject(a, -20,
            Greenfoot.getRandomNumber(getHeight()/2) + 30);
        }
    }
}
```

This method looks a lot like our other methods that generate actors. It will generate an item at a given random rate and place those items to emerge from either the left or the right of the screen towards a randomly generated place in the interior of the screen. The local variable `targetX` will be any valid *x* coordinate on the screen, except for a `40` pixel wide border on the left and right of the screen. We just want to ensure that it travels long enough to be seen and that it has an impact on the game. The variable `targetY` has slightly tighter constraints. We only want to generate a *y* value in the upper half of the screen, plus an initial `20` pixels to prevent the actor from traveling too close to the top of the screen. The inner `if-else` statement simply chooses from placing the object either on the left or the right of the screen for its initial location.

The real difference here, from how we generated other actors, is the call to `createPowerItem()`. Since we are using this method to generate any one of three power items, we can't hardcode the creation of a specific item, such as, `new Cupcake();`. We use `createPowerItem()` to create the right object that matches the type parameter of `generatePowerItems()`. Here's the implementation of `createPowerItem()`:

```
private Actor createPowerItem(int type, int targetX, int targetY, int
expireTime) {
  switch(type) {
    case 0: return new Cupcake(targetX, targetY,
    expireTime);
    case 1: return new Clover(targetX, targetY,
    expireTime);
    case 2: return new Rock(targetX, targetY,
    expireTime);
  }
  return null;
}
```

This method creates a new `Cupcake`, `Clover`, or `Rock` power item based on type.

We have really added a lot to this game, and now it's time to compile and test it out. Normally, you would not want to add this much code without testing small parts along the way. For example, we could have just implemented the `Rock` power-up completely and tested it before adding the other power items. For pedagogical reasons, it made sense to continue in the manner we did. I hope you don't encounter too many typos when you compile your code. By methodically checking your code against the code in this chapter and paying close attention to the compile error messages, you should be able to eliminate any mistakes quickly.

 If you need to refresh yourself on how a Java switch statement works, refer to the following link:

`http://docs.oracle.com/javase/tutorial/java/`
`nutsandbolts/switch.html`

Compile, debug, and play. This game is getting good. Check out my screenshot in *Figure 14.*

Figure 14: Here's Avoider Game complete with power-ups, power-downs, and all sorts of bling

# Avoider Game

Our Avoider Game is getting more complete and fun to play. In *Chapter 5, Interactive Application Design and Theory*, we will look at game design theory on how to build fun and engaging games. At that time, we will revisit our game and increase its playability.

# Your assignment

When an `Avatar` object is hit, it is invulnerable to being hit again for a short time. Unfortunately, we have provided no visual feedback to the player that indicates this is happening or when it expires. Your assignment is to make the hero blink while it cannot be hit. Look at the `Star` class for a hint on how to make an object blink.

# Summary

We covered a lot of material in this chapter. You learned several important techniques for animating actors, including image swapping, delay variables, parallax, and easing. Our enemies, our hero, and the background, all have more life. You should use all the techniques of this chapter when creating games, simulations, animated shots, or educational applications.

# 3

# Collision Detection

*"Live as if you were to die tomorrow. Learn as if you were to live forever."*

*– Mahatma Gandhi*

Often, you will need to determine whether two or more objects are touching in Greenfoot. This is known as *collision detection* and it is necessary for most simulations and games. Detection algorithms range from simple bounding-box methods to very complex pixel color analysis. Greenfoot provides a wide variety of simple methods to accomplish collision detection; you were introduced to some of them in *Chapter 1, Let's Dive Right in...*, and *Chapter 2, Animation*. In this chapter, you will learn how to use Greenfoot's other built-in collision detection mechanisms and then learn more accurate methods to use them to do collision detection. While pixel-perfect collision detection is beyond the scope of this book, the border-based and hidden-sprite methods of collision detection will be sufficient for most Greenfoot applications. The topics that will be covered in this chapter are:

- Greenfoot built-in methods
- Border-based methods
- Hidden-sprite methods

We will take a break from working on Avoider Game and use a simple zombie invasion simulation to illustrate our collision detection methods. Zombies seem apropos for this chapter. Judging from his quote above, I think Gandhi wanted you to learn as if you were a zombie.

# ZombieInvasion interactive simulation

In *Chapter 1*, *Let's Dive Right in...* and *Chapter 2*, *Animation*, we went step by step in building Avoider Game and ended up with playable versions of the game by the end of each chapter. In the zombie simulation, we will watch a horde of zombies break through a wall and make their way to the homes on the other side. The user will be able to interact with the simulation by placing explosions in the simulation, that will destroy both types of zombies and the wall. For our zombie simulation, I am going to supply most of the code in the beginning, and we will concentrate our efforts on implementing collision detection. All the code supplied uses concepts and techniques we covered in the last two chapters, and it should look very familiar. We will just provide an overview discussion of the code here. *Figure 1* provides a picture of our scenario.

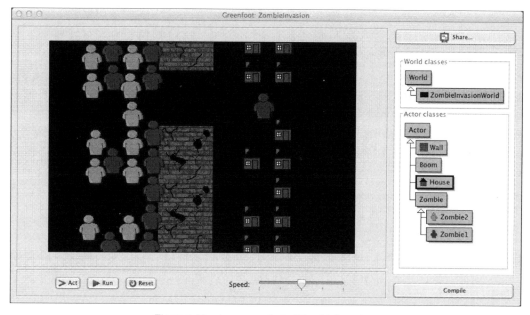

Figure 1: Here's a screenshot of ZombieInvasion

Let's create a new scenario called `ZombieInvasion` and then incrementally add and discuss the `World` subclass and `Actor` subclasses. Alternatively, you can download the initial version of **ZombieInvasion** at: `http://www.packtpub.com/support`

# Dynamically creating actors in ZombieInvasionWorld

This class has two main responsibilities: placing all the actors in the world and creating an explosion whenever the mouse is clicked. For the most part, the user will just observe the scenario and will only be able to interact with it by creating explosions. The `ZombieInvasionWorld` class is rather simple because we are creating an interactive simulation and not a game. Here's the code to accomplish this:

```java
import greenfoot.*;

public class ZombieInvasionWorld extends World {
  private static final int DELAY = 200;
  int bombDelayCounter = 0; // Controls the rate of bombs

  public ZombieInvasionWorld() {
   super(600, 400, 1);
   prepare();
  }

  public void act() {
   if( bombDelayCounter > 0 ) bombDelayCounter--;
   if( Greenfoot.mouseClicked(null) && (bombDelayCounter == 0) ) {
     MouseInfo mi = Greenfoot.getMouseInfo();
     Boom pow = new Boom();
     addObject(pow, mi.getX(), mi.getY());
     bombDelayCounter = DELAY;
   }
  }

  private void prepare() {
   int i,j;
   for( i=0; i<5; i++) {
     Wall w = new Wall();
     addObject(w, 270, w.getImage().getHeight() * i);
   }
   for( i=0; i<2; i++) {
     for( j=0; j<8; j++) {
      House h = new House();
      addObject(h, 400 + i*60, (12 +h.getImage().getHeight()) * j);
     }
   }
   for( i=0; i<2; i++) {
```

```
    for( j=0; j<8; j++) {
      Zombie1 z = new Zombie1();
      addObject(z, 80 + i*60, 15 + (2 +z.getImage().getHeight()) * j);
    }
  }
  for( i=0; i<2; i++) {
    for( j=0; j<7; j++) {
      Zombie2 z = new Zombie2();
      addObject(z, 50 + i*60, 30 + (3 +z.getImage().getHeight()) * j);
    }
  }
 }
}
```

When you right-click on the scenario screen and choose **Save the World** in the pop-up menu, Greenfoot will automatically create the prepare() method for you and will supply the appropriate code to add each Actor on the screen. This creates the initial state of your scenario (the one the user sees when they first run your scenario). In ZombieInvasionWorld, we are manually implementing the prepare() method and can do so in a more compact way than Greenfoot. We use for-loops to add our actors. Via this method, we add Wall, House, Zombie1, and Zombie2. We will implement these classes later in the chapter.

The act() method is responsible for listening for mouse-click events. If the mouse is clicked, we add a Boom object at the current position of the mouse. Boom is an actor we create just to display the explosion, and we want it placed exactly where the mouse was clicked. We use a delay variable, boomDelayCounter, to prevent the user from rapidly creating too many explosions. Remember, we explained delay variables in detail in the previous chapter, *Chapter 2, Animation*. If you want the user to have the ability to rapidly create explosions, then simply remove the delay variable.

# Creating obstacles

We will create two obstacles for our zombie horde: houses and walls. In the simulation, the House object has no functionality. It is simply an obstacle to zombie actors:

```
import greenfoot.*;

public class House extends Actor {
}
```

The code for the House class is extremely simple. Its sole purpose is just to add an image (buildings/house-8.png) of a house to Actor. It has no other functionality.

Walls are more complex than houses. As the zombies beat on the walls, they slowly crumble. The majority of the code for the `Wall` class implements this animation, as shown in the following code:

```
import greenfoot.*;
import java.util.List;

public class Wall extends Actor {
    int wallStrength = 2000;
    int wallStage = 0;

    public void act() {
     crumble();
    }

    private void crumble() {
      // We will implement this in the next section...
    }

}
```

The implementation of the animation of the `Wall` class crumbling is very similar to that of the `Avatar` class taking damage that we looked at, in the previous chapter, *Chapter 2, Animation*. The interesting code is all contained in the `crumble()` method, which is called repeatedly from the `act()` method. *Figure 1* shows the walls in various states of decay. We will implement and explain in detail the `crumble()` method in the *Detecting a collision with multiple objects* section.

# Creating our main actor framework

The `Zombie` class contains all the code that describes the behavior for zombies in our simulation. Zombies continually lumber forward trying to get to the humans in the houses. They beat on and eventually destroy any walls in the way, as shown in the following code:

```
import greenfoot.*;
import java.util.*;

public class Zombie extends Actor {
    int counter, stationaryX, amplitude;

    protected void addedToWorld(World w) {
      stationaryX = getX();
      amplitude = Greenfoot.getRandomNumber(6) + 2;
```

```
  }

  public void act() {
    shake();
    if( canMarch() ) {
      stationaryX = stationaryX + 2;
    }
  }

  public void shake() {
    counter++;
    setLocation((int)(stationaryX + amplitude*Math.sin(counter/2)),
 getY());
  }

  private boolean canMarch() {
    // We will implement this in the next section...
    return false; // Temporary return value
  }
}
```

The two important methods in this class are `shake()` and `canMarch()`. The `shake()` method implements the back-and-forth lumbering movement of the zombies. It calls `setLocation()` and leaves the *y* coordinate unchanged. It changes the *x* coordinate to have sinusoidal motion (back and forth). The distance it moves back and forth is defined by the `amplitude` variable. This type of motion was also used by one of the power-downs described in *Chapter 2, Animation* and is shown in *Figure 2*.

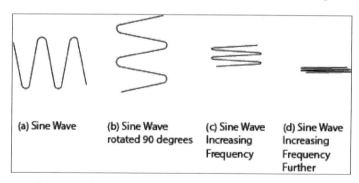

Figure 2: This is an illustration of using a sine wave to produce back and forth motion in Zombie objects. We start with a standard sine wave (a), rotate it 90 degrees (b), and reduce the amount we move in the y direction until the desired effect is achieved (not moving in the y-direction). Callouts (c) and (d) show the effects of reducing movement in the y direction.

We will fully implement and explain `canMarch()` in the *Detecting a collision with multiple objects* section. The method `canMarch()` checks surrounding actors (houses, walls, or other zombies) to see whether any are in the way of the zombie moving forward. As a temporary measure, we insert the following line at the end of `canMarch()`:

```
return false;
```

This allows us to compile and test the code. By always returning `false,` the `Zombie` objects will never move forward. This is a simple placeholder, and we will implement the real response later in the chapter.

We have two subclasses of the `Zombie` class: `Zombie1` and `Zombie2`:

```
public class Zombie1 extends Zombie {
}
public class Zombie2 extends Zombie {
}
```

This allows us to have two different-looking zombies but only write code for zombie behavior once. I chose to have a blue (`people/pp11.png`) zombie and a yellow-orange (`people/pp13.png`) zombie. If you have any artistic skill, you might want to create your own PNG images to use. Otherwise, you can continue to use the images provided with Greenfoot, as I have done.

# Creating an explosion

Here is the implementation of the `Boom` class we discussed previously in the description of the `ZombieInvasionWorld` class. The `Boom` class will immediately draw an explosion that will wipe out everything contained in the blast and then linger for a short time before disappearing. We create an explosion using the following code:

```
import greenfoot.*;
import java.awt.Color;
import java.util.List;

public class Boom extends Actor {
    private static final int BOOMLIFE = 50;
    private static final int BOOMRADIUS = 50;
    int boomCounter = BOOMLIFE;

    public Boom() {
        GreenfootImage me = new GreenfootImage
        (BOOMRADIUS*2,BOOMRADIUS*2);
```

```
      me.setColor(Color.RED);
      me.setTransparency(125);
      me.fillOval(0 , 0, BOOMRADIUS * 2, BOOMRADIUS*2);
      setImage(me);
  }

  public void act() {
     if( boomCounter == BOOMLIFE)
     destroyEverything(BOOMRADIUS);
     if( boomCounter-- == 0 ) {
        World w = getWorld();
        w.removeObject(this);
     }
  }

  private void destroyEverything(int x) {
     // We will implement this in the next section...
  }
}
```

Let's discuss the constructor (Boom()) and act() methods. The Boom() method creates an image manually using the drawing methods of GreenfootImage. We used these drawing methods in this way to draw the stars and eyes in AvoiderGame, which we presented over the last two chapters, *Chapter 1, Let's Dive Right in...*, and *Chapter 2, Animation*. The constructor concludes by setting this new image to be the image of the actor using setImage().

The act() method has an interesting use of a delay variable. Instead of waiting for a certain amount of time (in terms of the number of calls to the act() method) before allowing an event to occur, the boomCounter delay variable is used to control how long this Boom object lives. After a short delay, the object is removed from the scenario.

We will discuss the implementation of the destroyEverything() method in a later section.

# Test it out

You should now have a nearly complete zombie invasion simulation. Let's compile our scenario and make sure we eliminate any typos or mistakes introduced while adding the code. The scenario will not do much. The zombies will lumber back and forth but not make any forward progress. You can click anywhere in the running scenario and see the Boom explosion; however, it won't destroy anything yet.

Let's make this scenario a bit more interesting, using Greenfoot's collision detection methods.

# Built-in collision detection methods

We are going to go through all the methods provided by Greenfoot to do collision detection. First, we will go over some methods and discuss their intended use. Then, we'll discuss the remaining methods in the context of more advanced collision detection methods (border-based and hidden-sprite). We have already used a few collision detection methods in the implementation of Avoider Game. We will only briefly describe those particular methods here. Finally, we will not discuss `getNeighbors()` and `intersects()`, as those methods are only useful for Greenfoot scenarios that contain worlds that are created with a cell size greater than one.

> **Cell size and Greenfoot worlds**
>
> Until now, we have only created worlds (`AvoiderWorld` and `ZombieInvasionWorld`) that have set the `cellSize` parameter of the `World` constructor to 1. The following is an excerpt from Greenfoot's documentation on the `World` class:
>
> ```
> public World(int worldWidth, int worldHeight, int
> cellSize)
> ```
>
> Construct a new world. The size of the world (in number of cells) and the size of each cell (in pixels) must be specified.
>
> Parameters:
> worldWidth - The width of the world (in cells).
> worldHeight - The height of the world (in cells).
> cellSize - Size of a cell in pixels.
>
> The simple tutorials provided on Greenfoot's website mainly use large cell sizes. This makes game movement, trajectories, and collision detection very simple. We, on the other hand, want to create more flexible games that allow for smooth motion and more realistic animation. Therefore, we define our game cells to be 1 x 1 pixels (one pixel) and, correspondingly, will not discuss methods that target worlds with large cell sizes, such as `getNeighbors()` and `intersects()`.

As we go through our discussion, remember that we will, at times, add code to our `ZombieInvasion` scenario.

# Detecting a collision with a single object

The method `getOneIntersectingObject()` is great for simple collision detection and often used to see whether a bullet, or other type of enemy, hit the main protagonist of the game in order to subtract health, subtract life, or end the game. This is the method we used and explained in *Chapter 1, Let's Dive Right in...*, to build our first working version of Avoider Game. We will not discuss it again here and only mention it in the next section as a means to illustrate the use of `isTouching()` and `removeTouching()`.

## isTouching() and removeTouching()

The following is a common pattern for using `getOneIntersectingObject()`:

```
private void checkForCollisions() {
  Actor enemy = getOneIntersectingObject(Enemy.class);
  if( enemy != null ) { // If not empty, we hit an Enemy
    AvoiderWorld world = (AvoiderWorld) getWorld();
    world.removeObject(this);
  }
}
```

We used this basic pattern in Avoider Game several times. The `isTouching()` and `removeTouching()` methods provide a more compact way to implement the preceding pattern. Here is an equivalent function using `isTouching()` and `removeTouching()` instead of `getOneIntersectingObject()`:

```
private void checkForCollisions() {
  if( isTouching(Enemy.class) ) {
    removeTouching(Enemy.class);
  }
}
```

If all you're doing is removing an object that the object intersects with, all you need is the `isTouching()` and `removeTouching()` methods. However, if you want to do something with the object that you're intersecting with, which requires calling methods of the object's class, then you need to store the intersected object in a named variable, which requires using the `getOneIntersectingObject()` method.

In general, always use `getOneIntersectingObject()` instead of `isTouching()` and `removeTouching()`. It is more flexible and provides code that is easier to extend in the future.

# Detecting a collision with multiple objects

The collision detection method `getIntersectingObjects()` returns a list of all the actors in a given class that the calling actor is touching. This method is needed when you need to take an action on every object that is touching a specific actor, or you need to change the state of an actor based on the number of objects touching it. When using `getOneIntersectingObject()`, you are only concerned about being touched by at least one object of a given type. For example, in the game *PacMan*, you lose a life anytime you touch a ghost. It wouldn't matter if you ran into one, two, or three; the end result would be the same—you'd lose a life. However, in our zombie simulation, the `Wall` actors take damage based on how many zombies are presently beating on it. This is a perfect use for `getIntersectingObjects()`.

In the `Wall` code presented above, we left out the implementation of the `crumble()` method. Here is that code:

```
private void crumble() {
  List<Zombie> army = getIntersectingObjects(Zombie.class);
  wallStrength = wallStrength - army.size();
  if( wallStrength < 0 ) {
    wallStage++;
    if( wallStage > 4 ) {
      World w = getWorld();
      w.removeObject(this);
    }
    else {
      changeImage();
      wallStrength = 2000;
    }
  }
}

private void changeImage() {
  setImage("brick"+wallStage+".png");
}
```

Let's quickly go over the things we saw before. In the *Hurting the avatar* section of *Chapter 2, Animation*, we changed the image of the avatar to look damaged every time it was touched by an enemy. We are using the same animation technique here to make it look like walls are taking damage. However, in this code, we have given walls a durability property that is defined by the `wallStrength` variable. The value of `wallStrength` determines how many times a wall can be hit by a zombie before it visibly looks more crumbled and cracked.

The `wallStrength` variable is actually just an example of a delay variable that we discussed in the previous chapter, *Chapter 2, Animation*. Instead of this variable delaying a certain amount of time, it is delaying a certain number of zombie hits. When `wallStrength` is less than 0, we change the image using the method `changeImage()` unless this is the fourth time we have crumbled, which will cause us to remove the wall altogether. *Figure 3* shows the wall images I created and used for this animation.

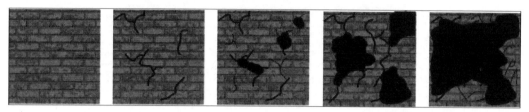

Figure 3: These are the four images used to animate the walls crumbling

Now, let's discuss the collision detection method `getIntersectingObjects()`. When called, this method will return all objects of a given class that intersect with the calling object. You specify the class of objects you are interested in by providing it as the argument to this method. In our code, I provided the argument `Zombie.class`, so the method would only return all the zombies that are touching the wall. Because of inheritance, we will get all of the `Zombie1` objects and all of the `Zombie2` objects that intersect. You can access, manipulate, or iterate through the objects returned using the methods defined in the `List` interface. For our purposes, we only wanted to count how many zombies we collided with. We get this number by calling the `size()` method on the `List` object returned from `getIntersectingObjects()`.

**Java interfaces and List**

The collision detection method `getIntersectingObjects()` introduces us for the first time to the `List` interface. In Java, interfaces are used to define a certain set of methods that two or more classes will have in common. When Java classes implement an interface, that class is promising that it implements all of the methods defined in that interface. So, the collection of `Actor` objects returned by `getIntersectingObjects()` could be stored in an array, linked list, queue, tree, or any other data structure. Whatever the data structure used for storing these objects, we know that we can access those objects via the methods defined in the `List` interface, such as `get()` or `size()`.

For more information, refer to the following link: `http://docs.oracle.com/javase/tutorial/java/IandI/createinterface.html`.

In our ZombieInvasion simulation, we need to use getIntersectingObjects() one more time. Earlier, we left the implementation of canMarch() incomplete when we looked at the code for the Zombie class. Let's implement that method now using getIntersectingObjects(). Here is the code:

```
private boolean canMarch() {
  List<Actor> things = getIntersectingObjects(Actor.class);
  for( int i = 0; i < things.size(); i++ ) {
    if ( things.get(i).getX() > getX() + 20 ) {
      return false;
    }
  }
  return true;
}
```

This method checks whether or not there are any actors in the way of this object moving forward. It accomplishes this by first getting all objects of the Actor class that are touching it and then checking each one to see if it is in front of this object. We do not care if Actor is touching the calling object at the top, bottom, or back as these actors will not prevent this object from moving forward. This line of code in canMarch() gives us the list of all intersecting actors:

```
List<Actor> things = getIntersectingObjects(Actor.class);
```

We then iterate through the list of actors using a for loop. To access an item in a list, you use the get() method. The get() method has one formal parameter that specifies the index of the object in the list that you want. For each actor in the list, we check to see if the x coordinate is in front of us. If it is, we return false (we can't move); otherwise, we return true (we can move).

We have added the implementation of the crumble() method to the Wall class (don't forget to add changeImage() too) and the implementation of canMarch() to the Zombie class. Let's compile our scenario and observe what happens. Our simulation is almost complete. The only thing missing is the implementation of the destroyEverything() method in the Boom class. We will look at that implementation next.

# Detecting multiple objects in range

The last method we need to implement to complete our simulation is
`destroyEverything()`. In this method, we will use the Greenfoot collision detection
method `getObjectsInRange()`. This method takes two parameters. We have seen the
second parameter in all of the rest of the collision detection methods, and it specifies
the class of actors we are testing for collision. The first parameter provides the radius
of a circle drawn around the actor that defines where to search for collision. *Figure
4* shows the relationship between the `radius` parameter and the search area. Unlike
`getIntersectingObjects()`, `getObjectsInRange()` returns a list of actors that are
within the range specified by the calling object.

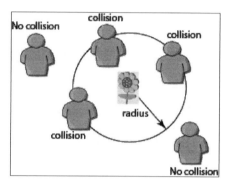

Figure 4: This shows the purpose of the radius parameter of the getObjectsInRange() method

Now that we know about the method `getObjectsInRange()`, let's look at the
implementation of `destroyEverything()`:

```
private void destroyEverything(int x) {
  List<Actor> objs = getObjectsInRange(x, Actor.class);
  World w = getWorld();
  w.removeObjects(objs);
}
```

This method is short, yet powerful. It calls `getObjectsInRange()` with a radius `x`,
the value that was passed to `destroyEverything()` when called, and `Actor.class`,
which in Greenfoot terms means everything. All objects within the circle defined
by the radius will be returned by `getObjectsInRange()` and stored in the `objs`
variable. Now, we could iterate through all the objects contained in `objs` and remove
them one at a time. Luckily, Greenfoot provides a function that can remove a list of
objects with one call. Here's its definition in Greenfoot's documentation:

```
public void removeObjects(java.util.Collection objects)
Remove a list of objects from the world.

Parameters:
objects - A list of Actors to remove.
```

# Time to test it out

The simulation is complete. Compile and run it and make sure everything works as anticipated. Remember, you can click anywhere to blow up buildings, walls, and zombies. Reset the scenario and move things around. Add walls and zombies and see what happens. Nice work!

# Border-based collision detection methods

Border-based collision detection involves incrementally searching outward from Actor until either a collision is detected, or it is determined there are no obstacles in the way. The method finds the edge (or border) of the item collided with. This method is especially useful when objects need to bounce off each other or one object is landing on another and needs to remain on that object for a certain amount of time, for example, when a user-controlled Actor is jumping on a platform. We will introduce this method of collision detection in this chapter, as well as use it in upcoming chapters.

# Detecting single-object collisions at an offset

The *at offset* versions of Greenfoot's collision detection methods are well suited to border-based collision detection. They allow us to check for a collision at a certain distance, or offset, from the center of the calling Actor. To demonstrate the use of this method, we will change the implementation of the canMarch() method in the Zombie class. Here is our revised version:

```
private boolean canMarch() {
   int i=0;
   while(i<=step) {
     int front = getImage().getWidth()/2;
     Actor a = getOneObjectAtOffset(i+front, 0, Actor.class);
     if( a != null ) {
       return false;
     }
     i++;
   }
   return true;
}
```

Typically, when an actor moves, it will change its position by a certain number of pixels. In the `Zombie` class, how far zombies will move, if they can, is stored in the `step` variable. We need to declare and initialize this instance variable by inserting the following line of code at the top of the `Zombie` class, as follows:

```
private int step = 4;
```

Using a `step` variable to store the length of movement for an actor is common practice. In the implementation of `canMarch()` above, we check each pixel in front of a zombie up to and including taking a full step. This is handled by the `while` loop. We increment the variable `i` from `0` to `step`, checking for a collision each time at the location `i + front`. Since the origin location of an object is its center, we set `front` to be half of the width of the image representing this actor. *Figure 5* illustrates this search.

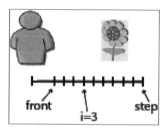

Figure 5: Using border-based detection, an object searches for a collision one pixel at a time. It starts from its front and then searches for an object starting at front + 0 all the way to front + step.

If we detect a collision any time in our while loop, we return `false`, indicating the actor cannot move forward; otherwise, we return `true`. Test out this new version of `canMarch()`.

# Detecting multiple-object collisions at an offset

The collision detection method `getObjectsAtOffset()` is very similar to `getOneObjectAtOffset()`. It just, as the name implies, returns all actors that collide at the given offset. To demonstrate its use, we are going to re-implement `canMarch()` as we did for `getOneObjectAtOffset()`. To take advantage of getting a list of actors that collide, we are going to add some additional functionality to `canMarch()`. For each actor blocking the forward movement of the zombie, we are going to shove them a little.

Here's the implementation of `canMarch()`:

```
private boolean canMarch() {
  int front = getImage().getWidth()/2;
  int i = 1;
  while(i<=step) {
    List<Actor> a = getObjectsAtOffset(front+i,0,Actor.class);
    if( a.size() > 0 ) {
      for(int j=0;j<a.size()&&a.get(j) instanceof Zombie;j++){
        int toss = Greenfoot.getRandomNumber(100)<50 ? 1 : -1;
        Zombie z = (Zombie) a.get(j);
        z.setLocation(z.getX(),z.getY()+toss);
      }
      return false;
    }
    i++;
  }
  return true;
}
```

In this version, we use a `while` loop and `step` variable in much the same way we did previously for the `getOneObjectAtOffset()` version of `canMarch()`. Inside the `while` loop is where we added the new "shoving" functionality. When we detect that there is at least one `Actor` in the list, we iterate through the list using a `for` loop to slightly push each actor we collided with. The first thing we do in the `for` loop is check whether or not the `Actor` class is a `Zombie` class using the `instanceof` operator. If it isn't, we skip over it. We don't want the ability to shove `Wall` or `House`. For each zombie we collided with, we set the `toss` variable to `1` or `-1` with equal probability We then move that zombie with `setLocation()`. The effect is interesting and gives the illusion that the zombies are trying to push and shove their way to the front. Compile and run the scenario with the changes to `canMarch()` and see for yourself. *Figure 6* shows how the zombies bunch up with the preceding changes.

**The instanceof Operator**

Java's `instanceof` operator checks whether the left-hand side argument is an object created from the class (or any of its subclasses) specified on the right-hand side. It will return `true` if it is and `false` otherwise. It will also return `true` if the left-hand side object implements the interface specified on the right-hand side.

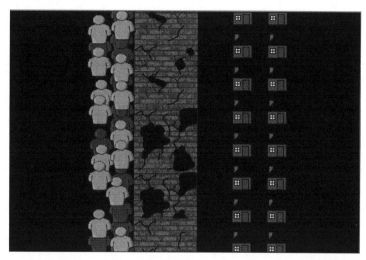

Figure 6: Here's a view of the zombies pushing and shoving to get to the humans in the houses first

# Hidden-sprite collision detection methods

One flaw with the `getOneObjectAtOffets()` and `getObjectsAtOffset()` methods is that they only check the granularity of a single pixel. If an object of interest is one pixel above or below the offset provided to these methods, then no collision will be detected. In fact, in this implementation, if you allow the simulation to run until the zombies reach the houses, you'll notice that some zombies can move past the houses. This is because the pixel-only check fails between houses. One way to handle this deficiency is to use hidden-sprite collision detection. *Figure 7* illustrates this method.

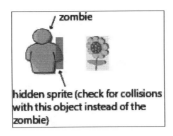

Figure 7: This shows the use of a hidden sprite to check for collisions.

In the hidden-sprite method, you use another `Actor` class to test for collisions. *Figure 7* shows a `Zombie` object using a smaller, auxiliary `Actor` class to determine if a collision occurred with the flower. While the hidden sprite is shown as a translucent red rectangle, in practice, we would set the transparency (using `setTransparency()` to `0`, so that it would not be visible. The hidden-sprite method is very flexible because you can create any shape or size for your hidden sprite, and it does not have the problem of only looking at a single pixel that the two previous collision detection methods had. Next, we will once again change the `canMarch()` method in the `Zombie` class, this time using hidden-sprite collision detection.

The first thing we need to do, is create a new `Actor` that will serve as the hidden sprite. Because we are going to use this hidden sprite for zombies, let's call it `ZombieHitBox`. Create this subclass of `Actor` now and do not associate an image with it. We will draw the image in the constructor. Here is the implementation of `ZombieHitBox`:

```java
import greenfoot.*;
import java.awt.Color;
import java.util.*;

public class ZombieHitBox extends Actor {
    GreenfootImage body;
    int offsetX;
    int offsetY;
    Actor host;

    public ZombieHitBox(Actor a, int w, int h, int dx, int dy, boolean
visible) {
        host = a;
        offsetX = dx;
        offsetY = dy;
        body = new GreenfootImage(w, h);
        if( visible ) {
            body.setColor(Color.red);
```

```
      // Transparency values range from 0 (invisible)
      // to 255 (opaque)
      body.setTransparency(100);
      body.fill();
    }
    setImage(body);
  }

  public void act() {
    if( host.getWorld() != null ) {
      setLocation(host.getX()+offsetX, host.getY()+offsetY);
    } else {
      getWorld().removeObject(this);
    }
  }

  public List getHitBoxIntersections() {
    return getIntersectingObjects(Actor.class);
  }
}
```

The constructor for ZombieHitBox takes six parameters. The reason it takes so many parameters is that we need to provide the Actor class to which it is attached (the a parameter), define the size of the rectangle to draw (the w and h parameters), provide the offset of the rectangle from the provided Actor (the dx and dy parameters), and check whether the hidden sprite is visible (the visible parameter). In the constructor, we use GreenfootImage(), setColor(), setTransparency(), fill(), and setImage() to draw the hidden sprite. We went over these methods previously in *Chapter 2, Animation*.

We use the act() method to ensure that this hidden sprite moves along with the Actor class it is attached to (we will call this the host actor). To do this, we simply call setLocation(), provide the current *x* and *y* position of the host actor and shift a little according to the offset values provided in the constructor. Before doing this, however, we check whether the host has not been deleted. If it has, we delete the hit box, as it only has meaning in relation to host. This handles the case where an explosion destroys host, but did not quite reach the hit box.

Finally, we provide one public method that the host actor will use to get all the actors that are colliding with the hidden sprite. We named this method as getHitBoxIntersections().

Next, we need to augment the `Zombie` class to use this new hidden sprite. We need a handle on this hidden sprite, so we need to add a new property to the `Zombie` class. Insert this line of code under the declaration of the `step` variable:

```
private ZombieHitBox zbh;
```

Next, we need to augment the `addedToWorld()` method to create and connect `ZombieHitBox` to `Zombie`. Here is the implementation of that method:

```
protected void addedToWorld(World w) {
    stationaryX = getX();
    amplitude = Greenfoot.getRandomNumber(6) + 2;
    zbh = new ZombieHitBox(this, 10, 25, 10, 5, true);
    getWorld().addObject(zbh, getX(), getY());
}
```

We create a 10 x 25 rectangle for our hidden sprite and initially make it visible, so that we can test it in our scenario. Once you are satisfied with the placement and size of your hidden sprite, you should change the `visible` parameter of `ZombieHitBox` from `true` to `false`.

Now that we have created, initialized, and placed `ZombieHitBox`, we can make our changes to `canMarch()` to demonstrate the use of the hidden-sprite method:

```
private boolean canMarch() {
   if( zbh.getWorld() != null ) {
     List<Actor> things = zbh.getHitBoxIntersections();
     if( things.size() > 1 ) {
       int infront = 0;
       for(int i=0; i < things.size(); i++ ) {
         Actor a = things.get(i);
         if( a == this || a instanceof ZombieHitBox)
         continue;
         if( a instanceof Zombie) {
           int toss =
           Greenfoot.getRandomNumber(100)<50 ? 1:-1;
           infront += (a.getX() > getX()) ? 1 : 0;
           if( a.getX() >= getX() )
           a.setLocation(a.getX(),a.getY()+toss);
         } else {
           return false;
         }
       }
     }
     if( infront > 0 ) {
       return false;
     } else {
```

```
            return true;
        }
    }
    return true;
} else {
    getWorld().removeObject(this);
}
    return false;
}
```

Unlike previous implementations of `canMarch()`, we need to first ask the hidden sprite for a list of actors colliding with this zombie. Once we get that list, we check that it has a size greater than one. The reason why it needs to be greater than one, is that `ZombieHitBox` will include the zombie it is attached to. If we are not colliding with any other zombies or actors, we return `true`. If we are colliding with a number of actors, then we iterate through them all and make some decisions based on the type of `Actor`. If `Actor` is this zombie or an instance of `ZombieHitBox`, we skip it and don't take any action. The next check is whether or not `Actor` is an instance of the `Zombie` class. If it isn't, then it is some other object, such as `House` or `Wall`, and we return `false`, so that we will not move forward. If it is an instance of the `Zombie` class, we check whether or not it is in front of this zombie. If it is, we shove it a little (just as we did in the previous implementation of `canMarch()`) and increment the `infront` variable. At the end of iterating through the list of actors, we check the `infront` variable. If there were any zombies in front of this zombie, we return `false` to prevent it from moving forward. Otherwise, we return `true`. The outermost `if` statement simply checks that the hitbox (`zbh`) associated with this object has not been previously destroyed by a `Boom` object. If it has, then we need to remove this object too.

Compile and run this version of the scenario. You should observe that the zombies bunch up nicely, push and shove each other, yet they are not able to move past the houses. Using the hidden-sprite method of collision detection is a bit more complex than the rest, but gives us good accuracy.

# Challenge

Okay, we have implemented several forms of collision detection in our zombie simulation. Which method of collision detection do you prefer for this simulation?

For a challenge, create an `Actor` ball that occasionally rolls in from the left and knocks zombies out of the way. If the ball hits `Wall`, have it do 1,000 damage to it. Which form of collision detection will you use to detect collisions between the ball and zombies and between the ball and a wall?

# Summary

Collision detection is a crucial component of any game, simulation, or interactive application. Greenfoot provides built-in methods of detecting collisions. In this chapter, we carefully explained each of these methods and then demonstrated how you could use them to do more advanced collision detection. Specifically, we discussed border-based and hidden-sprite techniques. Moving forward, we will use collision detection often and will choose a method appropriate for our example. In the next chapter, we will look at projectiles and will have ample opportunity to put into practice what you have learned in this chapter.

# 4
# Projectiles

*"Flying is learning how to throw yourself at the ground and miss."*

*– Douglas Adams*

Actors in creative Greenfoot applications, such as games and animations, often have movement that can best be described as *being launched*. For example, a soccer ball, bullet, laser, light ray, baseball, and firework are examples of this type of object. One common method of implementing this type of movement is to create a set of classes that model real-world physical properties (mass, velocity, acceleration, friction, and so on) and have game or simulation actors inherit from these classes. Some refer to this as creating a *physics engine* for your game or simulation. However, this course of action is complex and often overkill. As you learned in *Chapter 2, Animation*, there are often simple heuristics we can use to approximate realistic motion. This is the approach we will take here.

In this chapter, you will learn about the basics of projectiles, how to make an object bounce, and a little about particle effects. We will apply what you learn to a small platform game that we will build up over the course of this chapter. In this chapter, we will cover the following topics:

- Gravity and jumping
- Bouncing
- Particle effects
- Bullets and turrets

Creating realistic flying objects is not simple, but we will cover this topic in a methodical, step-by-step approach, and when we are done, you will be able to populate your creative scenarios with a wide variety of flying, jumping, and launched objects. It's not as simple as Douglas Adams makes it sound in his quote, but nothing worth learning ever is.

# Cupcake Counter

It is beneficial to the learning process to discuss topics in the context of complete scenarios. Doing this forces us to handle issues that might be elided in smaller, one-off examples. In this chapter, we will build a simple platform game called **Cupcake Counter** (shown in *Figure 1*). We will first look at a majority of the code for the **World** and **Actor** classes in this game without showing the code implementing the topic of this chapter, that is, the different forms of projectile-based movement. We will then present and explain the missing code in subsequent sections. This is the same approach we took in the preceding chapter, in order to study collision detection.

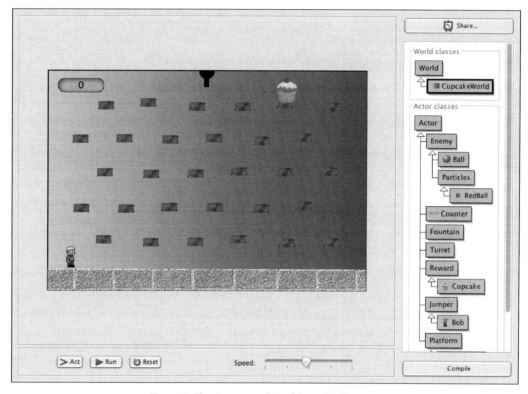

Figure 1: This is a screenshot of Cupcake Counter

# How to play

The goal of **Cupcake Counter** is to collect as many cupcakes as you can before being hit by either a ball or a fountain. The left and right arrow keys move your character left and right and the up arrow key makes your character jump. You can also use the space bar key to jump. After touching a cupcake, it will disappear and reappear randomly on another platform. Balls will be fired from the turret at the top of the screen and fountains will appear periodically. The game will increase in difficulty as your cupcake count goes up. The game requires good jumping and avoiding skills.

# Implementing Cupcake Counter

Create a scenario called `Cupcake Counter` and add each class to it as they are discussed. If you prefer, you can download the initial version of Cupcake Counter from: `http://www.packtpub.com/support`

# The CupcakeWorld class

This subclass of `World` sets up all the actors associated with the scenario, including a score. It is also responsible for generating periodic enemies, generating rewards, and increasing the difficulty of the game over time. The following is the code for this class:

```
import greenfoot.*;
import java.util.List;

public class CupcakeWorld extends World {
    private Counter score;
    private Turret turret;
    public int BCOUNT = 200;
    private int ballCounter = BCOUNT;
    public int FCOUNT = 400;
    private int fountainCounter = FCOUNT;
    private int level = 0;

    public CupcakeWorld() {
        super(600, 400, 1, false);
        setPaintOrder(Counter.class, Turret.class, Fountain.class,
        Jumper.class, Enemy.class, Reward.class, Platform.class);
        prepare();
    }

    public void act() {
        checkLevel();
```

```
}

private void checkLevel() {
  if( level > 1 ) generateBalls();
  if( level > 4 ) generateFountains();
  if( level % 3 == 0 ) {
    FCOUNT--;
    BCOUNT--;
    level++;
  }
}

private void generateFountains() {
  fountainCounter--;
  if( fountainCounter < 0 ) {
    List<Brick> bricks = getObjects(Brick.class);
    int idx = Greenfoot.getRandomNumber(bricks.size());
    Fountain f = new Fountain();
    int top = f.getImage().getHeight()/2 +
      bricks.get(idx).getImage().getHeight()/2;
    addObject(f, bricks.get(idx).getX(),
    bricks.get(idx).getY()-top);
    fountainCounter = FCOUNT;
  }
}

private void generateBalls() {
  ballCounter--;
  if( ballCounter < 0 ) {
    Ball b = new Ball();
    turret.setRotation(15 * -b.getXVelocity());
    addObject(b, getWidth()/2, 0);
    ballCounter = BCOUNT;
  }
}

public void addCupcakeCount(int num) {
  score.setValue(score.getValue() + num);
  generateNewCupcake();
}

private void generateNewCupcake() {
  List<Brick> bricks = getObjects(Brick.class);
  int idx = Greenfoot.getRandomNumber(bricks.size());
```

```
      Cupcake cake = new Cupcake();
      int top = cake.getImage().getHeight()/2 +
      bricks.get(idx).getImage().getHeight()/2;
      addObject(cake, bricks.get(idx).getX(),
      bricks.get(idx).getY()-top);
   }

   public void addObjectNudge(Actor a, int x, int y) {
      int nudge = Greenfoot.getRandomNumber(8) - 4;
      super.addObject(a, x + nudge, y + nudge);
   }

   private void prepare(){
      // Add Bob
      Bob bob = new Bob();
      addObject(bob, 43, 340);
      // Add floor
      BrickWall brickwall = new BrickWall();
      addObject(brickwall, 184, 400);
      BrickWall brickwall2 = new BrickWall();
      addObject(brickwall2, 567, 400);
      // Add Score
      score = new Counter();
      addObject(score, 62, 27);
      // Add turret
      turret = new Turret();
      addObject(turret, getWidth()/2, 0);
      // Add cupcake
      Cupcake cupcake = new Cupcake();
      addObject(cupcake, 450, 30);
      // Add platforms
      for(int i=0; i<5; i++) {
        for(int j=0; j<6; j++) {
           int stagger = (i % 2 == 0 ) ? 24 : -24;
           Brick brick = new Brick();
           addObjectNudge(brick, stagger + (j+1)*85, (i+1)*62);
        }
      }
   }
}
```

Let's discuss the methods in this class in order. First, we have the class constructor `CupcakeWorld()`. After calling the constructor of the superclass, it calls `setPaintOrder()` to set the actors that will appear in front of other actors when displayed on the screen. You were introduced to `setPaintOrder()` in *Chapter 2, Animation*. The main reason why we use it here, is so that no actor will cover up the `Counter` class, which is used to display the score. Next, the constructor method calls `prepare()` to add and place the initial actors into the scenario. We will discuss the `prepare()` method later in this section.

Inside the `act()` method, we will only call the function `checkLevel()`. As the player scores points in the game, the `level` variable of the game will also increase. The `checkLevel()` function will change the game a bit according to its `level` variable. When our game first starts, no enemies are generated and the player can easily get the cupcake (the reward). This gives the player a chance to get accustomed to jumping on platforms. As the cupcake count goes up, balls and fountains will be added. As the level continues to rise, `checkLevel()` reduces the delay between creating balls (`BCOUNT`) and fountains (`FCOUNT`). The `level` variable of the game is increased in the `addCupcakeCount()` method, which we will discuss in detail soon.

The `generateFountains()` method adds a `Fountain` actor to the scenario. The rate at which we create fountains is controlled by the delay variable (refer to, *Chapter 2, Animation* to review) `fountainContainer`. After the delay, we create a fountain on a randomly chosen `Brick` (the platforms in our game). The `getObjects()` method returns all of the actors of a given class presently in the scenario. We then use `getRandomNumber()` to randomly choose a number between one and the number of `Brick` actors. Next, we use `addObject()` to place the new `Fountain` object on the randomly chosen `Brick` object.

Generating balls using the `generateBalls()` method is a little easier than generating fountains. All balls are created in the same location as the `turret` at the top of the screen and sent from there with a randomly chosen trajectory. The rate at which we generate new `Ball` actors is defined by the delay variable `ballCounter`. Once we create a `Ball` actor, we rotate the `turret` based on its *x* velocity. By doing this, we create the illusion that the turret is aiming and then firing `Ball Actor`. Last, we place the newly created `Ball` actor into the scenario using the `addObject()` method.

The `addCupcakeCount()` method is called by the actor representing the player (`Bob`) every time the player collides with `Cupcake`. In this method, we increase `score` and then call `generateNewCupcake()` to add a new `Cupcake` actor to the scenario. The `generateNewCupcake()` method is very similar to `generateFountains()`, except for the lack of a delay variable, and it randomly places `Cupcake` on one of the bricks instead of a `Fountain` actor. In *Chapter 1, Let's Dive Right in...*, we demonstrated how to create a game score using the `Counter` class, a class you can import into your scenario. Please refer to that chapter for more details.

In all of our previous scenarios, we used a `prepare()` method to add actors to the scenario. The major difference between this `prepare()` method and the previous ones, is that we use the `addObjectNudge()` method instead of `addObject()` to place our platforms. The `addObjectNudge()` method simply adds a little randomness to the placement of the platforms, so that every new game is a little different. The random variation in the platforms will cause the `Ball` actors to have different bounce patterns and require the player to jump and move a bit more carefully. In the call to `addObjectNudge()`, you will notice that we used the numbers `85` and `62`. These are simply numbers that spread the platforms out appropriately, and they were discovered through trial and error.

I created a blue gradient background to use for the image of `CupcakeWorld`. Feel free to use this from the sample code you can download, create your own background image, or use one of the background images provided that come with Greenfoot.

# Enemies

In Cupcake Counter, all of the actors that can end the game if collided with are subclasses of the `Enemy` class. Using inheritance is a great way to share code and reduce redundancy for a group of similar actors. However, we often will create class hierarchies in Greenfoot solely for *polymorphism*. Polymorphism refers to the ability of a class in an object-orientated language to *take on many forms*. We are going to use it, so that our player actor only has to check for collision with an `Enemy` class and not every specific type of `Enemy`, such as `Ball` or `RedBall`. Also, by coding this way, we are making it very easy to add code for additional enemies, and if we find that our enemies have redundant code, we can easily move that code into our `Enemy` class. In other words, we are making our code extensible and maintainable.

Here is the code for our `Enemy` class:

```
import greenfoot.*;

public abstract class Enemy extends Actor {
}
```

The `Ball` class extends the `Enemy` class. Since `Enemy` is solely used for polymorphism, the `Ball` class contains all of the code necessary to implement bouncing and an initial trajectory. Here is the code for this class:

```
import greenfoot.*;

public class Ball extends Enemy {
    protected int actorHeight;
    private int speedX = 0;
```

```
    public Ball() {
      actorHeight = getImage().getHeight();
      speedX = Greenfoot.getRandomNumber(8) - 4;
      if( speedX == 0 ) {
        speedX = Greenfoot.getRandomNumber(100) < 50 ? -1 : 1;
      }
    }

    public void act() {
      checkOffScreen();
    }

    public int getXVelocity() {
      return speedX;
    }

    private void checkOffScreen() {
      if( getX() < -20 || getX() > getWorld().getWidth() + 20 ) {
        getWorld().removeObject(this);
      } else if( getY() > getWorld().getHeight() + 20 ) {
        getWorld().removeObject(this);
      }
    }
  }
```

The implementation of `Ball` is missing the code to handle moving and bouncing. As we stated earlier, we will go over all the projectile-based code after providing the code we are using as the starting point for this game. In the `Ball` constructor, we randomly choose a speed in the *x* direction and save it in the `speedX` instance variable. We have included one accessory method to return the value of `speedX` (`getXVelocity()`). Last, we include `checkOffScreen()` to remove `Ball` once it goes off screen. If we do not do this, we would have a form of memory leak in our application because Greenfoot will continue to allocate resources and manage any actor until it is removed from the scenario. For the `Ball` class, I choose to use the `ball.png` image, which comes with the standard installation of Greenfoot.

In this chapter, we will learn how to create a simple particle effect. Creating an effect is more about the use of a particle as opposed to its implementation. In the following code, we create a generic particle class, `Particles`, that we will extend to create a `RedBall` particle. We have organized the code in this way to easily accommodate adding particles in the future. Here is the code:

```
import greenfoot.*;

public class Particles extends Enemy {
  private int turnRate = 2;
```

```
    private int speed = 5;
    private int lifeSpan = 50;

    public Particles(int tr, int s, int l) {
        turnRate = tr;
        speed = s;
        lifeSpan = l;
        setRotation(-90);
    }

    public void act() {
        move();
        remove();
    }

    private void move() {
        move(speed);
        turn(turnRate);
    }

    private void remove() {
        lifeSpan--;
        if( lifeSpan < 0 ) {
            getWorld().removeObject(this);
        }
    }
}
```

Our particles are implemented to move up and slightly turn each call of the act() method. A particle will move lifeSpan times and then remove itself. As you might have guessed, lifeSpan is another use of a delay variable. The turnRate property can be either positive (to turn slightly right) or negative (to turn slightly left).

We only have one subclass of Particles, RedBall. This class supplies the correct image for RedBall, supplies the required input for the Particles constructor, and then scales the image according to the parameters scaleX and scaleY. Here's the implementation:

```
import greenfoot.*;

public class RedBall extends Particles {
    public RedBall(int tr, int s, int l, int scaleX, int scaleY) {
        super(tr, s, l);
        getImage().scale(scaleX, scaleY);
    }
}
```

For RedBall, I used the Greenfoot-supplied image red-draught.png.

# Fountains

In this game, fountains add a unique challenge. After reaching level five (see the World class CupcakeWorld), Fountain objects will be generated and randomly placed in the game. *Figure 2* shows a fountain in action. A Fountain object continually spurts RedBall objects into the air like water from a fountain.

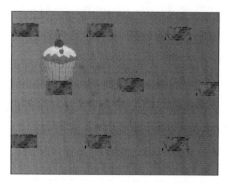

Figure 2: This is a close-up of a Fountain object in the game Cupcake Counter

Let's take a look at the code that implements the Fountain class:

```
import greenfoot.*;
import java.awt.Color;

public class Fountain extends Actor {
  private int lifespan = 75;
  private int startDelay = 100;
  private GreenfootImage img;

  public Fountain() {
    img = new GreenfootImage(20,20);
    img.setColor(Color.blue);
    img.setTransparency(100);
    img.fill();
    setImage(img);
  }

  public void act() {
    if( --startDelay == 0 ) wipeView();
    if( startDelay < 0 ) createRedBallShower();
  }

  private void wipeView() {
    img.clear();
```

```
    }

    private void createRedBallShower() {
    }
}
```

The constructor for Fountain creates a new blue, semitransparent square and sets that to be its image. We start with a blue square to give the player of the game a warning that a fountain is about to erupt. Since fountains are randomly placed at any location, it would be unfair to just drop one on our player and instantly end the game. This is also why RedBall is a subclass of Enemy and Fountain is not. It is safe for the player to touch the blue square. The startDelay delay variable is used to pause for a short amount of time, then remove the blue square (using the function wipeView()), and then start the RedBall shower (using the createRedBallShower() function). We can see this in the act() method. The implementation for createRedBallShower() is given and explained in the *Particle effects* section to come ahead in the chapter.

# Turrets

In the game, there is a turret in the top-middle of the screen that shoots purple bouncy balls at the player. It is shown in *Figure 1*. Why do we use a bouncy-ball shooting turret? *Because this is our game and we can!* The implementation of the Turret class is very simple. Most of the functionality of rotating the turret and creating Ball to shoot is handled by CupcakeWorld in the generateBalls() method already discussed. The main purpose of this class is to just draw the initial image of the turret, which consists of a black circle for the base of the turret and a black rectangle to serve as the cannon. Here is the code:

```
import greenfoot.*;
import java.awt.Color;

public class Turret extends Actor {
    private GreenfootImage turret;
    private GreenfootImage gun;
    private GreenfootImage img;

    public Turret() {
        turret = new GreenfootImage(30,30);
        turret.setColor(Color.black);
        turret.fillOval(0,0,30,30);

        gun = new GreenfootImage(40,40);
        gun.setColor(Color.black);
        gun.fillRect(0,0,10,35);
```

```
        img = new GreenfootImage(60,60);
        img.drawImage(turret, 15, 15);
        img.drawImage(gun, 25, 30);
        img.rotate(0);

        setImage(img);
    }
}
```

We previously talked about the `GreenfootImage` class and how to use some of its methods to do custom drawing. One new function we introduced is `drawImage()`. This method allows you to draw one `GreenfootImage` into another. This is how you compose images, and we used it to create our turret from a rectangle image and a circle image.

# Rewards

We create a `Reward` class for the same reason we created an `Enemy` class. We are setting ourselves up to easily add new rewards in the future. (later in the chapter, we will assign this as an exercise). Here is the code:

```
import greenfoot.*;

public abstract class Reward extends Actor {
}
```

The `Cupcake` class is a subclass of the `Reward` class and represents the object on the screen the player is constantly trying to collect. However, cupcakes have no actions to perform or state to keep track of; therefore, its implementation is simple:

```
import greenfoot.*;

public class Cupcake extends Reward {
}
```

When creating this class, I set its image to be `muffin.png`. This is an image that comes with Greenfoot. Even though the name of the image is a muffin, it still looks like a cupcake to me.

# Jumpers

The Jumper class is a class that will allow all subclasses of it to jump when pressing either the up arrow key or the spacebar. Most of the body of this class will be implemented in the *Gravity and jumping* section to come ahead in the chapter. At this point, we just provide a placeholder implementation:

```
import greenfoot.*;

public abstract class Jumper extends Actor
{
  protected int actorHeight;

  public Jumper() {
    actorHeight = getImage().getHeight();
  }

  public void act() {
    handleKeyPresses();
  }

  protected void handleKeyPresses() {
  }
}
```

The next class we are going to present is the Bob class. The Bob class extends the Jumper class and then adds functionality to let the player move it left and right. It also uses animation techniques discussed in *Chapter 2, Animation* to make it look as though it is actually walking. Here is the code:

```
import greenfoot.*;

public class Bob extends Jumper {
  private int speed = 3;
  private int animationDelay = 0;
  private int frame = 0;
  private GreenfootImage[] leftImages;
  private GreenfootImage[] rightImages;
  private int actorWidth;

  private static final int DELAY = 3;

  public Bob() {
    super();
```

```
      rightImages = new GreenfootImage[5];
      leftImages = new GreenfootImage[5];

      for( int i=0; i<5; i++ ) {
         rightImages[i] = new GreenfootImage("images/Dawson_Sprite_
Sheet_0" + Integer.toString(3+i) + ".png");
         leftImages[i] = new GreenfootImage(rightImages[i]);
         leftImages[i].mirrorHorizontally();
      }

      actorWidth = getImage().getWidth();
   }

   public void act() {
      super.act();
      checkDead();
      eatReward();
   }

   private void checkDead() {
      Actor enemy = getOneIntersectingObject(Enemy.class);
      if( enemy != null ) {
         endGame();
      }
   }

   private void endGame() {
      Greenfoot.stop();
   }

   private void eatReward() {
      Cupcake c = (Cupcake) getOneIntersectingObject(Cupcake.class);
      if( c != null ) {
         CupcakeWorld rw = (CupcakeWorld) getWorld();
         rw.removeObject(c);
         rw.addCupcakeCount(1);
      }
   }

   // Called by superclass
   protected void handleKeyPresses() {
      super.handleKeyPresses();
```

```
    if( Greenfoot.isKeyDown("left") ) {
      if( canMoveLeft() ) {moveLeft();}
    }
    if( Greenfoot.isKeyDown("right") ) {
      if( canMoveRight() ) {moveRight();}
    }
}

private boolean canMoveLeft() {
  if( getX() < 5 ) return false;
  return true;
}

private void moveLeft() {
  setLocation(getX() - speed, getY());
  if( animationDelay % DELAY == 0 ) {
    animateLeft();
    animationDelay = 0;
  }
  animationDelay++;
}

private void animateLeft() {
  setImage( leftImages[frame++]);
  frame = frame % 5;
  actorWidth = getImage().getWidth();
}

private boolean canMoveRight() {
  if( getX() > getWorld().getWidth() - 5) return false;
  return true;
}

private void moveRight() {
  setLocation(getX() + speed, getY());
  if( animationDelay % DELAY == 0 ) {
    animateRight();
    animationDelay = 0;
  }
  animationDelay++;
}
```

```
      private void animateRight() {
        setImage( rightImages[frame++] );
        frame = frame % 5;
        actorWidth = getImage().getWidth();
      }
    }
```

Like `CupcakeWorld`, this class is substantial. We will discuss each method it contains sequentially. First, the constructor's main duty is to set up the images for the walking animation. This type of animation was discussed in *Chapter 2, Animation* in the *Hurting the avatar* section and again in *Chapter 3, Collision Detection* in the *Detecting a collision with multiple objects* section. The images came from `www.wikia.com` and were supplied, in the form of a sprite sheet, by the user Mecha Mario. A direct link to the sprite sheet is `http://smbz.wikia.com/wiki/File:Dawson_Sprite_Sheet.PNG`. Note that I manually copied and pasted the images I used from this sprite sheet using my favorite image editor.

**Free Internet resources**

Unless you are also an artist or a musician in addition to being a programmer, you are going to be hard pressed to create all of the assets you need for your Greenfoot scenario. If you look at the credits for AAA video games, you will see that the number of artists and musicians actually equal or even outnumber the programmers.

Luckily, the Internet comes to the rescue. There are a number of websites that supply legally free assets you can use. For example, the website I used to get the images for the `Bob` class supplies free content under the Creative Commons Attribution-Share Alike License 3.0 (Unported) (CC-BY-SA) license. It is very important that you check the licensing used for any asset you download off the Internet and follow those user agreements carefully. In addition, make sure that you fully credit the source of your assets. For games, you should include a *Credits* screen to cite all the sources for the assets you used.

The following are some good sites for free, online assets:

- `www.wikia.com`
- `newgrounds.com`
- `http://incompetech.com`
- `opengameart.org`
- `untamed.wild-refuge.net/rpgxp.php`

Next, we have the `act()` method. It first calls the `act()` method of its superclass. It needs to do this so that we get the jumping functionality that is supplied by the `Jumper` class. Then, we call `checkDead()` and `eatReward()`. The `checkDead()` method ends the game if this instance of the `Bob` class touches an enemy, and `eatReward()` adds one to our score, by calling the `CupcakeWorld` method `addCupcakeCount()`, every time it touches an instance of the `Cupcake` class.

The rest of the class implements moving left and right. The main method for this is `handleKeyPresses()`. Like in `act()`, the first thing we do, is call `handleKeyPresses()` contained in the `Jumper` superclass. This runs the code in `Jumper` that handles the spacebar and up arrow key presses. The key to handling key presses is the Greenfoot method `isKeyDown()` (see the following information box). We use this method to check if the left arrow or right arrow keys are presently being pressed. If so, we check whether or not the actor can move left or right using the methods `canMoveLeft()` and `canMoveRight()`, respectively. If the actor can move, we then call either `moveLeft()` or `moveRight()`.

**Handling key presses in Greenfoot**

In the preface of the book, we explained that we assumed that you have some experience with Greenfoot and have, minimally, completed the tutorials located on the page: `http://www.greenfoot.org/doc`

The second tutorial explains how to control actors with the keyboard. To refresh your memory, we are going to present some information on the keyboard control here.

The primary method we use in implementing keyboard control is `isKeyDown()`. This method provides a simple way to check whether a certain key is being pressed. Here is an excerpt from Greenfoot's documentation:

```
public static boolean isKeyDown(java.lang.String
keyName)
Check whether a given key is currently pressed down.

Parameters:
keyName:This is the name of the key to check.

This returns : true if the key is down.

Using isKeyDown() is easy. The ease of capturing
and using input is one of the major strengths of
Greenfoot. Here is example code that will pause the
execution of the game if the "p" key is pressed:

if( Greenfoot.isKeyDown("p") {
  Greenfoot.stop();
}
```

Next, we will discuss canMoveLeft(), moveLeft(), and animateLeft(). The canMoveRight(), moveRight(), and animateRight() methods mirror their functionality and will not be discussed. The sole purpose of canMoveLeft() is to prevent the actor from walking off the left-hand side of the screen. The moveLeft() method moves the actor using setLocation() and then animates the actor to look as though it is moving to the left-hand side. It uses a delay variable to make the walking speed look natural (not too fast). The animateLeft() method sequentially displays the walking-left images. This is the same animation strategy we saw in *Chapter 2, Animation.*

# Platforms

The game contains several platforms that the player can jump or stand on. The platforms perform no actions and only serve as placeholders for images. We use inheritance to simplify collision detection. Here is the implementation of Platform:

```
import greenfoot.*;

public class Platform extends Actor {
}
```

Here's the implementation of BrickWall:

```
import greenfoot.*;

public class BrickWall extends Platform {
}
```

Here's the implementation of Brick:

```
import greenfoot.*;

public class Brick extends Platform {
}
```

# Test it out

You should now be able to compile and test Cupcake Counter. Make sure you handle any typos or other errors you introduced while inputting the code. For now, you can only move left and right. Check out Bob walking. *Pretty cool!* Everything else depends on some of the code we left out of the preceding implementations. We will fill out that missing code next. Let's launch some actors.

# Your assignment

Consider one of the locations we left out of the previous code. Try to supply the code yourself. How would you start? My suggestion would be to start with pencil and paper. Draw some figures and imagine the steps that you would need to perform to implement the functionality. Translate these steps to Java code and try them out. Doing this will help you better understand and process the upcoming solutions, even if your solution was incorrect.

# Launching actors

We are going to take the preceding incomplete implementation and turn it into a game by adding jumping, bouncing, a particle effect, and bullets fired from a turret.

# Gravity and jumping

Presently, our player character is stuck at the bottom of the screen. We are going to fill in the missing code in the `Jumper` class and the `Bob` class to enable our character to jump and finally have a way to reach the cupcake reward at the top of the screen. Jumping is applying a force to move an object upwards. We are also going to need a downwards force operating on the object, in order for it to fall back down. As in real life, we are going to call this force *gravity*. The changes to the `Jumper` class are so extensive that we are going to first look at the complete implementation and then discuss it afterwards. Here's the code:

```java
import greenfoot.*;

public abstract class Jumper extends Actor
{
  protected int actorHeight;
  private int fallSpeed = 0;
  private boolean jumping = false;

  // Class Constants
  protected static final int GRAVITY = 1;
  protected static final int JUMPSTRENGTH = 12;

  public Jumper() {
    actorHeight = getImage().getHeight();
  }

  public void act() {
    handleKeyPresses();
```

```
      standOrFall();
   }

   protected void handleKeyPresses() {
      if( (Greenfoot.isKeyDown("space") ||
      Greenfoot.isKeyDown("up")) && !jumping) {
         jump();
      }
   }

   private void jump() {
      fallSpeed = -JUMPSTRENGTH;
      jumping = true;
      fall();
   }

   private void standOrFall() {
      if( inAir() ) {
         checkHead();
         fall();
         checkLanding();
      } else {
         fallSpeed = 0;
         jumping = false;
      }
   }

   private void checkHead() {
      int actorHead = -actorHeight/2;
      int step = 0;
      while( fallSpeed < 0 && step > fallSpeed
      && getOneObjectAtOffset(0, actorHead + step,
      Platform.class) == null ) {
         step--;
      }
      if( fallSpeed < 0 ) {
         fallSpeed = step;
      }
   }

   private void checkLanding() {
      int actorFeet = actorHeight/2;
      int step = 0;
```

```
      while( fallSpeed > 0 && step < fallSpeed
      && getOneObjectAtOffset(0, actorFeet + step,
      Platform.class) == null ) {
        step++;
      }
      if( fallSpeed > 0 ) {
        fallSpeed = step;
      }
    }

    private boolean inAir() {
      Actor platform = getOneObjectAtOffset(0,
      getImage().getHeight()/2, Platform.class);
      return platform == null;
    }

    private void fall() {
      setLocation(getX(), getY() + fallSpeed);
      fallSpeed = fallSpeed + GRAVITY;
    }
  }
```

Please note that we have added two new instance variables (fallSpeed and jumping) and two static constants (GRAVITY and JUMPSTRENGTH). These new variables will be used throughout our code. In our act() method, we added the standOrFall() method. This method is responsible for applying gravity and detecting collisions (both for the head and feet of the actor). Before looking at that method further, let's look at the completed implementation of handleKeyPresses(). In this method, we detect whether the space bar or up arrow key was pressed and call jump() if it was. You will notice that the if statement also contains a check to see whether the Boolean variable jumping is false. We need this check to prevent double jumping (jumping again while in the middle of a jump). The jump() method changes fallSpeed to a negative value. This applies a force in the up direction on the actor. We set jumping to true (as we are now in a jumping state) and then call fall(). The fall() method applies gravity to an actor. In this method, we can see how a negative value of fallSpeed will propel the actor upwards.

The value of `fallSpeed` has GRAVITY added to it until it becomes positive. This will create a parabola-like motion, as shown in *Figure 3*.

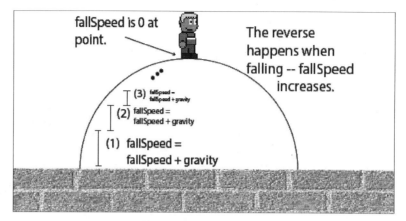

Figure 3: This is the implementation of falling

Let's look at the implementation of `standOrFall()`. The first thing we need to check is whether or not we are presently standing on a `Platform` object. We use the method `inAir()` to do this check. This method uses `getOneObjectAtOffset()` (see *Chapter 3, Collision Detection*) to check whether the bottom of the actor is touching a `Platform` object and returns `false` if it is. In `standOrFall()`, we do three things if we have determined that we are in the air. We check to see whether the top or bottom of the actor is colliding with `Platform` and call the `fall()` method if it is. The methods `checkHead()` and `checkLanding()` are similar. They are both used in border-based collision detection, as discussed in *Chapter 3, Collision Detection*, to detect at exactly which pixel location the collision occurred. They then change the value of `fallSpeed`, so that the actor stops at the point of collision. If we detect that we are not in the air in `standOrFall()`, then we are standing on a platform and can set `fallSpeed` to 0 (not falling) and `jumping` to `false` (not jumping).

# Bouncing

Bouncing actors look great and really add a nice dimension to any game. In the mind of the player, they propel your game from a flat arrangement of pixels to a rich world in which objects obey the natural laws of physics. In Cupcake Counter, the balls shot from the turret bounce. Bouncing is implemented in the `Ball` class. First, add the following instance variables to your existing `Ball` class:

```
private int fallSpeed = 0;
protected static final int GRAVITY = 1;
```

Next, we need to add code to the act() method that will cause an instance of the class to fall or bounce if it hits an object. Change your act() method to the following:

```
public void act() {
   fallOrBounce();
   checkOffScreen();
}
```

The fallOrBounce() method is going to be complex, but we are going to use functional decomposition (break it up into smaller methods) to manage the complexity and make our code more readable. Here is its implementation:

```
private void fallOrBounce() {
   if( fallSpeed <= 0) {
     checkHead();
   } else {
     checkLanding();
   }
}
```

We have reduced the implementation of fallOrBounce() to checking whether we are about to hit our head or checking whether we are about to land on a platform. We choose between the two checks based on the value of fallSpeed. If fallSpeed is negative, then we are moving upwards and there is no need to check for landing at this point. Here is the implementation of checkHead():

```
private void fallOrBounce() {
   if( fallSpeed <= 0) {
     checkHead();
   } else {
     checkLanding();
   }
}
private void checkHead() {
   int actorHead = -actorHeight/2;
   int step = 0;
   int oldFallSpeed;
   while( fallSpeed < 0 && step > fallSpeed &&
   getOneObjectAtOffset( 0, actorHead + step,
   Platform.class) == null ) {
     step--;
   }
   if( step > fallSpeed ) {
     if( fallSpeed < 0 ) {
       handleBounce(step);
```

```
      }
    } else {
      fall(speedX);
    }
  }
```

The `checkHead()` method uses border-based collision detection (discussed in *Chapter 3, Collision Detection*) to detect exactly when the top of the object touches a platform. If `step` ends up being greater than `fallSpeed`, then no collision occurred and we can continue letting gravity affect our trajectory by calling `fall()`. If `step` is less than `fallSpeed`, then we hit our head on a platform and we need to handle bouncing off this platform by calling `handleBounce()`. Here is the implementation of `handleBounce()`.

```
  private void handleBounce(int step) {
    int oldFallSpeed = fallSpeed;
    fallSpeed = step;
    fall(0);
    oldFallSpeed = (int)(oldFallSpeed * 0.7);
    fallSpeed = step - oldFallSpeed;
    fall(0);
    fallSpeed = -oldFallSpeed;
  }
```

This method handles a bounce by breaking it up into two main phases. The first phase handles the motion between the actor and the platform. The second phase handles travelling from the platform to the end location. The phases are shown in *Figure 4*.

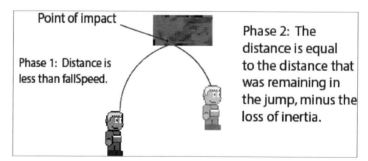

Figure 4: This shows the two main phases in handling a bounce. Phase 1 is the motion leading up to the impact and Phase 2 is the motion after impact

In the first phase, we move the ball to the point of collision by setting `fallSpeed` to `step` and calling `fall(0)`. We will look at the implementation of `fall()` soon. For now, it is enough to know that `fall(0)` calls `setLocation()` to move the ball and updates `fallSpeed` by applying the affects of gravity. In the second phase of `handleBounce()`, we multiply by `0.7` in order to simulate the loss of energy that occurs in an impact. There is nothing magical or scientific about `0.7`. It just looked right when tested. We then move the remaining distance of our inertia (`step` – `oldFallSpeed`) by calling `fall(0)` again. The bounce has changed our falling direction, so the last thing we do is update `fallSpeed` to reflect this change.

Since we just used the `fall()` method, let us look at that next:

```
private void fall(int dx) {
   setLocation(getX() + dx, getY() + fallSpeed);
   fallSpeed = fallSpeed + GRAVITY;
}
```

As mentioned earlier, `fall()` moves the actor using `setLocation()` according to its speed in the *x* direction and how fast it is falling. The instance variable `fallSpeed` is updated to account for the slowing (or accelerating) effects of gravity.

The only method left to complete the implementation of the `Ball` class is `checkLanding()`. Here it is:

```
private void checkLanding() {
   int actorFeet = actorHeight/2;
   int step = 0;
   int oldFallSpeed;
   while( fallSpeed > 0 && step < fallSpeed &&
   getOneObjectAtOffset(0, actorFeet + step,
   Platform.class) == null ) {
     step++;
   }
   if( step < fallSpeed ) {
     if( fallSpeed > 0 ) {
       handleBounce(step);
     }
   } else {
     fall(speedX);
   }
}
```

The implementation of `checkLanding()` exactly mirrors the implementation of `checkHead()` except that it handles moving downwards instead of moving upwards.

Bouncing is a great effect and can be applied to a wide variety of actors. You could combine the implementation of bouncing with the implementation of jumping we discussed in the previous section and make a bouncing, jumping hero for your game.

# Particle effects

Particle effects work by creating a bunch of small actors to make an animation. Previously, you learned to do animations mainly by rapid image swapping. You could imagine creating a water fountain by creating 4-6 images of a fountain shooting upwards and switching between those images. Instead of doing that, we will create a fountain using a particle effect. Conveniently, you already have all the information you need to create particle effects. Particles are simply small actors that you assign a pattern of motion to. You then create a lot of them to provide the desired effect. We will do this to complete our implementation of the `Fountain` class. The only part of the implementation we left out was the code for the `createRedBallShower()` method. Here is that missing code:

```
private void createRedBallShower() {
  lifespan--;
  if( lifespan < 0) {
    getWorld().removeObject(this);
  } else {
    int tr = Greenfoot.getRandomNumber(30) - 15;
    int s = Greenfoot.getRandomNumber(4) + 6;
    int l = Greenfoot.getRandomNumber(15) + 5;
    getWorld().addObject(new RedBall(tr, s, l, 10, 10), getX(),
getY());
  }
}
```

The instance variable `lifespan` is a delay variable that we use to determine how long the fountain will exist. Once `lifespan` is less than zero, we remove this fountain from the scenario. Otherwise, we create `RedBall` anew with a random lifespan and rate of turn and speed. These parameters to the constructor of the `RedBall` class were discussed in the *Enemies* section.

Creating `RedBall` anew for every call of the `act()` method with slightly different attributes creates a really interesting fountain effect, as shown in *Figure 2*.

# Bullets and turrets

We have already fully implemented bullets and turrets. The Turret class was complete and we finished the Ball class (our bullet) in the *Bouncing* section. What we will discuss here, are the basic steps to create a turret and a bullet and explain how what we have already done gives you the information you need to create a machine gun, cannon, tank, or other type of turret.

First, you need a turret with an image. You can dynamically create the image just as we did in the Turret class, or you can set it using setImage(). Then, turrets only need to be rotated in the direction they are firing. That is what we did in the generateBalls() method in CupcakeWorld. Bullets are just actors that are rotated in a certain direction and then continually call move() to move in that direction. If you rotate the turret and bullet by the same angle, place the bullet at the same starting location as the turret, and let the bullet move forward, then it will appear as if the turret fired the bullet. Does this make sense? *Figure 5* summarizes this strategy.

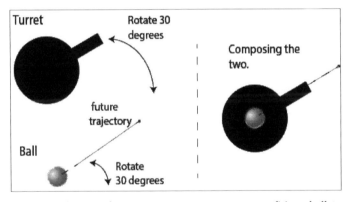

Figure 5: These are the steps necessary to create a turret firing a bullet

# Your assignment

Now, compile all of the code we just gave you and play Cupcake Counter for a while. You might start to notice why we started by having the platforms have some randomness to their placement. If we didn't, the player would quickly adapt to the falling patterns of the balls.

Your assignment for this section, is to code another random variation in the game. You could further randomize the platforms, mess with the ball speed or size, or change the power of the player's jump.

# Challenge

We have created a fairly functional game. We have a score, cool animations, collision detection, and levels in our game. After playing it, what would be the first thing you would improve? Let your friend play it. What did he/she think? Try to come up with a change that improves the game based on your experience playing it.

In addition, we designed our game so that it would be easy to add new rewards, enemies, and platforms. Add one of each to the game and add your own twist to them. For example, you could create a super cupcake that is worth five points but only lasts a short time. This will require the player to make some quick, meaningful decisions during the game.

# Summary

While we did not create a full physics engine, we did go over some simple techniques to give actors interesting movement. Our discussion was focused on projectile-based movement and included bouncing, jumping, firing, and particle effects. Until now, we acquired a number of creative program techniques that enable us to create a wide variety of animations, simulations, and games. However, creating a fun interactive experience is not trivial. In the next chapter, we are going to learn about game design and a process for game development that will help us create amazing interactive experiences.

# 5

# Interactive Application Design and Theory

*"If you never did, you should. These things are fun and fun is good."*

*– Dr. Suess*

Creating engaging and immersive experiences in Greenfoot is far more involving than compiling a collection of programming effects into one application. In this chapter, you will learn how to engage your user by understanding the relationship between user choice and outcome, conditioning the user, and including the right level of complexity into your work. You will be shown a proven iterative development process that will help you put theory into practice. The topics that will be covered in the chapter are as follows:

- Meaningful play
    - Choice, action, and outcomes
    - Complexity
    - Goals
- User conditioning
- Storytelling
    - Fictional worlds
    - Narrative descriptors
- Interactive entertainment iterative development process

As we discuss the topics of this chapter, we will refer to the Avoider game we created in *Chapter 1, Let's Dive Right in…* and *Chapter 2, Animation*. We will discuss items already implemented in the game to illustrate interactive design concepts and demonstrate other concepts by adding new features. In this chapter, we are discussing methods to engineer fun. That might sound strange, but creating fun is the main goal of the designers of games and other forms of interactive entertainment. And, as Dr. Suess so elegantly puts it, "These things are fun and fun is good."

# Meaningful play

Learning to create experiences that are meaningful to users is the most important skill needed by developers of interactive applications. It is the meaning of the interaction that drives players to invest time and energy in playing your application. We want to invoke feelings of happiness, anger, pride, relief, caring, astonishment, surprise, elation, or satisfaction in our users. To do this, *we need to provide immediate and long-term feedback to difficult choices and actions taken by the user.*

Let's look at a few clarifying examples that might take place in a role-playing game (RPG). Imagine that you are a wizard wondering through a forest-covered mountain when you come upon a cave. Peeking into the cave, you see in the dim light a sleeping dragon surrounded by treasure. The following are some possible interactions that could take place. We will discuss each, and determine if it created meaningful play.

**Scenario 1**:

- **User choice**: You look through your spell book and decide to cast the spell *Fireball*.
- **User action**: You cast the spell on the dragon.
- **System feedback/outcome**: The fireball hits the dragon. Nothing happens afterwards.

What!?!?? Did your spell fail? Is the game broken? Does the dragon have an aura of anti-magic? Did you actually miss? We get absolutely no meaning from this interaction. The player is left confused and disengaged. Let's look at another scenario.

**Scenario 2**:

- **User choice**: You look through your spell book and decide to cast the spell *Fireball*.
- **User action**: You cast the spell on the dragon.
- **System feedback/outcome**: The fireball hits the dragon. The dragon laughs and says, "Puny mortal. Go immediately, and I will let you live."

The meaning is perfectly clear here. You have little power and you have no chance against a creature as strong as a dragon. You could choose to talk to the dragon, but he has indicated extreme annoyance at your presence. Are you going to press your luck or flee? Maybe one day, you'll grow strong enough to come back and take that treasure from this dragon. For now, you might be feeling lucky, inspired to be better, frightened, or frustrated at your lack of progress. However, you are feeling something and the interaction definitely had meaning.

**Scenario 3**:

- **User choice**: You look through your spell book and decide to cast the spell *Fireball*.
- **User action**: You cast the spell on the dragon.
- **System feedback/outcome**: The fireball hits the dragon. The dragon screams in agony before disintegrating.

Ah, it is time to collect your loot. You marvel at your supreme power. Perhaps you should have allowed the dragon one chance to flee? Nah, it probably would not have done that for you. This interaction re-affirms your greatness.

The key to creating engaging applications is producing meaningful interactions on a moment-to-moment basis with the user. If a choice and action do not have a meaningful outcome, then why bother your users with it? *Every interaction in your interactive applications needs to be meaningful.* This is what Salen and Zimmerman refer to as *descriptive meaningful play* in their book, *Rules of Play*.

Another very important aspect to your application is the long-term outcome of a user's action. For example, in Scenario 3, the player could be referred to as Dragon Slayer, later in the game. The fine items purchased with the loot should be useful later in the game. *The outcomes of actions need to persist in the game.* Salen and Zimmerman refer to this as *evaluative meaningful play*.

Meaningful play is not only for games. The same thought process should be used to design any application. For example, if a user clicks on an item on an e-commerce site that they are interested in purchasing, there should be immediate visual feedback, such as the shopping cart icon displaying a 1 instead of a 0 or, going even further, the sound of a cheering crowd playing for a couple of seconds. If a user types in a word processing document, the word processing application should highlight the Save icon or put an asterisk by the filename to indicate that there are unsaved changes. If a person is taking a survey, there should a progress meter to let them know how many questions they have left to answer. Perhaps you could offer words of encouragement every time the user completes five survey questions.

# Complexity

There is a really funny game that demonstrates what a game plays like when the player's choices are overly simplistic. It is called *Super PSTW Action RPG*. In this RPG, you only have one control—the spacebar. For every given situation, you simply hit the spacebar. If you haven't guessed, the PSTW in the title stands for **Press Space To Win**.

Obviously, this game is a joke, but it is also an interesting experiment in game design. There is no meaningful play in the game, because the choice and action a player has to take is trivial. The actions and outcomes are well designed, but that is insufficient. Without complexity of choice, there is no meaningful play. We don't have to go to such an extreme example to demonstrate this point. Have you ever played the card game War? If not, you can quickly review the rules here: http://en.wikipedia.org/wiki/War_(card_game). This game also has no meaningful play. Throughout the game, the player either flips a card over or places three cards face down and then flips a card over. The current game state completely informs the player of which action they should take. There are no tradeoffs to consider and no risk analysis to be done. It is all mechanical play. For most players older than 10 years, Tic-Tac-Toe suffers from the same lack of meaningful play.

For meaningful play to exist, the decisions a player makes should require sufficient mental effort. A player must have several options available to them and each option should involve different tradeoffs, risks, and rewards. For example, in our RPG scenarios above, the player might have the following choices available to them: cast Fireball, cast Lightning Strike, cast Charm Monster, talk, or flee. Perhaps the player has learned previously in the game, that charm spells rarely work on dragons and that certain dragons are immune to either fire or lightning. The player could choose to flee. This is a low-reward, low-risk option.

When a player is making non-trivial decisions, taking action, and is provided with clear feedback, then the game becomes meaningful. When making decisions in an interactive application or game, the player needs to know what the goals of the interaction are. Is it to create custom pieces of music, become the most powerful wizard, or get the best deals on an e-commerce site? Setting up user goals is the next most important aspect of creating engaging applications.

# Goals

Goals provide the players the means to assess their decisions in their moment-to-moment and long-term interactions with your application. After each interaction, the user can ask, "Did my last choice and action bring me closer to completing my goal?" With this type of ongoing assessment, users can augment and optimize their decision processes, in order to more quickly achieve their goals. In essence, the players use goals as guides to learning optimal ways to interact with your application.

In writing an interactive application, you must set up clear goals and subgoals for your users. This is why high-score lists are so popular in many games. The simple fact of having one provides the goal of the game—score as many points as possible. As people play your game, they will constantly judge if their last course of action or long-term actions have led to the maximum amount of points. This enhances the meaningful play of the game.

In industry, companies will often try and gamify their applications or services. For example, the airline industry sets up programs to earn free flying miles. So, the customer is now engaged in making decisions that optimize their ability to gain free miles to earn a free airline flight. It often makes sense to establish subgoals to keep the customer invested along the way. If it takes a year or two to earn enough free flying miles, then the consumer could get discouraged. An airline might decide to offer intermediate goals, such as earning a free travel mug after achieving a certain, smaller amount of miles. Subgoals are very important to drive short-term behavior, as are rewards. We will talk further about methods of conditioning users next.

# User conditioning

In creating an interactive application or game, we want the user experience to be the best it can be. In creating meaningful play, we have given the user a rich set of options to choose from, and their path through the game has many possible states and outcomes. As the possible states and transitions in the game increase, it becomes harder as a game designer, to ensure that each path through the game states results in a positive interaction. We need to use user conditioning to help guide a user's behavior to interact with our application in predictable ways.

The effect of conditioning was clearly demonstrated by Ivan Pavlov in an experiment involving a dog and food. In this experiment, Pavlov would ring a bell every time he fed his dog. Eventually, he could get the dog to drool by just ringing a bell. The dog learned to associate a neutral stimulus, like the bell, with food. While it seems weird to say we want to manipulate our users like this, it will help us to guide the user into the most favorable interactions with our application.

There are three methods we will use to condition our users:

- **Positive reinforcement**: Give the user a reward for doing the behavior we want.

- **Negative reinforcement**: Take away something negative when the user does the desired behavior.

- **Punishment**: Take away something positive or add something negative when the users exhibit the wrong behavior.

We want to treat our users with respect, and we want them to have a good time; therefore, positive reinforcement should be the way we condition our users the most. We want to give them rewards for doing the correct behavior. In a game, we might give them points, an extra life, an extra ability, or access to a new part of the game. Whether you are creating a game or an interactive application, you should have a set reward schedule for your users. Some rewards could be given frequently, such as earning points for disposing of an enemy, while other rewards could be more rare, such as giving the character the ability to fly.

Giving rewards allows us to tell the player which behaviors are favored in the game. If we wanted the user to get through an area as fast as possible, we could give a reward for doing it under 30 seconds. If we wanted the user to explore the controls and find fighting move combinations, we could give extra points whenever three fighting combinations are done in a row. If we wanted our users to pick flowers, we could provide a 0.001 percent chance to receive the most powerful item in the game every time a flower is picked. If we wanted a customer to buy coffee at a store more often, we could give them every twelfth drink free. Rewards are a powerful mechanism to condition users.

Negative reinforcement is less used but still a powerful tool to condition users. In the last paragraph, I mentioned that you could encourage your player to move fast through an area by giving them a reward for making it through in under 30 seconds. Using negative reinforcement, we could drive the same behavior. Imagine that you are in very large room and the ceiling starts slowly moving down. You become aware that if you do not get out quickly, you will get squashed. By moving quickly to the other side of the room and leaving, you no longer have this pressure to move quick. This is negative reinforcement. Other examples of negative reinforcement include making the lighting dark in an area and playing creepy music, in order to encourage the player to get out of this area quickly (the game Bioshock is great at this), sounding a siren when the player is in a place they shouldn't be in, or blinking the screen until your health gets back to an acceptable level.

Ultimately, punishment is a necessary component of game play, although not usually included in the gamification of a non-game application. There eventually have to be hard consequences for not meeting game objects. This could include subtracting points, subtracting money, losing a life, and eventually losing the game. Punishment is necessary because there has to be some risk associated with the choices a player makes, in order to achieve meaningful play. Just try not to be too hard on your users. The whole point of making a game is to provide an engaging, recreational activity.

# Storytelling

Telling and appreciating stories has been engrained into our culture since the earliest times. We present stories in many different formats and mediums. They appear in oral traditions, the written word, theatre, cinema, and games. Games are one of the newest forms of storytelling but perhaps the most compelling for one simple reason—YOU are the main character of the story. In traditional methods of storytelling, the author must spend sufficient time building up a relatable character that the audience cares about. In games, you get this for free. You are the character.

# Fictional worlds

In games, stories have an additional role other than just pure entertainment. The story creates a fictional world for the player of the game that helps guide their experience. It provides context for the actions and the motivation to achieve goals. Why are we killing these aliens in this game? Well, given that they just wiped out all of South America and are heading north, we know we need to stop their advance soon if the world is to stand a chance of surviving this invasion. If a game takes place in outer space, you expect to have spaceships, lasers, and aliens. There is a whole wealth of information given to your player by just telling them that the story takes place in the Old West, under water, or on a soccer field.

For any game, you should have a rich and complete story that covers what happens in your game's fictional world before the game is played, what happens to it during the game, and what happens afterwards—even if the user will never experience the before and after. Your fictional world and story not only provide context and motivation for the player, but they also serve as a guide to the game designer. As you add and subtract features from the game, as you go through the interactive entertainment development process (described in the section by the same name), you need to make sure you stay true to both.

# Narrative descriptors

Everything in your game contributes to the story and your fictional world—the graphics on the box your game is shipped in, the manual, and the sounds and images in your game. You want your player to imagine a rich and vibrant world by providing appropriate and consistent narrative descriptors. Luckily, it does not take many prompts to get your user to imagine a complex world due to the principle of minimal departure. This principle states that people will use their knowledge of the world to fill in any missing gaps they see in an incomplete image. Take a few moments to look at *Figure 1*. What do you imagine lives in those mountains? Does this world have gravity? What else can you say about the world depicted in this figure? Whatever you come up with, you did so using the principle of minimal departure.

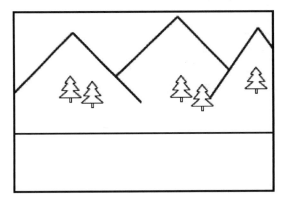

Figure 1: This is an example of the principle of minimal departure.

Now, take a look at *Figure 2*. What has been added to the picture? How does this change your perception of the world? What if I would have added a caveman instead of a robot?

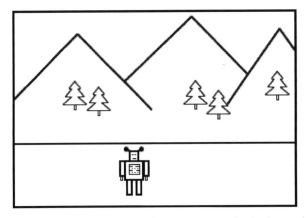

Figure 2: This shows the power of one narrative descriptor to completely change the fictional world

Just as in a movie, everything that appears in your game or interactive application should perpetuate the story. For example, if you create an interactive history simulation of medieval times, then you should use a font that matches the time period and not use Courier New. If you have a game that takes place during World War I, then perhaps instead of showing a vanilla health bar for your player, you could show the picture of a soldier that looks more injured as you take more damage.

**Disney**

Disney provides great stories and is a master of using narrative descriptors. Have you ever been to Disneyland? I once had the privilege to be given a tour of Disneyland by Disney Imagineers and artists. The first thing that struck me, is how every employee of Disney recites the same mantra, "Story, story, story". I was surprised to find that on the tour my guides continually pointed out their use of narrative descriptors. In the different lands, they would show me how the concrete, plants, trash cans, and lighting all contributed to the story of the area. They knew that one item out of place could confuse or destroy the fictional worlds that their customers were imagining.

# The interactive entertainment iterative development process

All of the design principles we have discussed thus far in this chapter will help you to create meaningful, engaging interactive applications. However, they are not enough. As you proceed with designing and building your game, you get to know the game deeply and lose your ability to be an unbiased judge of it. In addition, what you find fun and meaningful, could be confusing to others. You have to realize that if you have created a game with sufficient complexity, you will not be able to predict game play.

The only way to give your application the best chance of success, is to develop it using the interactive entertainment iterative development method shown in *Figure 3*.

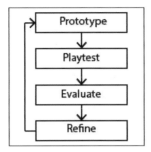

Figure 3: This is the interactive entertainment iterative development process

Next, we will talk about having an initial idea for a game and some upfront work you need to do to make an effective game pitch. In the gaming industry, game developers have to pitch their game and convince peers and management that this game is worth investing in. If you are working with a small team, you will still need to pitch the game to developers and artists that you want to recruit to work on your project. After talking about the upfront work, we will discuss each stage of the iterative design process in turn.

# Game pitch and initial design

So, you have an idea and a desire to build a game. What should you do next? You need to create a clear and concise way to describe your game to others. You need to be able to describe the world you are creating, the story behind this world, the major goal of the game, and a rough draft of the game rules. Here is a detailed process for creating this information:

1.  In one paragraph, write a description of your game. Try to keep it to five sentences or less. Be clear, specific, and concise. As your game evolves over time, be sure to update this paragraph.

2.  Write the story of your game, including what happened before your game, what happens during your game, and what happens after your game. This will end up being a guide that all developers, designers, and artists will consult as they consider new features and assets for the game. Again, keep this document up-to-date.

3.  In one sentence, state the game's goal. What is the player trying to achieve?

4. In one sentence, state how one player will know if he/she is better than another. Is the best player the one with the most points? Furthest progress? Best time?

5. Write a draft of the rules of the game. Try to come up with at least five major rules. Rules provide a formal description of your game. Every game has a concise set of rules.

6. Create a storyboard of your game. A storyboard reads like a comic book and depicts the main storyline and concept art for the game. Storyboards are a major design tool, used in both the gaming and movie industries.

After creating this information, make sure to keep it located in a central location that is shared among all team members and updated as the game evolves. When you are unsure what feature would be best to add to the game, or whether you should add a twist to the story, consult these documents and make sure everything stays consistent.

# Prototype

In this step, you implement a few features to your game that you have already decided upon in the last iteration's Refinement step. If this is your first iteration, pick a few simple things to implement, such as a main character, movement controls, and maybe one enemy. This step only contains coding and no design work. That was done through the last iteration.

# Playtest

This iterative development process encourages play-based design. In play-based design, you have volunteers playtest your game. They evaluate it, not based on a description you give them, but on how the game actually plays. Early stages will be simplistic and evaluators might only be able to comment on whether the controls feel natural or how the navigation feels. As the game evolves, so will their ability to provide feedback.

Your playtesting session should be well defined and repeatable. You want to make sure every playtester has the same experience, so that you can reliably compile and compare their feedback. To conduct a playtest, you should:

1. Have a computer available that has the prototype of your game ready to play.

2. Provide your tester with a short explanation of the playtesting procedure and then give them a short description of your game and what features are available for testing.

3. Allow your player 5–20 minutes of play time, depending on how many features you want tested during this iteration. Try not to interrupt your playtester (even if you notice them doing something very wrong) and only speak to them if they ask you a question. Provide short answers, but do not elaborate.

4. Observe the body language of your tester. Do they seem bored? Frustrated? Engaged? Are they looking at their watch or surprised when you tell them that their 10 minutes of playing are up?

5. When your playtester is done with the game, give them a short survey. Ask them questions about the game's controls, rules, goals, and story. Ask them whether they felt the challenge of the game was balanced. Did they think they had sufficient options to consider on a moment-to-moment basis? Was the look and feel of the game consistent? Did your choice of narrative descriptors work well? Were they ever confused on what to do next? Collect some demographics on your testers. How old are they? Are they casual or hardcore gamers?

6. Have an open question-and-answer period. Do they have any suggestions on how to improve the game? Were there aspects they did not enjoy?

Make sure to thank your playtester and go over the information you collected. This is your last chance to get clarification from the tester. After doing all of this, you are ready to move to the next stage.

# Evaluation

The evaluation stage is very mechanical. In this stage, you only compile the results you received from all of your playtesters. Compile all of the results from the survey. Is there a consensus on certain answers? For example, 80 percent of the playtesters felt the controls were awkward, or 100 percent of the players did not know what to do after killing the first enemy. For the open question-and-answer session, are there any suggestions that multiple testers made? From the body language observations, did a majority of the players ask if they were done playtesting before the time expired?

# Refinement

The real design work happens in this stage. Pick the top two or four issues with the game identified during playtesting and write them down. Now, brainstorm the changes, additions, or subtractions you could make to the game to address these issues. Your ideas could include suggestions playtesters gave you or not. You are not obligated at all to directly use the suggestions given to you by your playtesters; however, you should give them special consideration. While brainstorming, do not filter your, or your teammates' ideas. On a piece of paper, record at least twenty changes you could make to your game.

After brainstorming twenty ideas, prioritize them based on how effectively they address the top issues raised by your playtesters and also based on the scope of work needed to implement the idea. Choose your top two to five ideas and implement them in the upcoming prototype stage. The process begins again.

# Benefits

The interactive entertainment iterative development process allows you to incrementally grow your game in a way that is pleasing to users. By doing quick iterations, you quickly find development paths that should be abandoned and others that should be started. While it might seem initially to be time consuming, the process will actually save you a lot of development time in the long run and greatly increase the chances that you converge on a game that is truly fun to play.

# Avoider Game

In the first couple of chapters in this book, we worked on Avoider Game, then switched to a zombie invasion simulation, and then a platform game. We will go back to Avoider Game and use it to demonstrate the concepts discussed earlier in this chapter. You can either start with your version of Avoider Game or download this version: `http://www.packtpub.com/support`

## Avoider Game recap

Our version of Avoider Game which we created in *Chapter 1, Let's Dive Right in...* and *Chapter 2, Animation* is fairly functional. It has an introduction screen, a game-over screen, a moving star field, interesting actor animations, a score, power-ups, and power-downs. *Figure 4* shows a screenshot from the game.

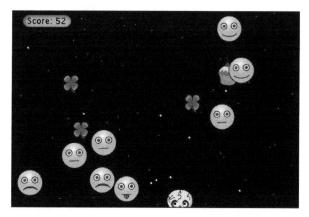

Figure 4: This is a snapshot of our version of Avoider Game

In the next several sections, we will augment this version of Avoider Game. Our changes will be based on the game design principles we just finished studying.

# High-score list

The first change we are going to make is to add a simple mechanism to record the highest score. We will then display this score on the game-over screen, so that players can see where they stand compared with each other. By adding a high score, we are clearly identifying the main goal of the game—score the most points. To add a high score, make the following changes to the `AvoiderGameOverWorld` class:

```java
import greenfoot.*;
import java.nio.*;
import java.nio.file.*;
import java.io.IOException;
import java.util.List;

public class AvoiderGameOverWorld extends World {
  public AvoiderGameOverWorld() {
    super(600, 400, 1);
  }

  public void act() {
    if( Greenfoot.mouseClicked(this) ) {
      AvoiderWorld world = new AvoiderWorld();
      Greenfoot.setWorld(world);
    }
  }

  public void setPlayerHighScore(String s) {
    Label scoreBoardMsg = new Label("Your Score: " + s, 35);
    Label highScoreMsg = new Label("Your Best: " +
recordAndReturnHighScore(s), 35);
    addObject(scoreBoardMsg, getWidth()/2, getHeight()*2/3);
    addObject(highScoreMsg, getWidth()/2, (getHeight()*2/3)+45);
  }

  private String recordAndReturnHighScore(String s) {
    String hs = null;
    try {
      Path scoreFile = Paths.get("./scoreFile.txt");

      if( Files.exists(scoreFile) ) {
```

```
            byte[] bytes = Files.readAllBytes(scoreFile);
            hs = new String(bytes);

            if( Integer.parseInt(s) > Integer.parseInt(hs) ) {
              Files.write(scoreFile, s.getBytes());
              hs = s;
            }
          } else {
            Files.write(scoreFile, s.getBytes());
            hs = s;
          }

        } catch( IOException e ) {
          System.out.println("IOException");
        }

      return hs;
    }
  }
```

The constructor and the `act()` method did not change. We added two new methods: `setPlayerHighScore()` and `recordAndReturnHighScore()`. The `setPlayerHighScore()` method is public and will be called by `AvoiderWorld` to pass the current player's score, in the form of `String`, to the game-over screen. Due to functional decomposition, this method is fairly simple. It creates two `Label` objects to display the player's score and the high score and then adds these objects to the current world, which is `AvoiderGameOverWorld`. The `Label` class is new and provides a way to easily create text-based images. We will look at the code for it shortly. First, we will look more closely at the `recordAndReturnHighScore()` method, which contains the functionality to retrieve and set the high score.

 The `java.nio.file` package requires that you have Java 1.7 or later installed.

The `recordAndReturnHighScore()` method introduces file I/O. To make the high score persist whether you have Avoider Game open or not, we need to store the high score in a file. Files provide persistent storage. We can use some very simple file I/O operations because we are only storing or retrieving a single `String`. First, we make a call to the `Paths.get()` static function. This provides the location of the file. Next, we check to see whether the file already exists using the `Files.exists()` static function. If the file does not exist, we create and write to it the current player's score using `Files.write()`.

This function will create the file and write to it and then close the file before returning. If the file does exist, then we read its contents using `Files.readAllBytes()` which will open the file, read the contents of the file, close the file, and then return the data it read. The last thing we need to do in this method, is to see if the current player's score is larger than the current high score. If it is, we update the file. `recordAndReturnHighScore()` then returns the highest score, which will either be the value read from the file or the current player's score. Please note the additional `import` statements we added to access these new file I/O classes.

> Greenfoot provides another mechanism to store and maintain high-score lists that only work after you have shared your game/application on the Greenfoot site. To learn more about this, read the Greenfoot online documentation on the `UserInfo` class provided by Greenfoot. You can access that documentation at `http://www.greenfoot.org/files/javadoc/`. To learn more about the Java file I/O, look at the tutorial at `http://docs.oracle.com/javase/tutorial/essential/io/index.html`.

Now, we can look at the code for the `Label` class. The `Label` class is a new class we are going to create to help us add text to our game. Create a new subclass of `Actor` and call it `Label`. Do not associate an image with this class. We will also use this class later in this chapter. Here is the code:

```java
import greenfoot.*;
import java.awt.Color;

public class Label extends Actor
{
  GreenfootImage msg;

  public Label(String s, int size) {
    this(s, size, Color.white);
  }

  public Label(String s, int size, Color c) {
    msg = new GreenfootImage(s, size, c, null);
    setImage(msg);
  }
}
```

This class is simple and only contains two constructors; the first one calls the second one with the default color, white. In the second constructor, `String`, which is supplied, is converted into an image using `GreenfootImage`, and then this image is set to be the default image for this instance of `Label`.

The last change that we need to make to get all this working, is add the code to `AvoiderWorld` to pass the player's current score to `AvoiderGameOverWorld`. We only need to add one line to the `endGame()` method in `AvoiderWorld`. Here is the complete implementation of `endGame()`:

```
public void endGame() {
   bkgMusic.stop();
   AvoiderGameOverWorld go = new AvoiderGameOverWorld();
   go.setPlayerHighScore(Integer.toString(scoreBoard.getScore()));
   Greenfoot.setWorld(go);
}
```

After making this change, compile the game to find and fix any typos that happened along the way. Play it. What's your top score? *Figure 5* demonstrates what your game-over screen should now look like.

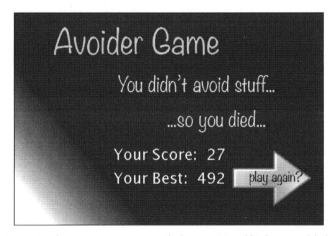

Figure 5: The game-over screen with the current and high score added.

# Achievement badges

Many games and gamification strategies use the notion of an achievement badge. This is a badge you earn for accomplishing something difficult or something out of the ordinary. In games and interactive applications, they are a convenient and popular technique of giving players subgoals to complete, conditioning their behavior, and adding complexity of choice. We will add achievement badges to accomplish all of those things in our version of Avoider Game.

First, we need to come up with a list of achievements. In practice, coming up with the right mix of achievements will take some careful thought, time, and playtesting. Here is the list of achievements I came up with:

- **Magically Delicious**: The player has to hit 20 clovers.

    ° This achievement adds complexity to the choices available to the player on a moment-to-moment basis. Do they dare risk collecting another clover and suffer the slow-down penalty?

- **Turkey**: The player must collect three rocks in a row. The user cannot touch any other object during this time.

    ° This achievement conditions the player to go after rocks even when they are at full health.

- **Unbreakable**: The player has to touch an enemy 10 times.

    ° This achievement adds to the complexity of choices available to the user and serves as a means to increase the challenge during certain slow parts of the game. In the game, you come across small periods of time where you are at full health and there is no immediate danger of being hit by an enemy. During these periods, the player could now choose to take a few hits to increase the number of **Unbreakable** badges they get.

- **Master Avoider**: The player finishes a game before hitting three cupcakes in total.

    ° This achievement reinforces the behavior that we want. We want the player to avoid cupcakes at all costs.

These achievements also serve as potential subgoals for the user. We will display the badges the player has earned on the game-over screen right next to the main goal—their score.

The first issue to consider when implementing achievement badges is that, the data needed to determine whether a badge was earned. In our case, this data is distributed between the `PowerItems` subclasses and `Avatar`. Also, the `AvoiderGameOverWorld` class will have to know which badges were earned, so that they can be displayed on the game-over screen. We would like to have a central location to collect this information. Because we need distributed access to a single class, we are going to use the **Singleton** design pattern.

### Design patterns

As you become more experienced in programming, you are going to recognize common patterns of coding that emerge in your work. Perhaps in the next game you create, you will also want achievements and think to yourself, "I can just reuse my design of achievements from my version of Avoider Game." In essence, you have a very small, personal design pattern that you can use to create achievements that you can improve upon over time.

Developers have created very useful design patterns since the inception of programming, that apply to many different types of applications. Design patterns provide a proven, tested method for coding certain functionality that you can easily adapt for your own uses.

Design patterns are also very useful to study. By examining them, you can see how some of the best programmers use abstraction to solve complex, recurring issues. They also serve as a concise language that developers can use to effectively communicate with each other. It is far more convenient to say that the `BadgeCenter` class in Avoider Game implements the Singleton design pattern rather than trying to describe it from scratch.

There are a lot of books published on design patterns, but the most famous and popular one is Design Patterns: Elements of Reusable Object-Oriented Software by *Gamma et al*. At some point in your development career, you should read it.

To keep track of player achievements, we are going to create a class called `BadgeCenter` that follows the Singleton design pattern. This new class will not be a subclass of `World` or `Actor`. To create it, click on **Edit** in the menu bar and then choose **New Class**. You should see the pop-up window shown in *Figure 6*. Type in `BadgeCenter` and press *Enter*. We are now ready to add the code.

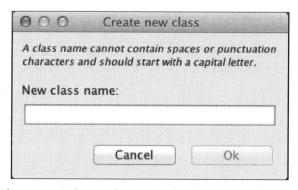

Figure 6: This is the popup window used to create a class that is not a subclass of Actor or World

# Here is the code for this class:

```java
import java.util.ArrayList;
import java.util.List;

public class BadgeCenter //Implemented as a Singleton
{
  private int clovers, rocks, enemies, cupcakes;
  int rockBadges;
  private String previous;
  private ArrayList<Badge> badges = new ArrayList<Badge>();
  private static final BadgeCenter INSTANCE = new BadgeCenter();

  private BadgeCenter() {
    clovers = rocks = enemies = cupcakes = 0;
    rockBadges = 0;
  }

  public static BadgeCenter getInstance() {
    return INSTANCE;
  }

  public void hitClover() {
    ++clovers;
    previous = "clover";
    if( clovers % 20 == 0 ) {
      if( clovers > 80 ) {
        awardBadge("Magically Delicious ");
      } else {
        awardBadge(clovers + " Clovers ");
      }
    }
  }

  public void hitRock() {
    if( previous != "rock" ) {
      rocks = 0;
    }
    ++rocks;
    previous = "rock";
    if( rocks > 2 ) {
      rockBadges++;
      rocks = 0;
    }
```

```
    }

    public void hitEnemy() {
      ++enemies;
      previous = "enemy";
      if( enemies % 10 == 0 ) {
        if( enemies > 60 ) {
          awardBadge( "Unbreakable " );
        } else {
          awardBadge("Hit " + enemies + " times ");
        }
      }
    }

    public void hitCupcake() {
      ++cupcakes; // Check if under 3 when return badges
      previous = "cupcake";
    }

    public List<Badge> getBadges() {
      if( cupcakes < 3 ) {
        awardBadge("Master Avoider ");
      }
      if( rockBadges > 0 ) {
        awardBadge("Turkey x " + rockBadges + " ");
      }
      cupcakes = 0;
      return badges;
    }

    private void awardBadge(String title) {
      badges.add(new Badge(title));
    }

}
```

Following the Singleton design pattern, we create a constructor that is `private` and provide a `static` method called `getInstance()` to manage access to the single instance of this class. Since `getInstance()` is `static`, all of our classes in our version of Avoider Game will have access to it.

 In practice, you should try and minimize your use of the keyword `static`. While it is very useful in several cases, abusing it can lead to poor design and hard-to-maintain code.

To collect all the data we need, we have four methods: `hitClover()`, `hitRock()`, `hitEnemy()`, and `hitCupcake()`. These methods will be called by the `Clover`, `Rock`, `Avatar`, and `Cupcake` classes, respectively, to report collisions. Each method tracks the number of hits, sets the `previous` variable, and then determines if a badge should be awarded. For example, `hitClover()` first increments the variable `clovers` and then sets `previous` to `Clover`. The method then checks to see if we have just hit another 20 clovers. If so, we award a badge using the `awardBadge()` method. If we hit over 80 clovers, we issue the grand prize—a *Magically Delicious* badge.

The `awardBadge()` method is used to record badges. It takes `String` that will be used as the title of the achievement, creates `Badge` anew, and then stores that badge in an array. The array will later be accessed using `getBadges()` by `AvoiderGameOverWorld`. The `getBadges()` method has a few duties other than returning the array of badges achieved until now. It looks at values maintained by `hitCupcakes()` and `hitRock()` and determines whether additional badges should be awarded. If you did not know, the term, *turkey*, comes from bowling and means you just got three strikes in a row.

Here is the code we need to add to the constructor of `AvoiderGameOverWorld`, in order to display the badges on the game-over screen:

```
public AvoiderGameOverWorld() {
   super(600, 400, 1);

   List<Badge> badgeList = BadgeCenter.getInstance().getBadges();
   int yPos = 130;
   while(!badgeList.isEmpty()) {
     Badge nextBadge = badgeList.remove(0);
     addObject(nextBadge, 60, yPos);
     yPos += 70;
   }

}
```

In the constructor, we use `BadgeCenter.getInstance()` to get access to the single instance of `BadgeCenter` and then immediately invoke `getBadges()`. We then iterate over `badgeList` (we discussed the `List` interface in *Chapter 3, Collision Detection*) and add each `Badge` to the world. We use the variable `yPos` to appropriately space out the badges.

Because we use the `List` interface, we need to add the following `import` statement to `AvoiderGameOverWorld`:

```
import java.util.List;
```

Last, we need to define the `Badge` class. It is a simple class that adds a text string onto an image for a badge. *Figure 7* shows the image I created for badges. I tried to make it look like a tombstone.

Figure 7: This is the image associated with the Badge class.

Create a new subclass of `Actor` and call it `Badge`. Assign the new image you created for badges or use mine. Add this code to it:

```
import greenfoot.*;
import java.awt.Color;

public class Badge extends Actor {
  GreenfootImage bkg;
  GreenfootImage msg;

  public Badge(String s) {
    bkg = getImage();
    msg = new GreenfootImage(s, 14, Color.white, null);
    bkg.drawImage(msg, 10, 20);
    setImage(bkg);
  }

}
```

We have already discussed the `Color` and `GreenfootImage` classes in the earlier chapters. The constructor uses the `drawImage()` method of `GreenfootImage` to draw one image on top of another. By doing this, we effectively add the text.

Compile the code, debug any mistakes, and try it out. What badges did you earn?

# Player conditioning

I would like to provide you with an example where some user conditioning I added to the game had to be removed as I determined, after playtesting, that it drove the wrong behavior. Initially, I thought of changing the game to provide 10 points for each clover you hit. This would help to increase the complexity of the game, as players would have to balance getting more points against the slowdown penalty of clovers.

However, this change really had an effect on the player. Because clovers are so plentiful and worth 10 points, it really became worthwhile to collect clovers as a means of getting high scores. This changed the whole feel of the game from one that encourages avoiding to one that encourages collecting. Therefore, the change was removed.

In addition, adding points to clovers broke some of the story elements of the game. In the game, things that look good are bad. But, by having a good item provide a direct benefit to the player, we broke our game's theme. Next, we will discuss theming and storytelling in Avoider Game.

# Storytelling

It is hard to build a deep, meaningful story for a game like ours. However, the player will still try to make sense of the world we threw them in, and we need to do as much as we can to help the player construct a meaningful world. Our story should motivate why we flee from smiley faces and cupcakes and welcome rocks.

## Adding a story screen

To help tell the story of our game, we are going to create a story screen the player can choose to view before playing the game. This screen will provide the background and context for our game, as well as set up its theme. While we are at it, we are going to add a credits screen. Adding comments to your code to credit artists and developers is a good start, but eventually you will need to formally recognize these people. Plus, you can give the person who worked hardest on this game credit—you!

First, we are going to add some buttons to our introduction screen that, when clicked, will either take you to the story screen, take you to the credits screen, or start the game. Here are the changes we need to make to AvoiderGameIntroScreen:

```
import greenfoot.*;

public class AvoiderGameIntroScreen extends World {
  Actor startButton, creditButton, storyButton;

  public AvoiderGameIntroScreen() {
    super(600, 400, 1);
    startButton = addButton("Start Game", getWidth()/2,
      getHeight()*2/3);
    creditButton = addButton("Credits Screen", getWidth()/2,
      (getHeight()*2/3)+40);
    storyButton = addButton("Story Screen", getWidth()/2,
      (getHeight()*2/3)+80);
  }
```

```
public void act() {
  if ( Greenfoot.mouseClicked(startButton) ) {
    AvoiderWorld world = new AvoiderWorld();
    Greenfoot.setWorld(world);
  } else if ( Greenfoot.mouseClicked(creditButton) ) {
    AvoiderGameCreditScreen world = new
      AvoiderGameCreditScreen();
    Greenfoot.setWorld(world);
  } else if ( Greenfoot.mouseClicked(storyButton) ) {
    AvoiderGameStoryScreen world = new AvoiderGameStoryScreen();
    Greenfoot.setWorld(world);
  }
}

private Actor addButton(String s, int x, int y) {
  Actor button = new Label(s, 24);
  addObject(button, x, y);
  return button;
}
}
```

The constructor function creates three buttons using the addButton() method. In the act() method, we simply listen for mouse clicks on those buttons and switch worlds appropriately if we get one. We covered all of this in *Chapter 1, Let's Dive Right in...,* except for the implementation of addButton().

The method addButton() creates a new Label and adds it to the screen. We discussed the Label class earlier in the chapter.

After running this code, your introduction screen will look like the one shown in *Figure 8.*

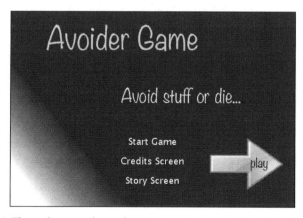

Figure 8: This is the revised introduction screen to our version of Avoider Game

Now, we just need to make the story screen (`AvoiderGameStoryScreen`) and the credits screen (`AvoiderGameCreditScreen`). You already learned how to do this (refer to *Chapter 1, Let's Dive Right in…*), and I will just show you what my screens look like in *Figure 9* and *Figure 10*. Feel free to use mine or make your own.

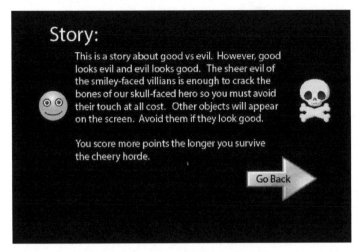

Figure 9: This is how our story screen will look

This is how the credits screen looks.

Figure 10: This is how the credits screen looks

# Changing the score

Getting points in the game is a good thing; therefore, our score indicator should look like a bad thing. Right now, it is neutral and does not contribute to the story or theme of the game. Let's change this narrative descriptor.

Presently, we are using the imported Counter class. To get a customized look for our score, we are going to need to create our own class and not rely on the Counter class. Create a new subclass of Actor and name it Score. Because points and badges are types of awards, I thought making them both tombstones made sense. *Figure 11* shows the image I used for the new Score actor. It is a smaller version of the tombstone used for achievement badges with the **Achievement Badge** text replaced with **R.I.P.**.

Figure 11: This is the image for our new Score class.

Here is the code for the Score class:

```
import greenfoot.*;
import java.awt.Color;

public class Score extends Actor{
  Label msg;
  int counter = 0;

  public Score() {
    msg = new Label("0", 24, Color.black);
  }

  protected void addedToWorld(World w) {
    w.addObject(msg, getX(), getY() + 5);
  }

  public void addScore(int i) {
    counter = counter + i;
    updateImage();
  }

  public int getScore() {
    return counter;
  }

  private void updateImage() {
    getWorld().removeObject(msg);
```

```
        msg = new Label(Integer.toString(counter), 24, Color.black);
        getWorld().addObject(msg, getX(), getY() + 5);
    }


}
```

This class stores the current score in the `counter` integer variable. You can increase the score by calling `addScore()` and retrieve the current score by calling `getScore()`. The `Score` class works by adding an image that contains the current score over the default image, which is a tombstone. Whenever the score changes, the `counter` variable is incremented and then `updateImage()` is called. The `updateImage()` method removes the old object containing the image of the score and then creates a new image based on the current value of `counter` using the `Label` class (as discussed previously). The `addedToWorld()` method is needed to display the initial score of 0.

We have made several changes. Make sure to compile and run your game to ensure that everything works properly.

# Adding sound effects

Sound effects can provide important and valuable feedback to players. Also, they can be important narrative descriptors. In this section, we are going to add some sound effects to both enhance meaningful play and the story of the game.

Because cupcakes, clovers, and rocks have a random, limited lifespan, it can be confusing to know whether you hit one or it just expired right before touching you. If you were at full health already, you have no idea whether you hit a rock or not. If you do not move, you cannot tell whether you really hit a cupcake or clover. We are going to solve this ambiguity by playing a sound whenever you collide with any `PowerItems`. This will also help players who are actively trying to gain achievement badges.

We will choose sounds appropriate for our game's story. If the player collides with a cupcake or clover, then we will play the sound of you saying, *Woot!*. If you, the player, collide with a rock, then we will play the sound of you saying, *Ahhh!*. This fits with the theme of the game.

You could play any sound effect you find on the Internet (assuming it is free for such use) or create your own using various audio editing programs. Fortunately, Greenfoot comes with a built-in audio recording and editing tool. To access it, click on **Controls** in the main menu and then choose **Show Sound Recorder**. You should see the window shown in *Figure 12*.

Figure 12: This is the sound recorder tool in Greenfoot

Using Greenfoot's sound recorder, record yourself saying *ahhh* and save it as `ahhh.`
`wav`. Then, record yourself saying *woot* and save it as `woot.wav`. To make your
recordings as concise as possible, you can use the **Trim to selection** button to
eliminate any beginning or ending silence or unnecessary noises.

We are going to add two methods to the `Avatar` class to play these sounds. Here is
the first method:

```
public void sayAhhh() {
  ahhh.play();
}
```

Here is the second method:

```
public void sayWoot() {
  woot.play();
}
```

We create two instance variables, `woot` and `ahhh`, at the top of the `Avatar` class:

```
private GreenfootSound woot;
private GreenfootSound ahhh;
```

Initialize them in the `AddedToWorld()` method. Here is this initialization code:

```
woot = new GreenfootSound("sounds/woot.wav");
ahhh = new GreenfootSound("sounds/ahhh.wav");
```

We have now set up Avatar to say *ahhh* or *woot!*. We just need to change PowerItems to call either of the two methods we just added to the Avatar class. In the Cupcake class, change checkHitAvatar() to this:

```
protected void checkHitAvatar() {
  Avatar a = (Avatar) getOneIntersectingObject(Avatar.class);
  if( a != null ) {
    bc.hitCupcake();
    a.sayWoot();
    a.stun();
    getWorld().removeObject(this);
  }
}
```

In the Clover class, we need to change checkHitAvatar() to this:

```
protected void checkHitAvatar() {
  Avatar a = (Avatar) getOneIntersectingObject(Avatar.class);
  if( a != null ) {
    bc.hitClover();
    a.sayWoot();
    a.lagControls();
    getWorld().removeObject(this);
  }
}
```

In the Health class, we need to change checkHitAvatar() to this:

```
protected void checkHitAvatar() {
  Avatar a = (Avatar) getOneIntersectingObject(Avatar.class);
  if( a != null ) {
    bc.hitRock();
    a.sayAhhh();
    a.addHealth();
    getWorld().removeObject(this);
  }
}
```

Compile your game and play. Enjoy all of the *wooting* and *ahhhing*!

# Playtesting

Playtest your game and see if you think the game needs any changes. After playing for a while, I decided to change the `increaseLevel()` method in `AvoiderWorld` to this:

```
private void increaseLevel() {
  int score = scoreBoard.getScore();

  if( score > nextLevel ) {
    enemySpawnRate += 4;
    enemySpeed++;
    cupcakeFrequency += 3;
    cloverFrequency += 3;
    healthFrequency += 1;
    nextLevel += 50;
  }
}
```

I felt that there were not enough enemies on screen and that the `Health` power-ups were too frequent after the player had increased several levels. To help with this, I increased the rate of change to the `enemySpawnRate` variable to 4 and reduced the rate of increase to the `healthFrequency` variable to 1. With these changes, the game play felt better. Do you agree with my changes? What changes do you feel improve the game? Of course, the way to best determine the appropriate values for these variables is to recruit more playtesters.

Refer to http://en.wikipedia.org/wiki/Balance_(game_design) for more information on game balance.

# Challenge

We added some nice features to our version of Avoider Game. Of course, it seems there are endless cool things we could try to implement in order to improve our game. As a programming challenge, let's try one more. Change the game, so that players are awarded bonus points for each achievement badge they get. This change will further encourage the users to attempt the achievements. This also potentially enhances long-term meaningful play. How many points are you going to assign for each badge? Will each badge be worth the same amount of points? How does this affect game play? Is this a change you would keep?

Let's spruce up our introduction screen. Add background music and play a *click* sound when the player clicks on a menu choice. Providing auditory feedback to player actions enhances those interactions.

# Additional readings

A good portion of my philosophy of game design came from many years of teaching game development and two key textbooks. The first textbook is *Rules of Play* by Eric Zimmerman and Katie Salen, published in 2003. This book provides an in-depth and thorough coverage of games, game history, and game design. The other book that heavily influenced me was *Half-real* by Jesper Juul, published in 2005. This book offers a more concise study of game design. If you have a passion for game design, I highly recommend that you read these two books.

# Summary

Creating meaningful play is the main goal for game designers. In this chapter, we defined meaningful play and learned many game design techniques for enhancing meaningful play. We also learned a process for creating interactive applications that will guide you in creating engaging applications. As you read the rest of this book, and eventually create your own applications, you should reflect on this chapter and apply the techniques provided.

In the next chapter, you will learn to create worlds for our games that expand far beyond the edges of the screen.

# 6

# Scrolling and Mapped Worlds

*"Already know you that which you need."*

*– Yoda*

In Greenfoot, we can build worlds that are much larger than the confines of a single screen. Through scrolling techniques and dynamic actor generation, we can build side-scrolling games and map worlds that can seem endless. When you combine these large worlds with the techniques learned in the previous chapters, you will be able to create a truly compelling and immersive experience for your audience.

The techniques you will learn in this chapter are similar to the ones you learned in *Chapter 2*, *Animation*, for animation. We will use illusion. Through very simple techniques, we can give the appearance that the user is moving through an expansive world. In this chapter, you will learn to create the following types of worlds:

- Dynamically generated
- Mapped
- Tile-based

As you learn more about Greenfoot and Java programming, you will notice repeating patterns and methods to accomplish specific tasks. While the content presented here warrants its own chapter, it is really a careful mixture of things you have already learned.

# Chapter scenario examples

In this chapter, we are going to look at four different methods to create large worlds for simulations, games, or animations. We are only going to present the code necessary to accomplish this and not elaborate further. *You should combine the methods learned here with the topics presented in the previous chapters to develop complete applications.* In addition, we will use very simple graphics in our scenarios and assume that you would spend more time on art and story (as described in *Chapter 5, Interactive Application Design and Theory*) for your own work.

# Dynamically generated worlds

It would seem creating worlds that are dynamically generated and potentially endless would be the concluding topic of this chapter, instead of the introductory one. On the contrary, dynamically creating a world is easy, and we have already seen all the coding necessary to do so. In *Chapter 1, Let's Dive Right in…*, we dynamically created enemies in Avoider Game that streamed down from the top, and later, in *Chapter 2, Animation*, we added a dynamically generated star field. We will use the same techniques to create a seemingly endless world. Imagine that the enemies in Avoider Game were generated less frequently and looked like planets. It would look like we were travelling through space. Imagine we had a green background and used an image of a tree for our enemies. It would look like we were walking through a forest. Next, we will create a Greenfoot scenario that displays a user-controlled rocket flying through a cloudy sky.

# Side-scrolling

We are going to create the flying game depicted in *Figure 1*. In this game, the user controls the rocket and attempts to avoid the walls. Why walls? Well, they are easy to draw and sufficiently illustrate the concepts. In your own scenario, you could spend some time and draw alien spaceships, birds, balloons, or anything else that makes sense to you.

Figure 1: This is a screenshot of the Clouds Greenfoot scenario.

Start by creating a new Greenfoot scenario, naming it Clouds, and saving it to disk. We will present the code for the world and actors next.

# The Rocket class

In this example scenario, the user controls a rocket. You move the rocket by pressing the arrow keys. The movement of the rocket is restricted to stay inside the area of the screen. If the rocket hits a wall (which we will add soon), then the scenario will stop. There is no code in the Rocket class specific to generating a dynamic world, and it is all code we saw in the previous chapters. Create a new subclass of Actor, name it Rocket, associate the image of a rocket provided by Greenfoot with it, and enter the following code in its class file:

```
import greenfoot.*;

public class Rocket extends Actor {
    private int speedX = 1;
    private int speedY = 0;
    private static final int SPEED = 2;
    private static final int BOUNDARY = 20;

    public void act() {
        handleKeyPresses();
        boundedMove();
        checkForCrash();
    }
```

```java
    private void handleKeyPresses() {
      handleArrowKey("down", 0, SPEED);
      handleArrowKey("up", 0, -SPEED);
      handleArrowKey("left", -SPEED, 0);
      handleArrowKey("right", SPEED, 0);
    }

    private void handleArrowKey(String k, int sX, int sY) {
      if( Greenfoot.isKeyDown(k) ) {
        speedX = sX;
        speedY = sY;
      }
    }

    private void boundedMove() {
      int newX = Math.max(BOUNDARY, speedX+getX());
      newX = Math.min(getWorld().getWidth()-BOUNDARY, newX);
      int newY = Math.max(BOUNDARY, speedY+getY());
      newY = Math.min(getWorld().getHeight()-BOUNDARY, newY);
      setLocation(newX,newY);
    }

    private void checkForCrash() {
      Actor w = getOneIntersectingObject(Obstacle.class);
      if( w != null ) {
        Greenfoot.stop();
      }
    }
}
```

You should be very familiar with the code to handle key presses and moving actors. One additional concept I have added here, is *functional decomposition* to remove code redundancy. Notice how the `handleArrowKey()` method can handle movement for all arrow keys. The code for `checkForCrash()` simply implements our standard template to detect collisions. We will add the `Obstacle` actor soon.

In `boundedMove()`, we have code that gets the user to not leave the screen. Without this code, the user could go off the screen and disappear from view in any direction. Using Java's `max()` and `min()` math library functions, `boundedMove()` ensures that the new *x* and *y* locations of the rocket stay within the confines of the screen. The `BOUNDARY` variable defines how close the rocket can get to an edge. We add this buffer to prevent the rocket from hiding a majority of its image off the sides.

# The CloudsWorld class

The main responsibility of our world class is to initially place the rocket on the screen and randomly generate clouds and walls. Create a new subclass of World, name it CloudsWorld, and assign a plain blue image to it for the background. You can either use the blue gradient background we used in *Chapter 4, Projectiles*, or create a new one using your favorite drawing program. As with the Rocket class, most of the code for CloudsWorld should be a review of previously provided code. Here is the code for CloudsWorld:

```
import greenfoot.*;

public class CloudsWorld extends World {

  public CloudsWorld() {
    super(600, 400, 1, false);
    prepare();
  }

  public void act() {
    generateBackgroundClouds();
    generateWalls();
  }

  private void generateBackgroundClouds() {
    generateActor(5, new Cloud1());
    generateActor(4, new Cloud2());
    generateActor(3, new Cloud3());
  }

  private void generateWalls() {
    generateActor(5, new Wall());
  }

  private void generateActor(int chance, Actor a) {
    if( Greenfoot.getRandomNumber(1000) < chance) {
      int randY = Greenfoot.getRandomNumber(300) + 50;
      addObject(a, getWidth()+20, randY);
    }
  }

  private void prepare(){
    Rocket rocket = new Rocket();
    addObject(rocket, 90, 200);
  }
}
```

Do you remember what the `act()` method looked liked in our latest version of Avoider Game? Here's what it looks like:

```
// NOTE: DO NOT PUT THIS CODE IN YOUR CLOUDSWORLD CLASS
public void act() {
  generateEnemies();
  generateStars(-1);
  generatePowerItems();
  increaseLevel();
}
```

Doesn't it look similar to the `act()` method for `CloudsWorld`? We are going to use the same technique we used to generate enemies in Avoider Game to generate clouds in the Clouds application.

Let's start by looking at the `generateActor()` method. This method takes an actor (type `Actor`) and an integer (type `int`) as parameters. The integer represents the chance that we add the supplied actor to the world. The higher the number, the more likely that the actor will appear on screen. With this method, we can easily implement the `generateBackgroundClouds()` method and the `generateWalls()` method. In these methods, we simply call `generateActor()`, providing the chance for the actor to appear on screen as well as a new instance of the desired actor.

## Side-scrolling actors

All of the other actors in our scenario are going to be subclasses of the `SideScrollingActor` class. Create this by subclassing `Actor`, but do not associate an image with it. With the following code, we are using inheritance to provide the side-scrolling behavior to a whole set of actors:

```
import greenfoot.*;

public abstract class SideScrollingActor extends Actor
{
  public int speed = -1; // Moves right to left
  private static final int BOUNDARY = 100;

  public void act()
  {
    move(speed);
    checkOffScreen();
  }

  private void checkOffScreen() {
```

```
     if( getX() < -BOUNDARY || getX() > getWorld().getWidth() +
BOUNDARY) {
        getWorld().removeObject(this);
     }
   }
}
```

To give the illusion that our rocket is moving from left to right, we make all of the scrolling actors move from right to left. That is why the speed variable is negative. In the act() method, we move the actor and then call checkOffScreen() to remove the actor after it has moved off screen. As we never intend to use the SideScrollingActor class to directly instantiate an object, we make it abstract. Next, we will discuss the actors that are going to the SideScrollingActor subclass.

## Clouds

We use three different images of clouds for our application, and we will make them travel at different, random speeds. This will provide enough variety to give a realistic feel to our flying rocket. The three images I used are shown in *Figure 2*. You can draw your own or the ones supplied at http://www.packtpub.com/support.

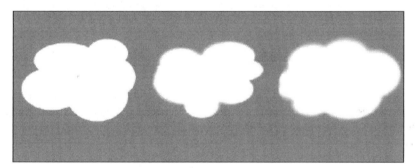

Figure 2: These are images of clouds

Create a cloud actor by subclassing SideScrollingActor, naming it Cloud1, and then assigning one of your cloud images to it. In the class file for Cloud1, put the following code:

```
import greenfoot.*;

public class Cloud1 extends SideScrollingActor {
  private static final int SPEEDRANGE = 3;
  public Cloud1() {
    speed = -(Greenfoot.getRandomNumber(SPEEDRANGE) + 1);
  }
}
```

In `Cloud1`, we assign a random value to the `speed` variable between 1 and 3. We inherited the `speed` variable from the `SideScrollingActor` parent class.

To create two more cloud actors, repeat the preceding steps once, substituting `Cloud1` with `Cloud2` and again substituting `Cloud1` with `Cloud3`. For further variety, you could change the SPEEDRANGE constant in each actor. I recommend setting SPEEDRANGE to 3 (as shown in Figure 2) for `Cloud1`, 2 for `Cloud2`, and 5 for `Cloud3`.

## Walls

The last thing we need to add is the wall obstacle. While we only have one obstacle in this example, we are going to write code that would allow us to easily add additional obstacles in the future. We are going to use inheritance, but this time, we are using it to group related types, as opposed to sharing code. In the `Rocket Actor` code, we check for a collision with an `Obstacle` class. We will now create this class by subclassing `SideScrollingActor`, naming the new subclass `Obstacle`, and not associating an image with it. Here is the code for the `Obstacle` actor:

```
import greenfoot.*;

public class Obstacle extends SideScrollingActor{
}
```

Again, we are not using inheritance for code reuse and, therefore, there is very little code to add.

Now, to create the `Wall` actor, we create a subclass of `Obstacle`. I simply created a dark gray rectangle image for my wall. I am sure you can come up with something better. Here is the code for the `Wall` class:

```
import greenfoot.*;
public class Wall extends Obstacle {
}
```

Since `Obstacle` inherits from `SideScrollingActor`, the `Wall` actor will have the same movement as the `Cloud` actors. However, the `Rocket` class can now detect collision with the `Obstacle` class. If we did collision detection with the `SideScrollingActor` class, then we would collide with clouds too.

# Try it out

We have finished creating the world and actor classes for our Greenfoot scenario. *Figure 3* shows the completed Greenfoot scenario. Make sure your class hierarchy is exactly the same.

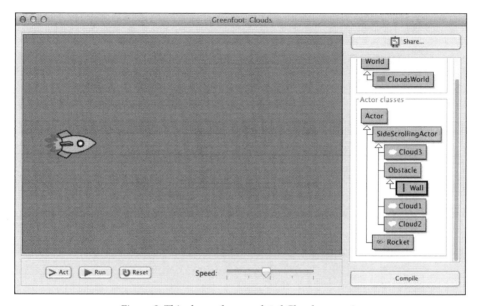

Figure 3: This shows the completed Clouds scenario

Compile it and take care of any typos you created along the way. Spend some time running the scenario and observing how the moving clouds give the illusion of travelling across an expansive sky. Even knowing how it is done, it is hard to imagine that your rocket is actually the actor on screen moving the least.

# Mapped worlds

There are definitely times when you are going to want a specific background for your game or simulation. In these cases, it is not sufficient to randomly generate actors to simulate a moving background. The methods we will explore next consist of creating a background image that is much larger than the dimensions of the screen and moving it appropriately to simulate motion. In addition, we will learn how to place actors in this larger world.

# Side-scrolling

Our side-scrolling example is a scenario that allows the user to walk through a mountain forest to find a lake at the end. The user will only be able to walk left and right, not up and down. *Figure 4* shows the completed application.

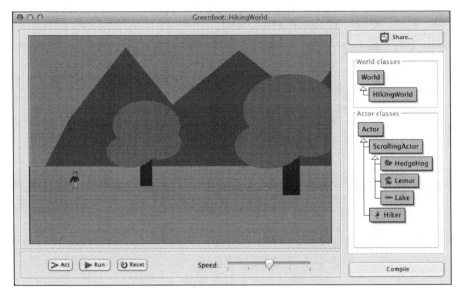

Figure 4: This is a screenshot of HikingWorld

To create this side-scrolling world, we are going to need a large image to serve as the background. For this example, I have created a 2400 x 400 image shown in *Figure 5*. Since our scenario has a viewable screen size of 600 x 400, the image is six times longer than our screen. Feel free to create your own 2400 x 400 image or use the one supplied at http://www.packtpub.com/support.

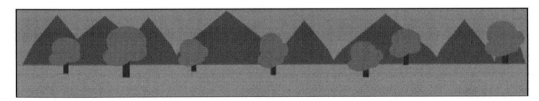

Figure 5: This is a background image for HikingWorld that is 2400 pixels long and 400 pixels high. Note that the image in this figure is one-fourth the original size in order to fit on a page

Next, we will describe the code for the world and actor classes.

# The HikingWorld class

The main responsibility of our world class, HikingWorld, is to shift everything in the world relative to the user-controlled Hiker class. We will allow the user to move normally within the confines of a screen, but when a user tries to move further than the left boundary or the right boundary of the screen, we will move everything to the right-hand side or left-hand side, respectively. Figure 6 demonstrates what we will do if the user is at the right edge of the screen and tries to move to the right-hand side.

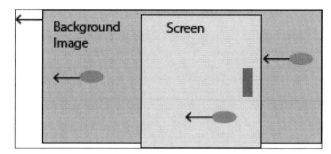

Figure 6: If the player moves right at the right edge of the screen, we will shift everything to the left

Now that we understand what the HikingWorld class must do, let's take a look at the code. First, subclass World and name the new subclass HikingWorld. Do not associate an image with this new class; we will do that in the constructor function. Here is the code for what the HikingWorld class must do:

```
import greenfoot.*;
import java.util.List;

public class HikingWorld extends World {
  private int xOffset = 0;
  private final static int SWIDTH = 600;
  private final static int SHEIGHT = 400;
  private final static int WWIDTH = 2400;
  private GreenfootImage bimg;

  public HikingWorld() {
    super(SWIDTH, SHEIGHT, 1, false);
    bimg = new GreenfootImage("HikingWorldBackground.png");
    shiftWorld(0);
    prepare();
  }

  public void shiftWorld(int dx) {
```

```
        if ( (xOffset + dx) <= 0 && (xOffset + dx) >= SWIDTH - WWIDTH) {
          xOffset = xOffset + dx;
          shiftWorldBackground(dx);
          shiftWorldActors(dx);
        }
    }

    private void shiftWorldBackground(int dx) {
      GreenfootImage bkgd = new GreenfootImage(SWIDTH, SHEIGHT);
      bkgd.drawImage(bimg, xOffset, 0);
      setBackground(bkgd);
    }

    private void shiftWorldActors(int dx) {
      List<ScrollingActor> saList =
      getObjects(ScrollingActor.class);
      for ( ScrollingActor a : saList ) {
        a.setAbsoluteLocation(dx);
      }
    }

    private void prepare() {
      HedgeHog hh1 = new HedgeHog();
      addObject(hh1, 900, 250);
      Lemur l = new Lemur();
      addObject(l, 1200, 300);
      HedgeHog hh2 = new HedgeHog();
      addObject(hh2, 1500, 250);
      Lake lake = new Lake();
      addObject(lake, 2100, 300);
      Hiker hiker = new Hiker();
      addObject(hiker, 90, 275);
    }
  }
```

At the beginning of the class, we create three constants to store the dimensions of the screen (SWIDTH and SHEIGHT) and the background image (WWIDTH). Since the image height and the screen height are the same, we don't need a WHEIGHT constant. We also declare the xOffset instance variable. We use this variable to keep track of how far the background image and actors are currently shifted. Last, we create an instance variable, bimg, to point to the background image.

In the constructor, we load our background image and call `shiftWorld()` with an offset of `0` to put everything at its starting location. We use the `prepare()` method in a standard way—to place our initial actors. One thing to notice is that we use *y* positions larger than the screen size. So, some of our actors will be created, but placed off screen. Eventually, they will be shifted to be on screen and viewable by the user. The real work to make this world large is done in `shiftWorld()`.

Notice the first `if` statement in the `shiftWorld()` method. This `if` statement prevents us from shifting the background image to the point where we would see the blank white space behind it.

If we are not at the edges of the background image, then we record the new offset by adding the current shift (`dx`) to the current offset (`xOffset`). Then, we proceed to shift the background image using the `shiftWorldBackground()` method and all actors in the world using `shiftWorldActors()`. The `shiftWorldBackground()` method is fairly simple. We start by creating a new image the size of the screen. We then draw our background image into it, offset by `xOffset` (which has just had `dx` added to it), and then set this new image to be the background image.

The `shiftWorldActors()` method may have few lines, but it does a lot of work. There is a `World` method called `getObjects()` provided to us that will return all of the actors in the world of the supplied class. For us, we call `getObjects(ScrollingActor.class)` to get all objects that should be shifted. The class the user controls, `Hiker`, is not a subclass of `ScrollingActor`; therefore, it will not be shifted in this method. We then iterate through the returned Java `List` and call `setAbsoluteLocation()` on each instance of `ScrollingActor`. We will look at the implementation of the `ScrollingActor` class and `setAbsoluteLocation()` soon.

The majority of the work for creating a side-scrolling world is done in `HikingWorld`. Make sure you understand this code before moving on. The rest of the code for the remaining actors in this scenario is pretty straightforward.

# The Hiker class

We will have one instance of the `Hiker` class that the user will control. In this scenario, we are only going to let the user move left and right. This amount of control is sufficient to demonstrate a side-scrolling scenario. The code for this class is almost identical to the code for the `Rocket` actor in the Clouds scenario we created at the beginning of this chapter. First, look at the code, and then we will discuss the differences:

```
import greenfoot.*;

public class Hiker extends Actor
```

```
{
  private int speedX = 1;
  private static final int SPEED = 2;
  private static final int BOUNDARY = 40;

  public void act() {
    handleKeyPresses();
    boundedMove();
    checkAtLake();
  }

  private void handleKeyPresses() {
    handleArrowKey("left", -SPEED);
    handleArrowKey("right", SPEED);
  }

  private void handleArrowKey(String k, int sX) {
    if( Greenfoot.isKeyDown(k) ) {
      speedX = sX;
    }
  }

  private void boundedMove() {
    if( speedX+getX() <= BOUNDARY ) {
      setLocation(BOUNDARY, getY());
      ((HikingWorld)getWorld()).shiftWorld(-speedX);
    } else if( speedX+getX() >= getWorld().getWidth()-BOUNDARY ) {
      setLocation(getWorld().getWidth()-BOUNDARY, getY());
      ((HikingWorld)getWorld()).shiftWorld(-speedX);
    } else {
      setLocation(getX()+speedX, getY());
    }
    speedX = 0;
  }

  private void checkAtLake() {
    // Do something cool if make it to the lake...
  }
}
```

The main difference occurs in boundedMove(). In the Rocket class presented earlier, we had a similar method that confined the user movement to a rectangular area slightly smaller than the screen. We are doing the same here for horizontal movement, but with one added feature. When we detect that the user is at the edge of the screen (either the left-hand side or the right-hand side), we will call shiftWorld() to make it look as though the actor is continuing to move.

We also have the checkAtLake() method that has no implementation. It is an example of how you could have a goal at the end of your world that the user must get to. In our case, we are going to place a lake at the end of the hike. We would use this method if we wanted to do something once the user arrived at the lake.

## The ScrollingActor class

All of the actors we want to shift will subclass the ScrollingActor class. It provides both a convenient way to group these actors and allows us to define the setAbsoluteLocation() method in one place. Here's how it's done:

```
import greenfoot.*;

public class ScrollingActor extends Actor {
  public void setAbsoluteLocation(int dx) {
    setLocation(getX()+dx, getY());
  }
}
```

In the HikingWorld class, we called setAbsoluteLocation() on all the actors we wanted to shift. This method is simply a wrapper for setLocation() and moves the actor by the dx amount.

The code for the HedgeHog, Lemur, and Lake actors are identical and very minimal. Those classes mainly exist to allow different images to be associated with them. The images for a hedgehog and lemur come with the default installation of Greenfoot. My lake is a simple blue oval created in a drawing program. These actors are placed in the world in the prepare() method of HikingWorld. Create each of these now and add the following code to each (make sure to substitute in the appropriate class name):

```
import greenfoot.*;

public class HedgeHog extends ScrollingActor {
}
```

# Try it out

Congratulations! You have created a side-scrolling, mapped world. Compile it and try it out. For an extra challenge, implement the `checkAtLake()` method found in the `Hiker` class to reward the hiker for reaching their destination. You can also download a completed version of the scenario at `http://www.packtpub.com/support`.

# 2D scrolling

Creating an application that allows a user to explore a large map in both the $x$ (left and right) and $y$ (up and down) directions is an easy extension of the side-scrolling world we just created. The code will be exactly the same except we will also handle the case for up and down movement. We also need an image that is both longer and wider than the screen size of our scenario. The image I created is 1200 x 1200 pixels and shown in *Figure 7*. You can create your own or download the image from *Figure 7* at `http://www.packtpub.com/support`. The picture is meant to represent a top-down view of a terrain with trees.

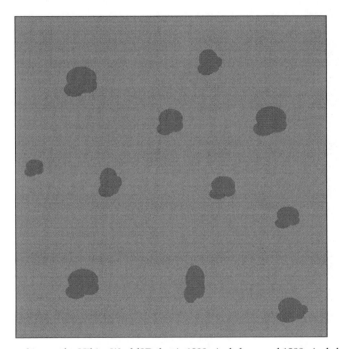

Figure 7: A background image for HikingWorld2D that is 1200 pixels long and 1200 pixels high. Note that the image shown in this figure has been scaled down to fit on the page.

Create a new scenario and name it `HikingWorld2D`. As this code is very similar to the `HikingWorld` scenario we just implemented in the previous section, we will only highlight the code necessary to handle up and down movement.

# The HikingWorld2D class

Subclass `World` and name the new class `HikingWorld2D`, but do not associate an image with it. We will add the image shown in *Figure 7* (or one like it that you create) in the constructor function of this class. Here is the code to accomplish all this:

```
import greenfoot.*;
import java.util.List;

public class HikingWorld extends World {
  private int xOffset = 0;
  private int yOffset = 0;
  private final static int SWIDTH = 600;
  private final static int SHEIGHT = 400;
  private final static int WWIDTH = 1200;
  private final static int WHEIGHT = 1200;
  private GreenfootImage bimg;

  public HikingWorld() {
    super(SWIDTH, SHEIGHT, 1, false);
    bimg = new GreenfootImage("HikingWorldBackground2D.png");
    shiftWorld(0,0);
    prepare();
  }

  public void shiftWorld(int dx, int dy) {
    if( (xOffset + dx) <= 0 && (xOffset + dx) >= SWIDTH - WWIDTH) {
      xOffset = xOffset + dx;
      shiftWorldBackground(dx, 0);
      shiftWorldActors(dx, 0);
    }
    if( (yOffset + dy) <= 0 && (yOffset + dy) >= SHEIGHT - WHEIGHT) {
      yOffset = yOffset + dy;
      shiftWorldBackground(0, dy);
      shiftWorldActors(0, dy);
    }
  }

  private void shiftWorldBackground(int dx, int dy) {
    GreenfootImage bkgd = new GreenfootImage(SWIDTH, SHEIGHT);
    bkgd.drawImage(bimg, xOffset, yOffset);
    setBackground(bkgd);
  }

  private void shiftWorldActors(int dx, int dy) {
```

```
    List<ScrollingActor> saList =
      getObjects(ScrollingActor.class);
    for( ScrollingActor a : saList ) {
      a.setAbsoluteLocation(dx, dy);
    }
  }

  private void prepare() {
    HedgeHog hh1 = new HedgeHog();
    addObject(hh1, 600, 600);
    Lemur l = new Lemur();
    addObject(l, 300, 900);
    HedgeHog hh2 = new HedgeHog();
    addObject(hh2, 900, 300);
    Lake lake = new Lake();
    addObject(lake, 900, 1100);
    Hiker hiker = new Hiker();
    addObject(hiker, 90, 275);
  }
}
```

First, we get WWIDTH and WHEIGHT to be the dimensions of the background image. Previously, we did not need WHEIGHT as it was the same as SHEIGHT. The main difference between this class and the HikingWorld class in HikingWorld, is that we add an extra parameter (dy) to shiftWorld(), shiftWorldBackground(), and shiftWorldActors() that provides the change in the *y* direction. The use of the new dy parameter mirrors the use of the dx parameter. We end up shifting the background image and other actors by both dx and dy.

# The Hiker class

Create a new subclass of Actor, name it Hiker, and associate one of the default people images provided by Greenfoot. Here is the code for this new class:

```
import greenfoot.*;

public class Hiker extends Actor {
  private int speedX = 1;
  private int speedY = 1;
  private static final int SPEED = 2;
  private static final int BOUNDARY = 40;

  public void act() {
    handleKeyPresses();
    boundedMove();
```

```
      checkAtLake();
   }

   private void handleKeyPresses() {
      handleArrowKey("left", -SPEED, 0);
      handleArrowKey("right", SPEED, 0);
      handleArrowKey("up", 0, -SPEED);
      handleArrowKey("down", 0, SPEED);
   }

   private void handleArrowKey(String k, int sX, int sY) {
      if( Greenfoot.isKeyDown(k) ) {
         speedX = sX;
         speedY = sY;
      }
   }

   private void boundedMove() {

      if( speedX+getX() <= BOUNDARY ) {
         setLocation(BOUNDARY, getY());
         ((HikingWorld)getWorld()).shiftWorld(-speedX, 0);
      } else if( speedX+getX() >= getWorld().getWidth()-BOUNDARY ) {
         setLocation(getWorld().getWidth()-BOUNDARY, getY());
         ((HikingWorld)getWorld()).shiftWorld(-speedX, 0);
      } else {
         setLocation(getX()+speedX, getY());
      }

      if( speedY+getY() <= BOUNDARY ) {
         setLocation(getX(), BOUNDARY);
         ((HikingWorld)getWorld()).shiftWorld(0, -speedY);
      } else if( speedY+getY() >= getWorld().getHeight()-BOUNDARY ) {
         setLocation(getX(), getWorld().getHeight()-BOUNDARY);
         ((HikingWorld)getWorld()).shiftWorld(0, -speedY);
      } else {
         setLocation(getX(), getY()+speedY);
      }
      speedX = 0;
      speedY = 0;
   }

   private void checkAtLake() {
   }
}
```

This class has also been augmented to handle moving in the $x$ and $y$ directions. In `handleKeyPresses()`, we added two more calls to `handleArrowKey()` to handle the up and down arrow keys being pressed. In `boundedMove()`, we add checks to make sure the actor does not move off the top or bottom of the screen and that it calls `shiftWorld()` at the appropriate times.

## The ScrollingActor class

Create a new subclass of `Actor` and name it `ScrollingActor`. You do not need to associate an image with it. As before, this class simply provides a wrapper for `setLocation()`. Now, it handles moving the actor in the $y$ direction as well. Here is the code:

```
import greenfoot.*;

public class ScrollingActor extends Actor {
  public void setAbsoluteLocation(int dx, int dy) {
    setLocation(getX()+dx, getY()+dy);
  }
}
```

The `HedgeHog`, `Lemur`, and `Lake` classes are exactly the same as they were in the `HikingWorld` scenario shown previously. Add them to `HikingWorld2D` as well.

## Try it out

With just a few changes, we have created a world worth exploring, and all it took were a few extensions to our already completed `HikingWorld` scenario. Now, it is time to compile and try your scenario out. Handle any typos/errors and then explore the map. You can also download a completed version of the scenario at `http://www.packtpub.com/support`.

# Tile-based worlds

Tile-based worlds are a happy incorporation between fully dynamically created worlds and worlds that use a large image for the background. With large images, you create a very detailed and predictable world, but it is very difficult to change. Dynamically created worlds are easy to generate but are often too random. Tile-based worlds let you easily create detailed, predictable worlds in a way such that they are easy to change or modify.

# Actors as tiles

Artists can create amazing images using small pieces of tile or glass. *Figure 8* shows a simple tile mosaic. By strategically placing small pieces of colored tiles, you can generate many different types of images.

Figure 8: This is a simple mosaic, courtesy of pixabay.com at http://pixabay.com/en/uzbekistan-mosaic-pattern-artfully-196875/

We will use a similar technique to create a world in Greenfoot, but we will use small actors instead of tiles. *Figure 9* demonstrates how we will do this. We will create a set of actors that will serve as our tiles. Then, we will specify how to compose these actors to create images using an array of strings that uses letters to code the type of actor to place. For example, the letter C corresponds to the actor displaying a cloud with a blue background, and the letter F corresponds to the actor displaying a flower on a green background. *Figure 9* shows a 4 x 3 matrix of letters that is used to specify the tile layout that creates the final image. In the matrix, the upper-left corner letter is an S; therefore, the upper-left corner of the image is solid blue.

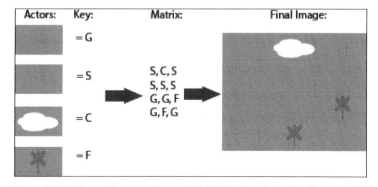

Figure 9: This shows the mapping of individual actors to create a larger world

Hopefully, you now have a sense of how tile-based world creation will work. In the coming snippet, we code the hiking world scenario again, but this time modified to use tile-based world creation. Much of the code is directly borrowed from the 2D-scrolling hiking world we built in the last section.

Create a new scenario and name it HikingWorldTiled. The world and actor classes for this scenario are described in the next section. We only highlight the additions pertinent to tile-based world creation. *Figure 10* shows a screenshot from the completed scenario. I provide this now, so that you can quickly see all the classes we will implement and get a glimpse of part of the image we will be creating.

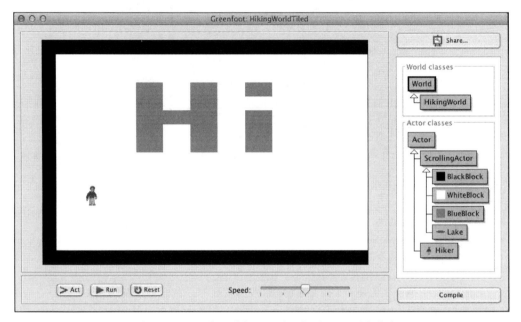

Figure 10: This is a screenshot of the completed HikingWorldTiled scenario

# The HikingWorld class

Create HikingWorld by subclassing World. We are dynamically creating a background image, so you don't want to associate an image with this class; here is the code to accomplish this:

```java
import greenfoot.*;
import java.util.List;

public class HikingWorld extends World {
    private int xOffset = 0;
    private final static int SWIDTH = 600;
    private final static int SHEIGHT = 400;
```

```
private final static int WWIDTH = 1200;
private final static int TWIDTH = 25;
private final static int THEIGHT = 25;

private final static String[] WORLD = {
  "BBBBBBBBBBBBBBBBBBBBBBBBBBBBBBBBBBBBBBBBBBB",
  "BWWWWWWWWWWWWWWWWWWWWWWWWWWWWWWWWWWWWWWWWWWB",
  "BWWWWWWWWWWWWWWWWWWWWWWWWWWWWWWWWWWWWWWWWWWB",
  "BWWWWWWUUWWUUWWUUWWWWWWWWWWWWWWWWWWWWWWWWWWB",
  "BWWWWWWUUWWUUWWWWWWWWWWWWWWWWWWWWWWWWWWWWWWB",
  "BWWWWWWUUUUUUWWUUWWWWWWWWWWWWWWWWWWWWWWWWWWB",
  "BWWWWWWUUWWUUWWUUWWWWWWWWWWWWWWWWWWWWWWWWWWB",
  "BWWWWWWUUWWUUWWUUWWWWWWWWWWWWWWWWWWWWWWWWWWB",
  "BWWWWWWWWWWWWWWWWWWWWWWWWWWWWWWWWWWWWWWWWWWB",
  "BWWWWWWWWWWWWWWWWWWWWWWWWWWWWWWWWWWWWWWWWWWB",
  "BWWWWWWWWWWWWWWWWWWWWWWWWWWWWWWWWWWWWWWWWWWB",
  "BWWWWWWWWWWWWWWWWWWWWWWWWWWWWWWWWWWWWWWWWWWB",
  "BWWWWWWWWWWWWWWWWWWWWWWWWWWWWWWWWWWWWWWWWWWB",
  "BWWWWWWWWWWWWWWWWWWWWWWWWWWWWWWWWWWWWWWWWWWB",
  "BWWWWWWWWWWWWWWWWWWWWWWWWWWWWWWWWWWWWWWWWWWB",
  "BBBBBBBBBBBBBBBBBBBBBBBBBBBBBBBBBBBBBBBBBBB"
};

public HikingWorld() {
  super(SWIDTH, SHEIGHT, 1, false);
  createWorldFromTiles();
  shiftWorld(0);
  prepare();
}

public void shiftWorld(int dx) {
  if( (xOffset + dx) <= 0 && (xOffset + dx) >= SWIDTH - WWIDTH) {
    xOffset = xOffset+dx;
    shiftWorldActors(dx);
  }
}

private void shiftWorldActors(int dx) {
  List<ScrollingActor> saList =
  getObjects(ScrollingActor.class);
  for( ScrollingActor a : saList ) {
    a.setAbsoluteLocation(dx);
  }
}
```

```
    private void createWorldFromTiles() {
      for( int i=0; i < WORLD.length; i++ ) {
        for( int j=0; j < WWIDTH/TWIDTH; j++ ) {
          addActorAtTileLocation(WORLD[i].charAt(j), j, i);
        }
      }
    }

    private void addActorAtTileLocation(char c, int x, int y) {
      Actor tile = null;
      switch(c) {
        case 'W':
        tile = new WhiteBlock();
        break;
        case 'B':
        tile = new BlackBlock();
        break;
        case 'U':
        tile = new BlueBlock();
        break;
      }
      if( tile != null)  addObject(tile, 12+x*TWIDTH, 12+y*THEIGHT);
    }

    private void prepare() {
      Lake lake = new Lake();
      addObject(lake, WWIDTH-300, 300);
      Hiker hiker = new Hiker();
      addObject(hiker, 90, 275);
    }
}
```

The two new parts of this class are the array of strings, WORLD, declared at the top
of the class, and the createWorldFromTiles() method, which uses the method
addActorAtTileLocation() to assist in building the world from the existing
actors. The WORLD array specifies where we are going to place each actor that makes
up part of the background. We have three actors we will use for our background
image; they are BlackBlock, WhiteBlock, and BlueBlock. These actors use images
that are 25 x 25 pixels. This is a decent size for a tile—any smaller and your WORLD
array will be too large and tedious to manage, and any larger and you will lose the
ability to create detail.

The WORLD array has sixteen strings in it that each contain forty-eight characters, thus the size of the image we are creating is 1200 (48 x 25) x 400 (16 x 25). The letter B corresponds to the BlackBlock actor, the letter W corresponds to the WhiteBlock actor, and the letter U corresponds to the BlueBlock actor. This mapping is captured in the switch statement in the addActorAtTileLocation() method. Knowing the mapping, you can look at the WORLD array and see that the image will have a black border and white background, and will spell the word Hi in blue.

OK, let's go through createWorldFromTilesMethod(). This method iterates through every character of every string in WORLD. For each character, it calls addActorAtTileLocation(), supplying parameters that specify the character that indicates which tile should be placed as well as the location for that tile. In addActorAtTileLocation(), we create a new actor based on the character passed to it and then use the provided x and y values to place the new actor in the world.

# The Hiker class

The code here is identical to the code we looked at earlier for the Hiker class in the dynamically created world. I reproduce it here for convenience and because it is relatively short:

```
import greenfoot.*;

public class Hiker extends Actor {
  private int speedX = 1;
  private static final int SPEED = 2;
  private static final int BOUNDARY = 40;

  public void act() {
    handleKeyPresses();
    boundedMove();
    checkAtLake();
  }

  private void handleKeyPresses() {
    handleArrowKey("left", -SPEED);
    handleArrowKey("right", SPEED);
  }

  private void handleArrowKey(String k, int sX) {
    if( Greenfoot.isKeyDown(k) ) {
```

```
          speedX = sX;
      }
  }

  private void boundedMove() {
    if( speedX+getX() <= BOUNDARY ) {
      setLocation(BOUNDARY, getY());
      ((HikingWorld)getWorld()).shiftWorld(-speedX);
    } else if( speedX+getX() >= getWorld().getWidth()-BOUNDARY ) {
      setLocation(getWorld().getWidth()-BOUNDARY, getY());
      ((HikingWorld)getWorld()).shiftWorld(-speedX);
    } else {
      setLocation(getX()+speedX, getY());
    }
    speedX = 0;
  }

  private void checkAtLake() {
  }
}
```

# The ScrollingActor class

This code is also identical to the code provided for the first scenario we created in this chapter. *It is important to note here, that the actors we are using to create the world could also have additional functionality and not simply be a passive background image.* For example, you could have a *Fire* tile that would burn the hiker if it collided with it. Here's the code we are discussing:

```
import greenfoot.*;

public class ScrollingActor extends Actor {
  public void setAbsoluteLocation(int dx) {
    setLocation(getX()+dx, getY());
  }
}
```

# Tiles

The code for the `BlackBlock`, `BlueBlock`, and `WhiteBlock` actors are nearly identical. The only difference is the name of the class and the associated image. Take a look at the code for `BlackBlock`:

```
import greenfoot.*;

public class BlackBlock extends ScrollingActor {
}
```

It is important that the images for these actors are all the same size, to make them easy to compose into a larger image. In our case, the images are 25 pixel x 25 pixel colored squares.

# The Lake class

The `Lake` class is the same as in the first scenario. It is important to note that not all subclasses of `ScrollingActor` have to serve as tiles for the background image. The `Lake` actor represents our final destination This is how the `Lake` class is used:

```
import greenfoot.*;

public class Lake extends ScrollingActor {
}
```

You can just copy it and its associated image from the previous scenario.

# Try it out

Compile the scenario and run it. It should feel similar to the side-scrolling example we provided after the Clouds scenario, except now it is very easy to change the image of the world. Instead of `Hi` being spelled in the background, spell your name. For a challenge, change the `Hiker` class such that if it touches a blue block, the game ends.

## Other game sprites

In our example, the tiles were very simple. The real strength of tile-based world creation comes from having a wide variety of tiles to choose from to create an interesting world. You can either create your own world, download some from sites that charge, such as http://cartoonsmartart.com, or download from 100 percent free sites, such as http://opengameart.org. *Figure 11* shows an example of a free tile set from http://opengameart.org.

Figure 11: This is a free tile sheet from opengameart.org provided by Kenny at http://opengameart.org/content/rpg-pack-base-set

## Summary

By combining the techniques of large-world creation presented in this chapter, with the other concepts and techniques presented in previous chapters, you are fully equipped to create endless forms of information, entertainment, and immersive experiences using Greenfoot. In the next chapter, we will explore making actors in your applications behave intelligently to further enhance user experience.

# 7
# Artificial Intelligence

*"Wisdom begins with Wonder."*

*– Socrates*

We looked at moving, controlling, detecting collisions between, and animating Greenfoot actors up to now in this book. What we will look at in this chapter, is giving our actors a semblance of intelligent behavior. Doing so will allow us to tell better stories and create more engaging user interactions.

Now, the field of **Artificial Intelligence (AI)** is very complex, and creating truly intelligent behavior for our actors is beyond the scope of this book. However, there are some simple techniques we can use to simulate various levels of intelligent behavior using probability and heuristics. We will then look at a popular algorithm (used in many AAA games) that will allow an actor to traverse a path through a set of obstacles. Specifically, you will learn how to apply the following to simulate intelligence:

- Randomness
- Behavior heuristics
- A* (pronounced A-star) pathfinding

Throughout this book, you have been acquiring the skills to create the *wow* factor in your applications, animations, and games. Adding simple AI techniques to your repertoire is going to elevate your ability to create and be creative. The more wisdom you have around Java programming, the more wonder you will be able to provide to your audience.

# The MazeWorld scenario

In the preceding chapter, we learned how to create tile-based worlds. We will augment the Hiking World scenario we created using the tile-based method to create our new scenario entitled `MazeWorld`. In this scenario, our hero will need to navigate around obstacles and avoid three intelligent actors, in order to reach the gold at the end of the maze. *Figure 1* contains a screenshot of the completed scenario.

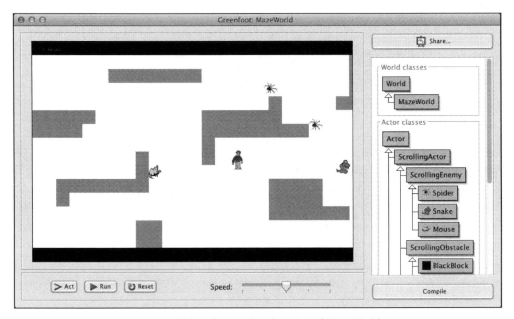

Figure 1: This is the completed version of MazeWorld

There are a few significant differences between the `HikingWorld` scenario from the previous chapter and the new `MazeWorld` scenario we are building in this chapter. The redundant area will be quickly explained, and we will slow down and explain in detail the changes necessary to create our intelligent actors. Please review *Chapter 6, Scrolling and Mapped Worlds*, if needed, for a full description of tile-based world creation.

# The MazeWorld class

Create a new scenario and call it `MazeWorld`. In the new scenario, create a subclass of the `World` class entitled `MazeWorld`. Choose **no image** as the image for this scenario. Here is the implementation of the `MazeWorld` class:

```
import greenfoot.*;
import java.util.List;
import java.util.Stack;
```

```
public class MazeWorld extends World {
  private int xOffset = 0;
  private Hiker hiker;
  private final static int SWIDTH = 600;
  private final static int SHEIGHT = 400;
  private final static int WWIDTH = 1200;
  private final static int TWIDTH = 25;
  private final static int THEIGHT = TWIDTH;
  private final static int TILEOFFSET = TWIDTH/2;
  private final static String validSpaces = "WG";

  private final static String[] WORLD = {
    "BBBBBBBBBBBBBBBBBBBBBBBBBBBBBBBBBBBBBBBBBBBBBBBBBB",
    "BWWWWWWWWWWWWWWWWWWWWWWWWWWWWWWWWWWWWUWWWWWB",
    "BWWWWWWWWWWWWWUUWWWWWWWWWWUUUUUUWWWWWWWWWWWWWWUWWWWB",
    "BWWWWWUUUUUWWWUUWWWWWWWWWWWWWWWWWWWWWWWWWWUWWWWB",
    "BWWWWWUUUUUWWWWWWWWWWWWWWWWWWWWWWWUWWWWUUUWWWB",
    "BWWWWWWWWWWWWWWWWUUUUUWWWWWWWWUUUUUWWWWWWWWWWB",
    "BWWWWWWWWWWWWWWWWUUUUUWWWWWWWWWWUUUUUUUUWWWWWWWWB",
    "BWWWWUUUUUUWWWUWWWWWWWWWWWWWWWWWWWWWWWWWWWB",
    "BWWWWWWWUUUWWWWUWWWWWWWWWWWUWWWWWUWWWWWWWWWWWWWWWWB",
    "BWWWWWWWWWWWWWWWWWWWWWUWWWWWWWWWWWWWWWWWWUWWB",
    "BWWWWWWWWWWWWWWWWWWUUUUUUWWWWWWWWWUUUUWWWWUWWB",
    "BWWWWWWWWWWWWWUUWWWWUWWWWWWWWWWUUUUWWWWWUWWB",
    "BWWWWWWWUUUUUUUUUWWWWWWWWWWWWWWUUUUUUWWUUWWB",
    "BWWWWWWWUUUUUUUUUWWWWWWWWWWUUWWWWWWWWWWWWWWUWWB",
    "BWWWWWWWUWWWWWWWWWWWWWWWUWWWWWWWWWWWWWWWWUWGB",
    "BBBBBBBBBBBBBBBBBBBBBBBBBBBBBBBBBBBBBBBBBBBBBBBBBB"
  };

  public MazeWorld() {
    super(SWIDTH, SHEIGHT, 1, false);
    createWorldFromTiles();
    shiftWorld(0);
    prepare();
  }

  public void shiftWorld(int dx) {
    if( (xOffset + dx) <= 0 && (xOffset + dx) >= SWIDTH - WWIDTH) {
      xOffset = xOffset+dx;
      shiftWorldActors(dx);
    }
  }
}
```

```
      private void shiftWorldActors(int dx) {
         List<ScrollingActor> saList =
           getObjects(ScrollingActor.class);
         for( ScrollingActor a : saList ) {
           a.setAbsoluteLocation(dx);
         }
      }

    private void createWorldFromTiles() {
       for( int i=0; i < WORLD.length; i++ ) {
         for( int j=0; j < WORLD[i].length(); j++ ) {
           addActorAtTileLocation(WORLD[i].charAt(j), j, i);
         }
       }
    }

    private void addActorAtTileLocation(char c, int x, int y) {
       Actor tile = null;
       switch(c) {
         case 'W':
           tile = new WhiteBlock();
           break;
         case 'B':
           tile = new BlackBlock();
           break;
         case 'U':
           tile = new BlueBlock();
           break;
         case 'G':
           tile = new GoldBlock();
           break;
       }
       if( tile != null) addObject(tile, TILEOFFSET+x*TWIDTH,
    TILEOFFSET+y*THEIGHT);

    }

   public int getTileWidth() {
      return TWIDTH;
   }

   public int getTileHeight() {
      return THEIGHT;
   }
```

```
    public int getTileOffset() {
      return TILEOFFSET;
    }

    public String[] getStringWorld() {
      return WORLD;
    }

    public int getXHiker() {
      return hiker.getX()-xOffset;
    }

    public int getYHiker() {
      return hiker.getY();
    }

    public String getValidSpaces() {
      return validSpaces;
    }

    private void prepare()
    {
      hiker = new Hiker();
      addObject(hiker, 80, 200);
      addObject(new Mouse(), 60,40);
      addObject(new Spider(), 1000,40);
      addObject(new Spider(), 120,340);
      addObject(new Spider(), 1050,250);
      addObject(new Snake(), 1050,250);
      addObject(new Mouse(), 1000,200);
      addObject(new Snake(), 400,260);
    }
  }
```

We first start by declaring all of the instance variables for this class. We added the TILEOFFSET constant (used to record half of the value of the width of a tile) and String validspaces (used to indicate which tiles our hero can walk on). The WORLD array defines the tile's type and placement in our world. We augmented the WORLD array to create various static obstacles with the letter U and added a goal destination in the lower-right corner via the letter G. The W character designates the walkable background area and B designates an impassable area.

The shiftWorld, shiftWorldActors, and createWorldFromTiles methods and the constructor are the same as they were in HikingWorld. The addActorAtTileLocation method simply had one case added to the switch statement to handle the creation and placement of gold tiles. Getting to the gold tiles is the goal of this scenario.

The following methods were added to provide an easy way to access information contained in our world: getTileWidth, getTileHeight, getTileOffset, getStringWorld, getXHiker, getYHiker, and getValidSpaces. We will see their use in the classes we define in this chapter. The last method provided in the implementation of MazeWorld is prepare(), which is, by default, used to place the initial actors in our world.

# The Hiker class

Our Hiker class is the same as the one we saw in the previous chapter in HikingWorld, except that we have expanded the ability of this class to move up and down as well. Moving in two dimensions was covered in previous chapters, and we will provide a summary explanation of this class. Here is the code:

```
import greenfoot.*;

public class Hiker extends Actor
{
  private static final int SPEED = 2;
  private static final int BOUNDARY = 40;
  private int speedX = SPEED;
  private int speedY = SPEED;

  public void act() {
    handleKeyPresses();
    handleCollisions();
    boundedMove();
  }

  private void handleKeyPresses() {
    handleArrowKey("left", -SPEED, 0);
    handleArrowKey("right", SPEED, 0);
    handleArrowKey("up", 0, -SPEED);
    handleArrowKey("down", 0, SPEED);
  }
```

```
    private void handleArrowKey(String k, int sX, int sY) {
      if( Greenfoot.isKeyDown(k) ) {
        speedX = sX;
        speedY = sY;
      }
    }

    private void handleCollisions() {
      if( isTouching(ScrollingEnemy.class) ) {
        Greenfoot.stop(); // Game Over
      }
    }

    private void boundedMove() {
      setLocation(getX()+speedX, getY()+speedY);
      if( isTouching(ScrollingObstacle.class) ) {
        setLocation(getX()-speedX, getY()-speedY);
      } else if( isTouching(GoldBlock.class) ) {
        Greenfoot.stop(); // Game over...you Win!!
      }else if( getX() > getWorld().getWidth() - BOUNDARY ) {
        ((MazeWorld)getWorld()).shiftWorld(-speedX);
        setLocation(getX()-speedX, getY()-speedY);
      } else if( getX() < BOUNDARY ) {
        ((MazeWorld)getWorld()).shiftWorld(-speedX);
        setLocation(getX()-speedX, getY()-speedY);
      }
      speedX = 0;
      speedY = 0;
    }
}
```

The code for the Hiker class handles the left, right, up, and down arrow key presses and ensures that the actor does not walk through obstacles and calls shiftWorld() appropriately. It also checks for collision with one of the ScrollingEnemy actors and stops the game if there is a collision.

The code for handling up and down movement mirrors the code to handle left and right movement. The handleKeyPresses() and boundedMove() methods have been extended by simply adding the cases for up and down movement.

# Scrolling actor

The ScrollingActor class is the same as it was in the previous chapter, and we reproduce it here for completeness:

```
import greenfoot.*;

public class ScrollingActor extends Actor {
  public void setAbsoluteLocation(int dx) {
    setLocation(getX()+dx, getY());
  }
}
```

There are four classes that subclass ScrollingActor. The first two are the implementations of GoldBlock and WhiteBlock. These two actors are the parts of the background world that are walkable and thus do not need any special handling. Make sure when you create them, that you associate an image of a gold block and an image of a white block, respectively. Here is the code for both:

```
import greenfoot.*;

public class GoldBlock extends ScrollingActor {
}

import greenfoot.*;

public class WhiteBlock extends ScrollingActor {
}
```

The other two subclasses of ScrollingActor are intended to be subclassed (note that they do not have an image associated with them) and help us group actors into one of two categories: obstacles or enemies. We will discuss these two subclasses next.

## The ScrollingObstacle class

This class does not add any additional functionality. It merely serves as a convenient way to group tiles that instances of the Hiker class cannot pass through. This makes it easier to perform collision detection in the Hiker class. Here is the code:

```
import greenfoot.*;

public class ScrollingObstacle extends ScrollingActor {
}
```

We only have two obstacle tiles: `BlackBlock` and `BlueBlock`. When you create these, make sure you associate the appropriate images (as we did in the previous chapter) with each other. Here is the code for both:

```
import greenfoot.*;

public class BlackBlock extends ScrollingObstacle {
}

import greenfoot.*;

public class BlueBlock extends ScrollingObstacle {
}
```

We are now in a position to describe the implementation of the classes that exhibit intelligent behavior.

# Intelligently behaving actors

We are now going to add enemies to our `MazeWorld` scenario that implement different methods of simulating intelligent behavior. The first method we will discuss uses probabilistic movement, the second method uses simple heuristics, and the last method uses the **A\* pathfinding** algorithm to guide actor movement. Before discussing each method, we present the `ScrollingEnemy` class that implements a common structure for intelligently behaving actors.

# The ScrollingEnemy class

The class `ScrollingEnemy` inherits from `ScrollingActor`, so it will be placed properly within a scrolling world. Then, it sets up a pattern of behavior that is conducive to intelligently moving actors. Modeling actual sentient animals, `ScrollingEnemy` provides a three-phase action-taking process in its `act()` method. First, it calls a method that requires the actor to sense its environment, then it calls a method to choose a course of action based on what it has sensed, and then it calls a method to move the actor. Please note that this class is abstract and cannot be instantiated directly.

Here is the code for `ScrollingEnemy`:

```
import greenfoot.*;

abstract public class ScrollingEnemy extends ScrollingActor {
```

```
protected static final int SPEED = 1;
private static final int BOUNDARY = 40;
protected int speedX = SPEED;
protected int speedY = SPEED;

protected void addedToWorld(World w) {
  MazeWorld mw = (MazeWorld) w;
  GreenfootImage img = getImage();
  img.scale(mw.getTileWidth(),mw.getTileHeight());
  setImage(img);
}

public void act() {
  sense();
  reaction();
  boundedMove();
}

protected void sense() {
  // No smarts
}

protected void reaction() {
  // No reaction
}

protected void boundedMove() {
  setLocation(getX()+speedX, getY()+speedY);
  if( isTouching(ScrollingObstacle.class) ) {
    setLocation(getX()-speedX, getY()-speedY);
  }
}
}
```

The sense() and reaction() methods are empty, as they are intended to be overridden by subclasses implementing one of our strategies for intelligent movement. The end result of these methods are that they will change the values of the variables speedX and speedY to affect movement. The last method, boundedMove(), is fully implemented as once the values of speedX and speedY are set, the movement for every subclass of ScrollingEnemy is the same.

# Randomness

Algorithms using pure probability to determine solutions to problems are surprisingly effective and not uncommon in computer science. While they are almost never the best answer, they make for good comparisons against new algorithms developed for things such as memory management or scheduling.

For games, an actor that moves randomly provides a unique challenge for players to avoid or capture. We are going to add an actor to our `MazeWorld` scenario that moves around the world randomly.

# Spider

Let us create a new actor by right-clicking on `ScrollingEnemy`, choosing **New subclass…**, entering **Spider** as the new class name, and then selecting the image `spider.png` in the animals category. Add the following code to this new class:

```
import greenfoot.*;

public class Spider extends ScrollingEnemy {
   private final static int SPEEDVARIATION = 3;
   private final static int SPEEDCHANGECHANCE = 20;

   protected void reaction() {
      speedX = Greenfoot.getRandomNumber(1000) < SPEEDCHANGECHANCE ?
Greenfoot.getRandomNumber(SPEEDVARIATION)-1 : speedX;
      speedY = Greenfoot.getRandomNumber(1000) <    SPEEDCHANGECHANCE ?
Greenfoot.getRandomNumber(SPEEDVARIATION)-1 : speedY;
   }
}
```

One of the first things to notice, is that we do not provide an implementation for the empty `sense()` method defined in `ScrollingEnemy`. Since we are moving randomly, we do not need to do any sensing of the environment. The `reaction()` method randomly sets both the `speedX` and `speedY` variables to `1`, `0`, or `-1`. It only changes the values of those variables 2 percent of the time so that movement is not too sporadic.

You can now test the scenario. First, comment out the additions of the `Mouse` and `Snake` objects in the `prepare()` method in `MazeWorld`, and then compile and run the scenario. Observe the movements of the Spider objects. Can you get around them? Play with the values in the `Spider` class and see how they affect the movement of `Spider` objects.

With a little code, we have constructed an enemy that is hard to avoid.

# Behavior heuristics

In this method, we supply some simple rules for movement that provide pretty good intelligence without complex coding. A good example of an animal in nature that follows simple behavior heuristics, is an ant. Ants follow a few rules of movement that provide a proven method of finding food in the environment and returning to the hive.

Examples of these simple heuristics are:

- If you hit an obstacle, turn left
- Follow the sun
- If you are close to prey, run at it
- Walk in a circular path

Let us create an actor that will attack the hiker if the hiker gets too close; otherwise, it paces back and forth.

# The Snake class

Create a class called Snake in the same way that we created the previous Spider class. Of course, you will need to choose the image for a snake, snake2.png, instead of the spider image.

Here is the code for the Snake class:

```
import greenfoot.*;
import java.util.List;

public class Snake extends ScrollingEnemy {
    private static final int PATHLENGTH = 200;
    private static final int INRANGE = 100;
    private int pathCounter = PATHLENGTH;
    private boolean pathing = false;
    private int rememberSpeedX = 0;
    private List<Hiker> lse;

    public Snake() {
        speedX = rememberSpeedX = SPEED;
        speedY = 0;
    }

    protected void sense() {
        // If near, move towards enemy
```

```
      lse = getObjectsInRange(INRANGE,Hiker.class);
      pathing = lse.isEmpty();
  }

  protected void reaction() {
    if( pathing ) {
      speedX = rememberSpeedX;
      speedY = 0;
      if( --pathCounter == 0 ) {
        pathCounter = PATHLENGTH;
        speedX = rememberSpeedX = -speedX;
      }
    } else {
      speedX = lse.get(0).getX() > getX() ? 1 : -1;
      speedY = lse.get(0).getY() > getY() ? 1 : -1;
    }
  }
}
```

The sense() method for the Snake actor is simple. It looks to see whether the hiker is within range using the getObjectsInRange() collision detection method. If the hiker is within range, then getObjectsInRange() will return a list containing a reference to the Hiker object; otherwise, the list will be empty. Next, we check whether the returned list is empty by calling the isEmpty() method and saving the result in the pathing variable. We will use the value of pathing to determine whether the snake should move back and forth or chase the hiker.

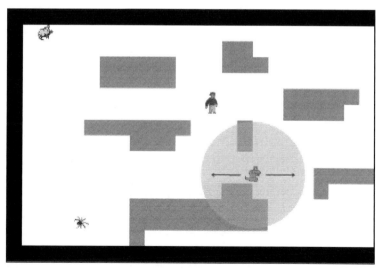

Figure 2: This shows the movement decision made by the Snake actors. The snake moves back and forth, as shown by the arrows, unless the hiker is within the green circle. In that case, the snake will move towards the hiker.

In the `reaction()` method, we have the snake march back and forth if `pathing` is true; otherwise, we have the snake chase the hiker. *Figure 2* shows the two cases. To march back and forth, we use a delay variable, `pathCounter`, to define how long the snake marches in each direction. When the variable expires (has a value of `0`), we have the snake switch directions and reset the delay variable. To chase the hiker, we simply set the `speedX` and `speedY` variables using a simple calculation. If the hiker is to the right of the snake, we set `speedX` to be `1`; otherwise, it is set to `-1`. If the hiker is below the snake, then we set `speedY` to be `1`; otherwise, we set it to `-1`.

Let's test the scenario. Because we have not yet implemented the `Mouse` class, you will need to comment out the addition of `Mouse` objects in the `prepare()` method present in the `MazeWorld` class. Compile and run the scenario. Observe the movements of the `Snake` objects. Try getting close to one. Are the `Spider` objects or `Snake` objects harder to avoid?

# A* pathfinding

The A* pathfinding algorithm finds a path between a start location and an end location that intelligently avoids obstacles. This algorithm is used heavily in the gaming industry. *Ever wonder how enemies in games you have played are able to chase you while avoiding obstacles?* Their movement is programmed using this algorithm. While the algorithm is fairly complex (as we will soon see), understanding it is fairly straightforward. *Figure 3* shows the different areas considered by the A* algorithm when determining a path between the mouse actor and the hiker.

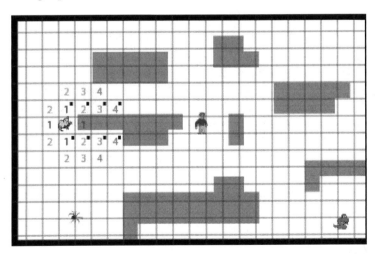

Figure 3: The first round of comparisons is done on the areas containing a red "1", the second round on the areas containing a green "2", the third round on the areas containing a blue "3", and the fourth round on the areas containing a purple "4". The competing paths are shown with a black square in the upper-right corner. After round four, the upper path continues to progress until it reaches the goal destination

# Overview

Before starting the algorithm, you need to divide the world into a grid of uniform-sized areas. Each individual area immediately surrounding an actor defines a potential location the actor could move to. With this in place, we can start. The A* algorithm works by comparing the areas an actor could move to using a heuristic that approximates the remaining distance to the goal location (often referred to as the H value) and combines that with the distance traveled thus far (referred to as the G value). For example, in *Figure 3*, the mouse can initially move to any of the squares marked with a red 1. When an area contains an obstacle, it is not used in the comparison. Therefore, we calculate H + G (referred to as F) for the squares above, below, and to the left of the mouse. The H value is approximated by just counting how far away we are from the goal destination, ignoring any obstacles in the way. The G value is determined by counting the number of squares back to the starting location of the mouse. Knowing that, we can calculate the F value (G+H) for each of the walkable squares around the mouse. For our example, the F value for each square is 10 (H=9, G=1). The algorithm will then pretend that the actor has moved to the most favorable current location (the one with the lowest F value) and then repeat the process. If there is a tie for the best F values, the algorithm will just choose one at random. *Figure 3* depicts this and a few more iterations of the algorithm pictorially. *Our mouse can only move up, down, left, and right – not diagonally.* However, the algorithm works just as well for actors that can move diagonally.

# Algorithm

Given that we now have a base understanding of the algorithm, we can state it a bit more formally. Here are the steps:

1. Add the starting location to the open list.
2. Pick the node in the open list that has the minimum F value. Let's call that *n*.
3. Remove *n* from the open list and add it to the closed list.
4. For every neighbor of *n* not already in the closed list and not containing an obstacle, perform the following steps:
    1. Calculate its F value, set its parent to be *n*.
    2. Add it to the open list if not already in that list.
    3. Update its F value and its parent node if it is in the open list.
5. If you have not reached the destination, go back to step 2.
6. If you have reached the destination node, then construct the path from the start location to the end location by backtracking through the parent links.

In our algorithm, these are the definitions of G, H, and F:

- G: This is the number of locations we need to traverse from the start location to get to this node.
- H: This is approximately how far we are from the destination node. This is calculated by summing the absolute value of the difference in the $x$ location of the current node and the destination node with the absolute value of the difference in the $y$ location of the current node and the destination node. This is known as the *Manhattan distance*.
- F: This is the sum of H and G.

Now, let's look at the implementation of this algorithm in our MazeWorld scenario.

To learn more about A* pathfinding, refer to the following resources:

- http://www.policyalmanac.org/games/aStarTutorial.htm
- http://theory.stanford.edu/~amitp/GameProgramming/
- http://www.raywenderlich.com/4946/introduction-to-a-pathfinding
- http://en.wikipedia.org/wiki/Pathfinding

# The Mouse class

We are going to create a Mouse actor that will use A* pathfinding to track down the hiker. Start by right-clicking on ScrollingEnemy, select **New subclass…**, then enter Mouse as the new class name, and then select the mouse.png image in the **animals** category. Open Greenfoot's editor for this new class and enter the following code:

```
import greenfoot.*;
import java.util.Stack;

public class Mouse extends ScrollingEnemy {
  private TiledWorldPathfinding twp;
  private Stack<Point> apath;
  private int walkDelay = -1;
  private final static int WALKDELAY = 40;
  private int searchDelay = -1;
  private final static int SEARCHDELAY = 130;
  private int prevRow = 0;
  private int prevCol = 0;

  /* initilization */
```

```
protected void addedToWorld(World w) {
  MazeWorld mw = (MazeWorld) w;
  super.addedToWorld(w);
  twp = new TiledWorldPathfinding
  (mw.getStringWorld(),mw.getValidSpaces());
  prevRow = getY()/mw.getTileWidth();
  prevCol = getX()/mw.getTileWidth();
  setLocation(prevCol*mw.getTileWidth()+mw.getTileWidth()/2,
  prevRow*mw.getTileWidth()+mw.getTileWidth()/2);
}

protected void sense() {
  // A* pathfinding determines direction
  if( --searchDelay < 0) {
    MazeWorld w = (MazeWorld) getWorld();
    int hikerCol = w.getXHiker()/w.getTileWidth();
    int hikerRow = w.getYHiker()/w.getTileWidth();
    apath = twp.findShortestFeasiblePath(new
    Point(prevRow,prevCol), new Point(hikerRow,hikerCol));
    if( apath != null && !apath.isEmpty() ) apath.pop();
    searchDelay = SEARCHDELAY;
  }
}

protected void reaction() {
  // Move in direction chosen by A* pathfinding
  if( --walkDelay < 0 ) {
    walkDelay = WALKDELAY;
    if( apath != null && !apath.isEmpty() ) {
      Point p = apath.pop();
      MazeWorld w = (MazeWorld) getWorld();
      speedX = (p.col-prevCol) * w.getTileWidth();
      speedY = (p.row-prevRow) * w.getTileWidth();
      prevCol = p.col;
      prevRow = p.row;
    }
  } else {
    speedX = 0;
    speedY = 0;
  }
}

}
```

In the implementation of the Mouse class, the sense() method runs the A* algorithm to find a path to the hiker, and the reaction() method sets speedX and speedY to move the Mouse object along the found path. As the hiker can move, the Mouse class will need to update its calculated path periodically.

The Mouse class needs to perform a one-time initialization of the A* pathfinding algorithm code in the addedToWorld() method. First, a call to the parent's addedToWorld() method is performed to ensure any initialization needed in that class, for example, scaling the actor's image is not skipped. Next, we create a new instance of the TiledWorldPathfinding class. This is the class that implements A* pathfinding, and we will go over it in detail soon. For now, we can just assume it works flawlessly. To create a new instance of TiledWorldPathfinding, we need to provide the string representation of the world defined in the MazeWorld class and the set of spaces in this representation that are walkable, also defined in MazeWorld. The last thing this method accomplishes is making sure the actor is aligned to be at the center of a grid in the new grid-view of the world needed by the A* algorithm.

The sense() method runs the A* pathfinding algorithm. It is wrapped in a delay variable in order to lower the rate at which we rerun the algorithm, in order to be more efficient as the hiker will not really be able to move very far during the delay. When searchDelay is less than zero, we ask our world for the location of the Hiker object and determine what row and column the hiker is on. We pass our location and the location of the hiker to the findShortestFeasiblePath() method of TiledWorldPathfinding. For convenience, we have chosen to represent locations in the world as points defined by the Point class. We will look at the implementation of Point soon. The findShortestFeasiblePath() method then returns the shortest feasible path from the location of the mouse to the location of the hiker. The path returned contains our current location, so we remove that from the path and then reset the searchDelay value.

In the reaction() method, we just move the Mouse object according to the path determined in the sense() method. First, we check to see whether walkDelay has become less than zero. We need this delay variable so that the mouse moves at a reasonable pace towards the hiker. Inside the if statement, we pop off the next location from the path to the hiker and then set speedX and speedY to values that will properly move the mouse.

The Mouse class actually has a straightforward implementation. The real heavy coding is done in the TiledWorldPathfinding class—the class that implements A* pathfinding.

The `TiledWorldPathfinding` class is not going to be a subclass of `Actor`. It is a non-graphical class that will be used solely to encapsulate the implementation of A* pathfinding. To create this class, click on **Edit** in Greenfoot's main menu bar and then select **New class…**. In the pop-up window, type `TiledWorldPathfinding`. You will see the new class appear below all of the `Actor` classes in Greenfoot's main scenario window. Later in this chapter, you will create the `Point` class and the `Tile` class in the same way.

Here is the code:

```java
import java.util.PriorityQueue;
import java.util.Queue;
import java.util.Stack;

public class TiledWorldPathfinding {
  private String []world;
  private String validSpaces;
  private int worldColumns;
  private int worldRows;
  private Tile[][] tiledWorld;

  public TiledWorldPathfinding(String []w, String vs) {
    world = w;
    worldColumns = w[0].length(); // number of columns
    worldRows = w.length; // number of rows
    tiledWorld = new Tile[worldRows][worldColumns];
    validSpaces = vs;
    resetWorld();
  }

  public void changeWorld( String []w ) {
    world = w;
    resetWorld();
  }

  public Stack<Point> findShortestFeasiblePath(Point start,
    Point end) {
    Queue<Tile> openList = new PriorityQueue<Tile>();
    Queue<Tile> closedList = new PriorityQueue<Tile>();
    Stack<Point> answer = new Stack<Point>();

    // Check for trivial case
    if( start.equals(end) ) {
      answer.push(start);
```

```
      return answer;
    }

    // Check that both start and end are walkable
    if( !tiledWorld[start.row][start.col].isWalkable() ) {
      return null;
    }
    if( !tiledWorld[end.row][end.col].isWalkable() ) {
      return null;
    }

    // Mark location of end point
    tiledWorld[end.row][end.col].setEndNode();

    // Add starting node to open list
    openList.add(tiledWorld[start.row][start.col]);

    // A* algorithm
    runAStar(openList, closedList, end);

    // derive the answer area from the marked up TileWorld
    if( tiledWorld[end.row][end.col].getParent() == null ) {
      resetWorld();
      return null;
    } else {
      deriveWaypoints(answer, end);
    }

    // Prepare for next time
    resetWorld();

    // return result
    return answer;
  }

  /* private methods */
  private void runAStar(Queue<Tile> openList,
  Queue<Tile> closedList, Point end) {
    boolean done = false;
    Tile t;

    while( !openList.isEmpty() && !done ) {
      t = openList.remove();
```

```
      done = done || processNeighbor(t, t.getUp(),
        openList, end);
      done = done || processNeighbor(t, t.getDown(),
        openList, end);
      done = done || processNeighbor(t, t.getLeft(),
        openList, end);
      done = done || processNeighbor(t, t.getRight(),
        openList, end);
      t.setDone();
      closedList.add(t);
    }
  }

  private boolean processNeighbor( Tile parent, Tile node,
    Queue<Tile> openList, Point end) {
    boolean retval = false;

    if( node != null && !node.isDone() && node.isWalkable()) {
      if( node.isEndNode() ) { // Are we done?
        node.setParent(parent);
        retval = true; // FOUND THE END NODE
      } else {
        node.setParent(parent);
        node.setG(1 + parent.getG());
        node.setH(calculateManhattenDistance(
        node.getPoint(), end));
        openList.add(node);
      }
    }
    return retval;
  }

  private int calculateManhattenDistance(Point start,Point end)
  {
    return Math.abs(start.row - end.row) +
      Math.abs(start.col - end.col);
  }

  private void deriveWaypoints(Stack<Point> a, Point end) {
    Tile tp = tiledWorld[end.row][end.col];

    while( tp != null ) {
      a.push(tp.getPoint());
      tp = tp.getParent();
```

```
      }
  }

  private void resetWorld() {
    for( int i = 0; i<worldRows; i++ ) {
      for(int j = 0; j<worldColumns; j++) {
        tiledWorld[i][j] = new Tile();
        tiledWorld[i][j].setPoint(i,j);
      }
    }
    for( int i = 0; i<worldRows; i++ ) {
      for(int j = 0; j<worldColumns; j++) {
        Tile t = tiledWorld[i][j];;
        if( validSpaces.indexOf(world[i].charAt(j)) == -1) {
          t.setNotWalkable();
        } else {
          if( i == 0 ) {
            t.setUp(null);
          } else {
            t.setUp(tiledWorld[i-1][j]);
          }
          if( i == worldRows-1 ) {
            t.setDown(null);
          } else {
            t.setDown(tiledWorld[i+1][j]);
          }
          if( j == 0 ) {
            t.setLeft(null);
          } else {
            t.setLeft(tiledWorld[i][j-1]);
          }
          if( j == worldColumns-1 ) {
            t.setRight(null);
          } else {
            t.setRight(tiledWorld[i][j+1]);
          }
        }
      }
    }
  }
}
```

The main method of this class is findShortestFeasiblePath(). The other methods in the class support this method, so let's first look at it. The method findShortestFeasiblePath() accepts two locations in the form of Point. The Point class is very simple. It simply records the row and column values of a location. The findShortestFeasiblePath() method starts by checking the simple case where the start and end locations are the same using the equals() method defined in the Point class. If so, we can return a path that just contains the starting node, and we are done. Next, we check that both the starting and end locations are walkable; if they are not, then we really can't run the algorithm as it ignores locations that are not walkable, so we return null. We then set the end node as our destination, add the start node to the open list (openList), and then run the A* algorithm. We will now look into the implementation of runAStar().

Because we use good functional decomposition, the implementation of runAStar() is fairly concise. We remove a node from openList, process all of its valid neighbors, set the node to done, and add it to closedList. As we are processing the neighbors, we add new nodes to openList. If we encounter the end node, we set done to true and break out of the loop. This is a straightforward implementation of the A* pathfinding algorithm we discussed previously. To complete our discussion, we need to look at the implementation of processNeighbor().

In processNeighbor(), we check for two things. If the node is not valid (we have already processed it or it is not walkable), we skip it. We then check whether the node is our target destination. If so, we set the node we just came from as the parent and return true. If not, we calculate G, H, and F, set the parent node, and then add this node to openList.

After runAStar() completes, we return to the findShortestFeasiblePath() method. We now have either found a path to the target location or have determined that there is no feasible path. If we have found a valid path, we construct a list of points stored in Stack (see the information box after the following two paragraphs) using deriveWaypoints(), reset the state of this class so that we can be called again, and return the answer to the caller.

The deriveWaypoints() method is small. It derives the path from the tiledWorld matrix by following the parent pointers from the destination back to the start. Along the way, it pushes each node onto a stack. This is why we set parent references in processNeighbor().

The last method we discuss in this class is `resetWorld()`. It has the responsibility of initializing the `tiledWorld` matrix and making sure it accurately represents the current state of the game (where obstacles are and where the destination is). We run the A* pathfinding algorithm on `tiledWorld` and not the actual screen of the game.

**Stacks and priority queues**

In programming, you will use many different types of data structures to store your data. We have already used arrays and lists (The List class was first used in *Chapter 3, Collision Detection*). Sometimes, we want the ordering to occur in a certain way when storing data, as lists and arrays are unordered. In the implementation of A* pathfinding, we use two new data structures: a stack and a priority queue. A stack stores data in the **Last-in First-out (LIFO)** order, while a priority queue stores data in sorted order. To learn more about these two data structures, refer to the following links:

- http://docs.oracle.com/javase/7/docs/api/java/util/PriorityQueue.html
- http://docs.oracle.com/javase/7/docs/api/java/util/Stack.html
- http://www.oopweb.com/Java/Documents/ThinkCSJav/Volume/chap16.htm
- http://www.tutorialspoint.com/java/java_stack_class.htm

We have two classes that we used to support the running of the A* pathfinding algorithm: `Tile` and `Point`. Let's first discuss the `Tile` class. This class is used to represent an area of the screen and is stored in the `tiledWorld` matrix. As we progress through the pathfinding algorithm, we need to track information about each area. For example, we need to store the G, H, and F values for that area; note whether it is the destination node and whether it is walkable and record parent information. The class is set up to store that information and allow easy access to it. The code is as follows:

```java
import java.util.Comparator;

public class Tile implements Comparable<Tile> {
  private int g = 0, h = 0;
  private Tile up, down, left, right, parent;
  private Point location;
  private boolean walkable = true;
  private boolean done = false;
  private boolean isEndNode = false;

  public Tile() {
    parent = up = down = left = right = null;
```

```
        location = new Point(0,0);
    }

    public Tile(Tile u, Tile d, Tile l, Tile r) {
        up = u;
        down = d;
        left = l;
        right = r;
        parent = null;
        location = new Point(0,0);
    }

    /* state methods */
    public boolean isWalkable() {
        return walkable;
    }

    public void setNotWalkable() {
        walkable = false;
    }

    public boolean isDone() {
        return done;
    }

    public void setDone() {
        done = true;
    }

    public boolean isEndNode() {
        return isEndNode;
    }

    public void setEndNode() {
        isEndNode = true;
    }

    /* neighbors */
    public void setParent(Tile t) {
        parent = t;
    }

    public Tile getParent() {
        return parent;
```

```
    }

    public void setUp(Tile t) {
      up = t;
    }

    public Tile getUp() {
      return up;
    }

    public void setDown(Tile t) {
      down = t;
    }

    public Tile getDown() {
      return down;
    }

    public void setRight(Tile t) {
      right = t;
    }

    public Tile getRight() {
      return right;
    }

    public void setLeft(Tile t) {
      left = t;
    }

    public Tile getLeft() {
      return left;
    }

    /* accessor methods */
    public void setPoint(int _row, int _col) {
      location.row = _row;
      location.col = _col;
    }

    public Point getPoint() {
      return location;
    }
```

```java
public void setG(int n) {
   g = n;
}

public int getG() {
   return g;
}

public void setH( int n) {
   h = n;
}

public int getH() {
   return h;
}

public int getF() {
   return g+h;
}

// needed for Comparable interface
public int compareTo(Tile t) {
   return getF()-t.getF();
}

}
```

**Comparable interface**

In *Chapter 3, Collision Detection*, we already discussed Java interfaces in general. The Comparable interface is an interface that requires the implementing class to provide a compareTo() method. This method will then be used in classes such as PriorityQueue to help determine ordering within the queue.

As mentioned earlier, the Point class gives us a convenient way to refer to locations in tiledWorld. It concisely tracks the row and column position and also provides an easy way to compare points (see whether they are equal). Here is the code to accomplish this:

```java
public class Point {
   public int row;
   public int col;

   public Point() {
```

```
        row = col = 0;
    }

    public Point( int _row, int _col) {
        row = _row;
        col = _col;
    }

    public boolean equals(Point p) {
        return (p.row == row) && (p.col == col);
    }
}
```

We have now fully implemented the `Mouse` class. That was quite a bit of coding! But now, we have an actor that can effectively chase our hiker. Compile the scenario and fix any typos you made along the way. We now have a very interesting scenario.

## Play test

We have spent a long time on this scenario. Time to play!

Uncomment all of the actors in the `prepare()` method, compile the scenario, and then try it out. Can you reach the gold square? Which enemy is hardest to avoid?

# Summary

We really covered a lot of ground in this chapter. As we saw, adding intelligent behavior to an actor can range from very simple to very complex. Quite often, using randomness or heuristics, or a combination of both can create some very challenging enemies and will suffice for many of the games/simulations you create. However, there is no substitute for an enemy that knows how to track you down through the A* pathfinding algorithm. I hope you find new and creative ways to bring challenge, intrigue, and surprise into the behavior of your actors.

At this point in the book, we have really covered a lot of topics to help you create an interesting and engaging interactive application. Next, we will look at creating user interfaces to accept more information from our user and to provide them with more feedback.

# 8
# User Interfaces

*"If you can dream it, you can do it."*

*— Walt Disney*

Aside from user controls for games and simulations, you will, at times, want your user to click buttons, view text, and select items from menus. Imagine that you are creating a physics simulation and want to have your user set certain simulation parameters or that you have a store in your game where players can purchase upgrades. Or perhaps you want to create a dialogue between two actors in your scenario. In this chapter, we are going to explore techniques to provide various types of **user interfaces** (UIs). Specifically, we will look at the following topics:

- Buttons and labels
- Menus
- Heads-up display (HUD)

Greenfoot provides little direct support to create user interfaces. There are only a few classes, such as `Label` and `Counter`, packaged with Greenfoot to help in this regard. So, we will have to build our own support. We will use Greenfoot `Actors` and the `GreenfootImage` class to create user interfaces and classes that will support the creation of user interfaces. Luckily, Greenfoot allows us to build just about anything we can dream up, including user interfaces.

## UIWorld

In this section, we will explain how to write the following user interface elements: buttons, textboxes, menus, and **heads-up displays** (HUDs). We are going to work through a Greenfoot scenario (shown in *Figure 1*) that only contains user interface elements, so we can discuss each element independently.

Some of the code we write will be general and able to be applied to many different scenarios. In other cases, we will write user interface code that will only need minor modification to be used across scenarios. In the next section, we will add these elements to the MazeWorld scenario that we wrote in the previous chapter, to make it a more polished and playable game.

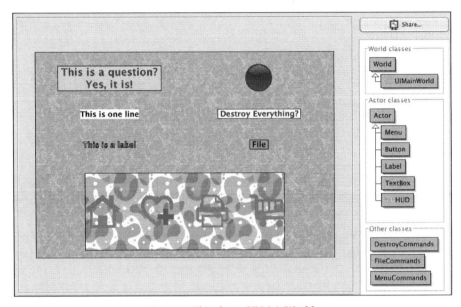

Figure 1: This shows UI MainWorld

To work through this scenario, start with a new Greenfoot scenario named UIMainWorld, create a subclass of World named UIMainWorld, and then associate a plain background to it. The background I chose was bluerock.jpg. Here is the code for UIMainWorld:

```
import greenfoot.*;
import java.awt.Color;

public class UIMainWorld extends World {

  public UIMainWorld() {
    super(600, 400, 1);
    testActors();
  }

  private void testActors() {
    /*    ⊠Begin comment
    TextBox t1 = new TextBox(
    " This is a question?\n Yes, it is! ",
    24, true, Color.BLUE, Color.YELLOW);
```

```
        addObject(t1, 150, 50);
        TextBox t2 = new TextBox("This is one line",
        18, false, Color.BLACK, Color.WHITE);
        addObject(t2, 150, 120);
        Button b1 = new Button("button-blue.png",
        "button-green.png");
        addObject(b1, 450, 50);
        Menu m1 = new Menu(" Destroy Everything? ",
        "Are you sure?", 18,
        Color.BLUE, Color.WHITE
        Color.BLACK, Color.WHITE,
        new DestroyCommands());
        addObject(m1, 450, 120);
        Menu m2 = new Menu(" File ",
        "New\nOpen\nSave\nClose\nExit", 18,
        Color.BLACK, Color.lightGray,
        Color.WHITE, Color.BLUE,
        new FileCommands());
        addObject(m2, 450, 180);
        HUD h = new HUD();
        addObject(h, 300, 310);
        Label l = new Label("This is a label", 18);
        addObject(l, 150, 180);
        End Comment ▨ */
    }
}
```

For now, the lines of code in the testActors() method are commented out. Uncomment them as we implement the associated actor, so that you can test and play with each one in turn. If you prefer, you can download the complete UI scenario from http://www.packtpub.com/support.

# The Button class

Is there a more prolific UI element than the humble button? It is hard to imagine any interface that does not contain several of these buttons. Luckily for us, they are very easy to implement in Greenfoot. In your UI scenario, subclass the Actor class and call this new subclass Button. Choose **No Image** for the image of Button. We will dynamically add the images necessary for this actor. Here is the code for the Actor class:

```
import greenfoot.*;

public class Button extends Actor {
  protected String first;
```

```
    protected String second;

    public Button(String f, String s) {
        first = f;
        second = s;
        setImage(f);
    }

    public void act() {
        handleMouseClicks();
    }

    private void handleMouseClicks() {
        if( Greenfoot.mousePressed(this) ) {
            setImage(second);
        } else if( Greenfoot.mouseClicked(this) ) {
            setImage(first);
            clickedAction();
        }
    }

    protected void clickedAction() {
        // Can either fill this in or have subclasses override.
    }
}
```

For a button, you need to have one image for the normal state and one image for the pressed state. The `first` and `second` instance variables store the names of these images. Their values are provided to the class's constructor as input parameters. The constructor sets the initial image to the `first` image.

The `act()` method only contains one method call to handle mouse events for this actor—`handleMouseClicks()`. This method displays the `second` image when the mouse is pressed and then goes back to displaying the `first` image when the click completes. In Greenfoot, the `Greenfoot.mousePressed()` method returns `true` when the left mouse button is held down on the given object. The `Greenfoot.mouseClicked()` method returns `true` when the left mouse button is pressed down and released on the given object. *Figure 2* demonstrates these two mouse events. When we detect that the mouse is pressed, we simply change the image to the `second` image. When the mouse is released, a full click has occurred, and we do two things. First, we set the image back to normal, and then we perform an action by calling the `clickedAction()` method. This method is currently empty and serves as a placeholder where you could put the code for your own custom action. Another option, would be to subclass this class and override the `clickedAction()` method in your new subclass.

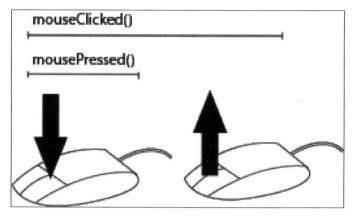

Figure 2: In Greenfoot, a mouse is considered clicked when the left mouse button is both pressed and released

The button was added to the screen in the `UIMainWorld` subclass of `World` with the following two lines of code:

```
Button b1 = new Button("button-blue.png", "button-green.png");
addObject(b1, 450, 50);
```

The `button-blue.png` and `button-green.png` images are the images that come with the default installation of Greenfoot (not available in version 2.2). You can quickly get these images into your project by creating temporary actors that have them as their default image or by copying them from the installation of Greenfoot. Uncomment the two lines shown in the `testActors()` method in `UIMainWorld`, compile your scenario, and test out your new button.

# The TextBox class

The functionality of `TextBox` is very similar in functionality to the `Label` class that is supplied with Greenfoot. Note that in `UIMainWorld`, we added one instance of the `Label` class to our scenario for demonstration and comparison purposes. To add the `Label` class to your UI scenario, click on **Edit** in Greenfoot's main menu and then click on **Import Class...**. Click on **Label** on the left-hand side of the pop-up window that appears, read the documentation on the `Label` class (if you are interested), and then click on the **Import** button. We will implement our own version of `Label` and call it `TextBox`. The `Textbox` class we will write is a bit more concise and provides us with a reason to discuss how to work with text in Greenfoot.

In *Figure 1*, we can see two examples of the `TextBox` class. This class allows us to display text on the screen with a custom font, color, background color, and optional border. Here is the code for `TextBox`:

```
import greenfoot.*;
import java.awt.Color;

public class TextBox extends Actor {
    private GreenfootImage img;
    private boolean border = false;
    private int fontSize;
    private Color foreground;
    private Color background;

    public TextBox(String s, int fs, boolean b,
    Color fg, java.awt.Color bg) {
        super();
        fontSize = fs;
        foreground = fg;
        background = bg;
        img = new GreenfootImage(s, fontSize,
        foreground, background);
        border = b;
        display();
    }

    public void setText(String s) {
        img = new GreenfootImage(s, fontSize,
        foreground, background);
        display();
    }

    private void display() {
        setImage(img);
        if( border ) {
            img.setColor(Color.BLACK);
            img.drawRect(0, 0, img.getWidth()-1,
            img.getHeight()-1);
            setImage(img);
        }
    }
}
```

In `TextBox`, we can configure the foreground color, background color, font size, and whether or not to draw a border around the textbox. In addition to the actual text to display, the constructor accepts and stores these values. The `display()` method is responsible for actually creating our new textbox. First, it creates a new image based on the earlier configuration information using Greenfoot's `GreenfootImage()` method.

When you supply text as the first parameter to `GreenfootImage()`, it will create an image of that text. Then, we can just use `setImage()` to display that text. The `display()` method checks the `border` instance variable and draws a border in the new image we created, if needed. We also supplied a `setText()` method, in case we need to dynamically change the text. This method creates a new `GreenfootImage` based on the new text and then uses the `display()` method to properly set the image of the textbox to the new image created.

To test our new `TextBox` class, uncomment all the lines in `testActors()` in `UIMainWorld` that deal with adding instances of `TextBox`, compile the scenario, and run it.

# The Menu class

Menus are amazing at accepting user commands. I am sure you have had plenty of experience using them and understand their utility. Our implementation of a menu involves using the `TextBox` class we just created and a new Java interface named `MenuCommands` that we will implement soon. The `TextBox` instances display the text, and the actions of the menu choice are performed by classes that implement the `MenuCommands` interface. We will explain that more thoroughly soon.

*Figure 3* provides an overview of the functionality of our `Menu` class. Our menu initially looks like `TextBox`, as shown in *Figure 3(a)*. When the user clicks on the menu, a pop-up menu appears with a set of actions the user can choose from. The pop-up menu is shown in *Figure 3(b)*. Both the menu title and set of commands are configurable.

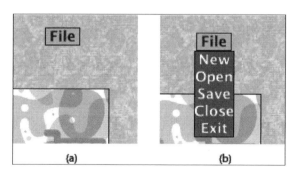

Figure 3: Initially, menu objects look like TextBox (see (a)). When the user clicks on the text, a drop-down menu appears, giving the user multiple items to choose from (see (b))

Here is the code for Menu:

```
import greenfoot.*;
import java.awt.Color;

public class Menu extends Actor
{
  private TextBox titleBar;
  private TextBox menuItems;
  private MenuCommands menuCommands;
  private int fontSize = 24;
  private boolean visible = false;
  private Color mainFG;
  private Color mainBG;
  private Color secondFG;
  private Color secondBG;
  int th, mh;  /* title and menu height */

  public Menu(String tb, String i, int fs,
  Color fg1, Color bg1, Color fg2, Color bg2,
  MenuCommands mc) {
    mainFG = fg1;
    mainBG = bg1;
    secondFG = fg2;
    secondBG = bg2;
    titleBar = new TextBox(tb, fs, true, mainFG, mainBG);
    menuItems = new TextBox(i, fs, true, secondFG, secondBG);
    menuCommands = mc;
    fontSize = fs;
  }

  public Menu() {
    this("not initialized", "none", 24,
    Color.BLACK, Color.lightGray, Color.BLACK,
    Color.WHITE, null);
  }

  protected void addedToWorld(World w) {
    w.addObject(titleBar, getX(), getY());
    th = titleBar.getImage().getHeight();
    mh = menuItems.getImage().getHeight();
  }

  public void act() {
```

```
        handleMouse();
    }

    private void handleMouse() {
      if( Greenfoot.mouseClicked(titleBar) ) {
        if( !visible ) {
          getWorld().addObject(menuItems,
          getX(), getY()+(th+mh)/2);
        } else {
          getWorld().removeObject(menuItems);
        }
        visible = !visible;
      }

      if( Greenfoot.mouseClicked(menuItems)) {
        MouseInfo mi = Greenfoot.getMouseInfo();
        int menuIndex =
        ((mi.getY()-menuItems.getY()+mh/2)-1)/fontSize;
        menuCommands.execute(menuIndex, getWorld());
        visible = !visible;
        getWorld().removeObject(menuItems);
      }
    }
  }
}
```

An instance of Menu is composed of two TextBox instances and one implementation of the MenuCommands interface. The first TextBox instance represents the menu title (shown in *Figure 3(a)*), and the second TextBox instance represents the collection of commands (shown in *Figure3(b)*). The Menu constructor creates both TextBox instances and stores the supplied MenuCommands object for later use.

When Menu is added to World, we use the addedToWorld() method to place the menu title bar in the scenario and collect height information needed to properly place the pop-up window later.

The act() method calls one method, handleMouse(), that places the menu item popup when the title text is clicked on. For the menu item popup, the method handleMouse() determines whether it was clicked on and where it was clicked and then calls the appropriate command. The following code determines the click location:

```
((mi.getY()-menuItems.getY()+mh/2)-1)/fontSize
```

This is based on the current font size and the height of the TextBox menu item. *Figure 4* shows the calculation pictorially.

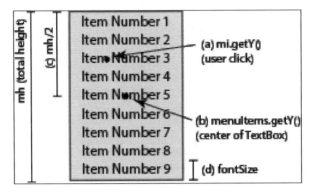

Figure 4: To determine which menu item was clicked on, use this formula: $((a)-(b)+(c))/(d)$. This formula determines the distance between the center of the image (b) and the click location (a), adjusts the value so that it is relative to the top of the figure by adding half the height (c) and then dividing by the font size (d) to get the actual index of the item

Now that we know the index of the menu item clicked on by the user, we need to run the command associated with it. To do this, we simply call the execute() method on the MenuCommands object that was passed to us via the constructor. MenuCommands is a Java interface that guarantees that any Java class that implements this interface will have the execute() method.

We first encountered Java interfaces in *Chapter 3, Collision Detection.* Remember that a class that implements a Java interface is promising to provide an implementation of every method defined in that interface. For more information, review *Chapter 3, Collision Detection.*

Here is the code for MenuCommands:

```
import greenfoot.*;

public interface MenuCommands {
   public void execute(int idx, World w);
}
```

As we can see, this interface only defines one method, execute(), that must accept an integer parameter (representing the index of the menu item) and a reference to the current World instance.

In our UI scenario, we provide two examples of using the `Menu` class. The first is the one that has the menu title bar text, **Destroy Everything?**. The menu that pops up only has one option, **Are you sure?**. Here is the code for the `DestroyCommands` class, which implements the `MenuCommands` interface:

```
import greenfoot.*;

public class DestroyCommands implements MenuCommands {
  public void execute(int idx, World w) {
    System.out.println("Boooom!!!!");
  }
}
```

Because the pop-up menu only has one choice, we do not need to use the supplied `idx` value. We implement the `execute()` method by simply printing **Boooom!!!!** to the console window.

The second `Menu` class example mimics the types of commands you would see in an application that works with files. This example is shown in *Figure 3*. Here is the code for `FileCommands`, which implements the `MenuCommands` interface:

```
import greenfoot.*;

public class FileCommands implements MenuCommands {
  public void execute(int idx, World w) {
    switch(idx) {
      case 0:
      System.out.println("Running New command");
      break;
      case 1:
      System.out.println("Running Open command");
      break;
      case 2:
      System.out.println("Running Save command");
      break;
      case 3:
      System.out.println("Running Close command");
      break;
      case 4:
      System.out.println("Running Exit command");
      break;
    }
  }
}
```

This code uses the `idx` value to run one of several available options. For simplicity, we simply print messages to the console window to demonstrate that the code is working properly. In your own applications, you would substitute the print messages with actual relevant code.

In *Chapter 3, Collision Detection*, we used interfaces because we needed to conform to the Greenfoot API. In this case, we choose to use interfaces because they provided a clean and simple way to provide many different types of menu actions without having to change the `Menu` class. We have effectively abstracted the need to know about the contents of the custom menus and made our `Menu` class applicable to a wide variety of uses.

Now, uncomment the `Menu` actors in the `testActors()` method in `UIMainWorld` and test out the menus we created previously.

The `Menu` class is fairly complicated as it involves managing two `TextBox` classes and implementing a `MenuCommands` interface. To improve your understanding of it, try creating your own menu and adding it to the UI scenario now.

# Heads-up display

Often, you want to create a completely custom UI that involves various shapes and graphics. In this section, we will learn how to do exactly that. The title of this section is heads-up display (HUD) because games often have custom interfaces (called HUDs) that provide critical information and controls to their players. However, the methodology discussed here applies to any custom UI. For our example, we will create the custom user interface element shown in *Figure 5*. In our HUD, the user will be able to click the home, favorite, print, and cart icons to perform actions of our choosing.

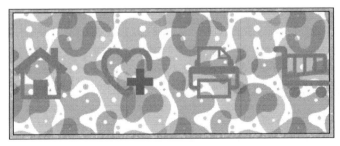

Figure 5: This shows a custom user interface element

The graphic shown in *Figure 5* was created in Adobe Illustrator. Use any graphic editor to create something that looks similar. In the UI scenario, create a new HUD actor and associate the image you created with it. In general, you can create any graphic you want in any editor you want. Our method of creating a custom interface involves us overlaying invisible Greenfoot actors over the custom graphic, and the graphic is not required to be any certain shape or size.

Here is the code for the HUD class in our UI scenario:

```
import greenfoot.*;

public class HUD extends Actor {
  private TransparentRectangle home;
  private TransparentRectangle favorite;
  private TransparentRectangle print;
  private TransparentRectangle cart;
  private static final int W = 70;
  private static final int H = 70;

  protected void addedToWorld(World w) {
    home = new TransparentRectangle(W,H);
    w.addObject(home,
    getX()-getImage().getWidth()/2+W/2,
    getY());
    favorite = new TransparentRectangle(W,H);
    w.addObject(favorite, getX()-W+20, getY());
    print = new TransparentRectangle(W,H);
    w.addObject(print, getX()+W-10, getY());
    cart = new TransparentRectangle(W,H);
    w.addObject(cart,
    getX()+getImage().getWidth()/2-W/2,
    getY());
  }

  private class TransparentRectangle extends Actor {
    public TransparentRectangle(int w, int h) {
      GreenfootImage img = new GreenfootImage(w,h);
      setImage(img);
    }
  }

  public void act() {
    handleMouseClicks();
  }
```

```
private void handleMouseClicks() {
  if( Greenfoot.mouseClicked(home) ) {
    System.out.println("Clicked Home");
  }
  if( Greenfoot.mouseClicked(favorite) ) {
    System.out.println("Clicked Favorite");
  }
  if( Greenfoot.mouseClicked(print) ) {
    System.out.println("Clicked Print");
  }
  if( Greenfoot.mouseClicked(cart) ) {
    System.out.println("Clicked Cart");
  }
}
}
```

As illustrated in the preceding snippet, there is not a lot of code associated with this class. The code creates four new invisible actors and places them over objects we want the user to be able to click on in our custom UI. In the addedToWorld() method, we create home, favorite, print, and cart actors to cover the home, favorite, print, and cart icons shown in *Figure 5*. The part of this method that is specific to the graphic shown in *Figure 5* is the placement of the invisible actors. If you created a different graphic than the one I have shown, then you will need to determine the correct locations to place the new actors yourself.

You have probably noticed that the invisible actors we created were instances of an inner class named TransparentRectangle. This is the first time we have used an inner class in this book, and they warrant some discussion. At the simplest level, an inner class is just a class that was defined inside another class and, thus, not generally accessible to other classes in the project. The following information box contains additional information about inner classes.

**More about inner classes**

In object-oriented design, you solve a problem by breaking it up into smaller objects and then carefully constructing how those objects communicate or cooperate. This is an example of top-down design (discussed in *Chapter 1, Let's Dive Right in...*) where we break a problem up into smaller and smaller subproblems. Sometimes, a class's internal state may be quite complex and using inner classes may help manage that internal complexity. In essence, this is a form of hierarchical object-oriented design.

Another use of inner classes is encapsulating classes that only have a very specific use for only one class in the project. For example, our HUD class is the only class in our scenario that uses the TransparentRectangle class. By hiding TransparentRectangle within HUD, no other class is exposed to TransparentRectangle. You will notice that in Greenfoot, TransparentRectangle does not appear in the **Actor classes...** section of the main scenario window.

For more information on inner classes (and nested classes), refer to the article at: http://www.javaworld.com/article/2077411/core-java/inner-classes.html

The last two methods, act() and handleMouseClicks(), follow a common pattern to handle mouse clicks on actors, which we have seen several times in this book and discuss again here. As with the Menu actors we created in this scenario, we print a message to the console when the user clicks on one of the icons.

Let us test the whole scenario now. Remember to uncomment the HUD actor created and added to the scenario in the testActors() method in UIMainWorld. Compile and ensure that messages are being sent to the console when you click on the various icons.

# Adding a UI to MazeWorld

Now that we have some experience in creating various UI elements, we are going to enhance the MazeWorld scenario from the previous chapter. This will give us the opportunity to practice what we have learned in a more realistic context.

Specifically, we will add:

- A start screen with a button to start the game and a menu the player can use to indicate the difficulty mode of the game
- A game over screen with a button the player can use to restart the game
- A HUD the player can use to temporarily stun the enemies, slow them, or make the snake enemies say, "sssssssss"

Start with the code for MazeWorld you ended with in the previous chapter, or download it from `http://www.packtpub.com/support`.

# Adding menus and buttons

In this section, we will add an introduction screen and game over screen to `MazeWorld`. We will add a button, textbox, and menu to the introduction screen (shown in *Figure 6*) and just a button to the game over screen (shown in *Figure 7*).

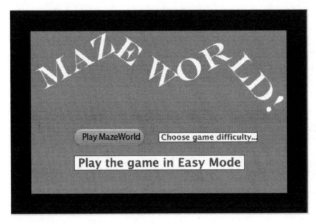

Figure 6: This is the new introduction screen we are adding to MazeWorld

This is how the game over screen will look.

Figure 7: This is the new game over screen we are adding to MazeWorld

We created an introduction screen and game over screen in *Chapter 1, Let's Dive Right in...* and augmented the game over screen in *Chapter 5, Interactive Application Design and Theory* for Avoider Game, so the addition of these screens to MazeWorld will only be quickly covered here.

To start with, we are going to create a new class that both screens will inherit from. Create a new subclass of the `World` class and name it, `MazeWorldScreens`; don't associate an image with this class, and add the following code to it:

```
import greenfoot.*;

public class MazeWorldScreens extends World
{
  int playMode = 0;

  public MazeWorldScreens() {
    super(600, 400, 1);
  }

  public void startGame() {
    MazeWorld mw = new MazeWorld(playMode);
    Greenfoot.setWorld(mw);
  }

}
```

Both the introduction screen and the game over screen will need to store the difficulty level the user selects (in the `playMode` instance variable) and implement a method to start the game, as both have a **Play MazeWorld** button on them. That commonality is captured in the `MazeWorldScreens` class. The `startGame()` method passes the mode of play to a new instance of MazeWorld and then switches the scenario to that world.

Create the `MazeWorldIntro` and `MazeWorldGameOver` classes as subclasses of `MazeWorldScreens`. Make sure to create an image (minus the UI elements) for the introduction screen that looks like *Figure 6* and an image (minus the UI elements) for the game over screen that looks like *Figure 7*, and select them as the images for your new classes. Our images do not need to contain the UI elements as we will be adding them to these screens dynamically.

Once you have created these `World` classes, you should see what is shown in *Figure 8* in the **World classes** area of your main Greenfoot scenario screen.

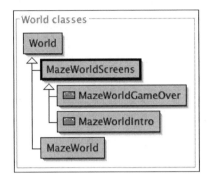

Figure 8: This shows the class hierarchy for World classes in MazeWorld

Here is the code you need to add to the `MazeWorldIntro` class:

```
import greenfoot.*;
import java.awt.Color;

public class MazeWorldIntro extends MazeWorldScreens {
  TextBox mode;

  public MazeWorldIntro() {
    super();
    prepare();
  }

  public void setMode(String s, int i) {
    mode.setText(s);
    playMode = i;
  }

  private void prepare() {
    PlayButton pb = new PlayButton(
    "playButton1.png", "playButton2.png");
    addObject(pb, 200, 250);
    Menu m = new Menu(" Choose game difficulty...",
    "Easy\nMedium\nHard ", 18,
    Color.BLUE, Color.WHITE,
    Color.BLACK, Color.WHITE,
    new GameDifficultyCommands());
    addObject(m, 400, 250);
    mode = new TextBox(" Play the game in Easy Mode ",
```

```
        28, true, Color.BLUE, Color.WHITE);
        addObject(mode, 300, 300);
    }

}
```

The `prepare()` method adds the UI elements to the introduction screen. For clarity, *Figure 9* shows a close-up view of the specific elements added. The play button uses two images I created (one for the pressed state and the other for the normal state of the button). You will need to create your own images or use two of the default ones provided with Greenfoot. An instance of the `Menu` class is placed next to the button. This menu will allow the user to specify whether they want to play in easy, medium, or hard mode (later, we will change the `MazeWorld` class to honor these selections). To complete the functionality of the menu, we need to provide a class that implements the `MenuCommands` interface. In this case, we pass a `GameDifficultyCommands` object. Lastly, we add an instance of `TextBox` to display the current difficulty level of the game. The message changes if the user selects a different difficulty level.

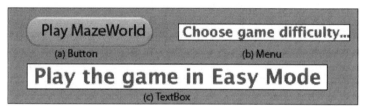

Figure 9: This is a close-up view of the UI elements on the introduction screen in MazeWorld.

As with the UI example scenario, you will need to add the `MenuCommands` interface to your scenario. For convenience, I have replicated the code for the `MenuCommands` interface here:

```
import greenfoot.*;

public interface MenuCommands {
    public void execute(int idx, World w);
}
```

The `GameDifficultyCommands` class implements the `MenuCommands` interface and provides the appropriate commands for the menu choices provided in the popup. Here is the code for `GameDifficultyCommands`:

```
import greenfoot.*;

public class GameDifficultyCommands implements MenuCommands {
```

```
    public void execute(int idx, World w) {
      MazeWorldIntro mwi = (MazeWorldIntro) w;
      switch(idx) {
        case 0:
        mwi.setMode(" Play the game in Easy Mode ", idx);
        break;
        case 1:
        mwi.setMode(" Play the game in Medium Mode ",
        idx);
        break;
        case 2:
        mwi.setMode(" Play the game in Hard Mode ", idx);
        break;
      }
    }
  }
```

For each menu choice, the execute() method in the GameDifficultyCommands class calls the setMode() method that we defined in the MazeWorldIntro class. This method changes the message of TextBox in the introductory screen, as well as stores the difficulty mode for later use.

The MazeWorldGameOver class is simpler, as it only needs to add a play button. Here is the code for the MazeWorldGameOver class:

```
import greenfoot.*;
public class MazeWorldGameOver extends MazeWorldScreens {

  public MazeWorldGameOver(int pm) {
    super();
    prepare();
    playMode = pm;
  }

  private void prepare() {
    PlayButton pb = new PlayButton("playButton1.png",
    "playButton2.png");
    addObject(pb, 420, 330);
  }
}
```

The game over screen needs the difficulty level passed to it in its constructor via the pm parameter variable, so that it can pass it to MazeWorld when the player hits the **Play MazeWorld** button to play again.

Of course, this will not work as we have not added the `Menu`, `TextBox`, and `Button` classes we created in `UIWorldScenario`. These classes will be identical or very similar to the ones we already discussed earlier in the chapter. We will look at the code here now and only discuss the differences.

First, to easily group the UI classes together, let's create an empty class, named `UI`, they all can inherit from. This is a useful organizational technique in Greenfoot where you may have projects with hundreds of actors in them. As we progress through this section and the next section, we will be creating the class hierarchy shown in *Figure 10*.

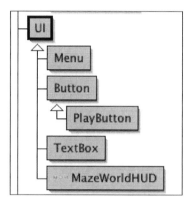

Figure 10: This shows the class structure of the UI elements in MazeWorld

Here is the code for `UI`:

```
import greenfoot.*;

public class UI extends Actor {
}
```

The code for `TextBox`, `Button`, and `Menu` are exactly the same as they were in the UI example scenario we worked on at the beginning of this chapter. Add them now to the `MazeWorld` scenario in exactly the same way you added them to the UI scenario except for one small change. These classes will subclass `UI` instead of `Actor`.

Last, we need to create the `PlayButton` class. This class extends the `Button` class (as shown in *Figure 9*) and contains the following code:

```
import greenfoot.*;

public class PlayButton extends Button {

  public PlayButton(String f, String s) {
    super(f,s);
```

```
    }

    protected void clickedAction() {
      MazeWorldScreens mws = (MazeWorldScreens) getWorld();
      mws.startGame();
    }
  }
```

This class overrides the empty `clickedAction()` method found in the `Button` class. When the user clicks on an instance of `PlayButton`, the `startGame()` method is called. This is the method we implemented in `MazeWorldScreens` earlier.

We just added a ton of code. We went through it fairly quickly as most of the code we added was explained in the first part of this chapter and in earlier chapters. We have a few more things to add to complete this new version of MazeWorld. We need to add a heads-up display and then augment the `MazeWorld` class to allow the game to be played according to the difficulty mode selected by the user.

You should always test your code as often as you can. Sometimes, you will need to make small, simple/temporary changes to your code to be able to test it. For example, if we change the constructor of the `MazeWorld` class to accept an integer parameter, then we can compile and run the code at this point in time.

# Adding a HUD

We are going to add a simple set of actions for the main character in the game. *Figure 11* shows the three controls we are adding. If the user clicks on the first icon, then the enemies will be temporarily stunned. If the user clicks on the second icon, then the enemies will move slower for a short period of time. If the user clicks on the last icon, then the snake enemies say, "sssssssss". Having the snakes hiss does not really help the player beat the game. I just thought it was something fun we could add.

Figure 11: This shows a set of controls we are adding to MazeWorld

*Figure 12* is a close-up view of the controls when placed in the game; we are adding them to the bottom-middle of the screen.

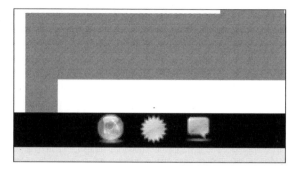

Figure 12: This shows the HUD in the game

Using your favorite graphics editor, create something similar to the picture shown in *Figure 12*. I made my graphic fairly small so that it would be fully contained in the bottom black border of the game.

Once you have an appropriate graphic, create the MazeWorldHUD class as a subclass of UI. Associate the graphic you just made with it and add the following code:

```
import greenfoot.*;

public class MazeWorldHUD extends UI {
  private TransparentRectangle stun;
  private TransparentRectangle slow;
  private TransparentRectangle talk;
  private static final int W = 29;
  private static final int H = 22;

  protected void addedToWorld(World w) {
    stun = new TransparentRectangle(W,H);
    w.addObject(stun, getX()-W, getY());
    slow = new TransparentRectangle(W,H);
    w.addObject(slow, getX(), getY());
    talk = new TransparentRectangle(W,H);
    w.addObject(talk, getX()+W, getY());

  }

  private class TransparentRectangle extends Actor {
    public TransparentRectangle(int w, int h) {
      GreenfootImage img = new GreenfootImage(w,h);
      setImage(img);
```

```
      }
   }

   public void act() {
     handleMouseClicks();
   }

   private void handleMouseClicks() {
     MazeWorld mw = (MazeWorld) getWorld();
     if( Greenfoot.mouseClicked(stun) ) {
       mw.stunAllEnemies();
     }
     if( Greenfoot.mouseClicked(slow) ) {
       mw.slowAllEnemies();
     }
     if( Greenfoot.mouseClicked(talk) ) {
       mw.makeSnakesTalk();
     }
   }
}
```

The code differs from the HUD we added in the UI example scenario, in that we now have three controls instead of four and the `handleMouseClicks()` method performs the appropriate actions for this scenario. In `addedToWorlds()`, we create three `TransparentRectangle` objects and place them over the three icons (stun, slow, and talk) in our image. In `handleMouseClicks()`, we obtain a reference to the current `World` object and call one of the following three methods on it: `stunAllEnemies()`, `slowAllEnemies()`, and `makeSnakesTalk()`.

This concludes adding a HUD to MazeWorld. Next, we need to modify the `MazeWorld` class to change the game, based on the play mode selected by the player and implement the `stunAllEnemies()`, `slowAllEnemies()`, and `makeSnakesTalk()` methods.

# Implementing game difficulty settings and HUD controls

We have a few things to take care of before our new version of MazeWorld is ready. First, we need to incorporate the difficulty level chosen by the player on the introduction screen, and we need to implement the functionality of the HUD we added to the game. These changes involve three classes: `MazeWorld`, `ScrollingEnemy`, and `Snake`.

Here is the code for `MazeWorld` where the changes needed are highlighted:

```java
import greenfoot.*;
import java.util.List;
import java.util.ListIterator;
import java.util.Stack;

public class MazeWorld extends World {
  private int xOffset = 0;
  private Hiker hiker;
  private final static int SWIDTH = 600;
  private final static int SHEIGHT = 400;
  private final static int WWIDTH = 1200;
  private final static int TWIDTH = 25;
  private final static int THEIGHT = TWIDTH;
  private final static int TILEOFFSET = TWIDTH/2;
  private final static String validSpaces = "WG";
  private int playMode = 0;

  private final static String[] WORLD = {
    "BBBBBBBBBBBBBBBBBBBBBBBBBBBBBBBBBBBBBBBBBBBBBBBBBB",
    "BWWWWWWWWWWWWWWWWWWWWWWWWWWWWWWWWWWWWWWWUWWWWB",
    "BWWWWWWWWWWWWWUUWWWWWWWWWUUUUUUUWWWWWWWWWWWUWWWWB",
    "BWWWWWUUUUUWWWUUWWWWWWWWWWWWWWWWWWWWWWWWWUWWWWB",
    "BWWWWWUUUUUWWWWWWWWWWWWWWWWWWWWWWWUWWWWWUUUWWWWB",
    "BWWWWWWWWWWWWWWWWUUUUUWWWWWWWWWUUUUUUWWWWWWWWWWB",
    "BWWWWWWWWWWWWWWWWUUUUWWWWWWWWWWWUUUUUUUUWWWWWWWWWB",
    "BWWWWUUUUUUWWWUWWWWWWWWWWWWWUWWWWWWWWWWWWWWWWWB",
    "BWWWWWWWUUWWWWUWWWWWWWWWWWUWWWWUWWWWWWWWWWWWWWWWB",
    "BWWWWWWWWWWWWWWWWWWWWWWWWUWWWWWWWWWWWWWWWWWWUWWB",
    "BWWWWWWWWWWWWWWWWWWWUUUUUUUWWWWWWWWWUUUUWWWWWUWWB",
    "BWWWWWWWWWWWWWUUWWWWWUWWWWWWWWWWWWWWWUUUUWWWWWUWWB",
    "BWWWWWWWUUUUUUUUUWWWWWWWWWWWWWWWWUUUUUUUWWUWWB",
    "BWWWWWWWUUUUUUUUUWWWWWWWWWUUWWWWWWWWWWWWWWWUWWB",
    "BWWWWWWWUWWWWWWWWWWWWWWWWWUUWWWWWWWWWWWWWWWWUWGB",
    "BBBBBBBBBBBBBBBBBBBBBBBBBBBBBBBBBBBBBBBBBBBBBBBBBB"
  };

  /* constructors */
  public MazeWorld() {
    this(0);
  }

  public MazeWorld(int pm) {
```

```java
    super(SWIDTH, SHEIGHT, 1, false);
    playMode = pm;
    createWorldFromTiles();
    shiftWorld(0);
    prepare();
}

/* ability methods */
public void shiftWorld(int dx) {
  if( (xOffset + dx) <= 0
  && (xOffset + dx) >= SWIDTH - WWIDTH) {
    xOffset = xOffset+dx;
    shiftWorldActors(dx);
  }
}

/* accessor methods */
public int getTileWidth() {
  return TWIDTH;
}

public int getTileHeight() {
  return THEIGHT;
}

public int getTileOffset() {
  return TILEOFFSET;
}

public String[] getStringWorld() {
  return WORLD;
}

public int getXHiker() {
  return hiker.getX()-xOffset;
}

public int getYHiker() {
  return hiker.getY();
}

public String getValidSpaces() {
  return validSpaces;
}
```

```
public void stunAllEnemies() {
  List<ScrollingEnemy> le =
  getObjects(ScrollingEnemy.class);
  ListIterator<ScrollingEnemy> listItr = le.listIterator();
  while( listItr.hasNext() ) {
    ScrollingEnemy se = listItr.next();
    se.stun();
  }
}

public void slowAllEnemies() {
  List<ScrollingEnemy> le =
  getObjects(ScrollingEnemy.class);
  ListIterator<ScrollingEnemy> listItr = le.listIterator();
  while( listItr.hasNext() ) {
    ScrollingEnemy se = listItr.next();
    se.slow();
  }
}

public void makeSnakesTalk() {
  List<Snake> le = getObjects(Snake.class);
  ListIterator<Snake> listItr = le.listIterator();
  while( listItr.hasNext() ) {
    Snake s = listItr.next();
    s.talk();
  }
}

public void gameOver() {
  MazeWorldGameOver mwgo = new MazeWorldGameOver(playMode);
  Greenfoot.setWorld(mwgo);
}

/* private methods */
private void shiftWorldActors(int dx) {
  List<ScrollingActor> saList =
  getObjects(ScrollingActor.class);
  for( ScrollingActor a : saList ) {
    a.setAbsoluteLocation(dx);
  }
}
```

```
private void createWorldFromTiles() {
  for( int i=0; i < WORLD.length; i++ ) {
    for( int j=0; j < WORLD[i].length(); j++ ) {
      addActorAtTileLocation(WORLD[i].charAt(j), j, i);
    }
  }
}

private void addActorAtTileLocation(char c, int x, int y) {
  Actor tile = null;
  switch(c) {
    case 'W':
    tile = new WhiteBlock();
    break;
    case 'B':
    tile = new BlackBlock();
    break;
    case 'U':
    tile = new BlueBlock();
    break;
    case 'G':
    tile = new GoldBlock();
    break;
  }
  if( tile != null) addObject(tile, TILEOFFSET+x*TWIDTH,
  TILEOFFSET+y*THEIGHT);

}

private void prepare()
{
  hiker = new Hiker();
  addObject(hiker, 80, 200);
  addObject(new MazeWorldHUD(), 300, 387);
  addObject(new Mouse(), 60,40);
  addObject(new Spider(), 1000,40);
  addObject(new Spider(), 120,340);
  addObject(new Spider(), 1050,250);
  addObject(new Snake(), 1050,250);
  addObject(new Mouse(), 1000,200);
  addObject(new Snake(), 400,260);
  if( playMode >= 1 ) {
    addObject(new Snake(), 80,40);
    if( playMode == 2 ) {
```

```
            addObject(new Mouse(), 50,350);
        }
    }
  }
}
```

We are going to implement the different difficulty levels by changing the number of enemies you have to avoid in the maze. First, we create the `playMode` instance variable to store the difficulty level. Next, we need to add another constructor that accepts an integer parameter. To do this, we need to change the old constructor that had no parameters to have one and add one line of code that sets the `playMode` instance variable to that parameter—everything else remains the same. We can then add a new constructor that has no parameters and simply calls the other constructor method passing in a value of `0` (which corresponds to the easy mode). Finally, in the `prepare()` method, we add code at the end of the method to check whether to add more actors to the game depending on the value of `playMode`. If `playMode` is `1`, then we add an additional snake. If it is `2`, then we add an additional snake and mouse to the game.

Next, we need to add the `stunAllEnemies()`, `slowAllEnemies()`, and `makeSnakesTalk()` methods to `MazeWorld`. Each method uses the Greenfoot `World` method `getObjects()` to get a list of all the objects of the supplied type. When `ScrollingEnemy.class` is supplied to `getObjects()`, we get a list of all current enemies. When `Snake.class` is passed as a parameter to the `getObjects()` method, we get a list of all the `Snake` objects currently in the scenario. We then loop through the list of objects and call `stun()`, `slow()`, and `talk()`, respectively, on the objects.

Because all of the enemies inherit from `ScrollingEnemy`, we can implement both `stun()` and `slow()` in that class.

Here is the code for `ScrollingEnemy` with the required changes highlighted:

```
import greenfoot.*;

abstract public class ScrollingEnemy extends ScrollingActor {
  protected static final int SPEED = 1;
  private static final int BOUNDARY = 40;
  protected int speedX = SPEED;
  protected int speedY = SPEED;
  private int stunTime = 0;
  private int slowTime = 0;
  private boolean stunned = false;
  private boolean slowed = false;

  /* initialization */
```

```java
protected void addedToWorld(World w) {
  MazeWorld mw = (MazeWorld) w;
  GreenfootImage img = getImage();
  img.scale(mw.getTileWidth(),mw.getTileHeight());
  setImage(img);
}

public void stun() {
  if( stunned == false ) {
    stunned = true;
    stunTime = 100;
  }
}

public void slow() {
  if( slowed == false ) {
    slowed = true;
    slowTime = 400;
  }
}

/* ability methods */
public void act() {
  if( !stunned ) {
    if( slowTime > 0 ) {
      slowed = (slowTime-- % 2) == 0;
    }
    if( !slowed ) {
      sense();
      reaction();
      boundedMove();
    }
  } else {
    if( stunTime-- < 0 ) {
      stunTime = 0;
      stunned = false;
    }
  }
}

protected void sense() {
  // No smarts
}
```

```
    protected void reaction() {
      // No reaction
    }

    protected void boundedMove() {
      setLocation(getX()+speedX, getY()+speedY);
      if( isTouching(ScrollingObstacle.class) ) {
        setLocation(getX()-speedX, getY()-speedY);
      }
    }
  }
```

At the beginning of the Snake class, we add four instance variables. Two of the variables store information about how long the enemies are stunned (stunTime) and slowed (slowTime) and the other two variables track whether or not we are presently in a stunned (stunned) or slowed (slowed) state.

When a ScrollingEnemy object is stunned by the player, the stun() method is invoked on that object (as we saw in our discussion on MazeWorld). The stun() method will do nothing if the object is presently stunned. If not, the method will set stunned to true and set stunTime to 100. These values are used in the act() method to implement stunning the object. The slow() method is nearly identical to the stun() method, except that slowTime is set to 400. This equates to the slowing of an object lasting longer than a stun.

In act(), we check the values of the stunned Boolean variable and skip calling the sense(), reaction(), and boundedMove() methods if stunned is true. The stunTime variable serves as a delay variable (covered in *Chapter 2, Animation*). If we are not stunned, then the act() method proceeds to check the slowed variable. If not slowed, we proceed as normal. The slowTime variable serves as a delay variable; however, as it is counting down, it toggles the values of slowed. This toggling will constrain the sense(), reaction(), and boundedMove() methods to only be invoked on every other call of the act() method. This makes the enemies move at half speed when slowed.

Since snakes are the only ones that need to talk, we put the implementation of the talk() method directly into the Snake class.

Here is the code for Snake with the required changes highlighted:

```
import greenfoot.*;
import java.util.List;
import java.awt.Color;

public class Snake extends ScrollingEnemy {
```

```
private static final int PATHLENGTH = 200;
private static final int INRANGE = 100;
private int pathCounter = PATHLENGTH;
private boolean pathing = false;
private int rememberSpeedX = 0;
private List<Hiker> lse;
private boolean talking = false;
private int talkTime = 0;
private TextBox sss;

/* constructors */
public Snake() {
  speedX = rememberSpeedX = SPEED;
  speedY = 0;
}

public void talk() {
  if( talking == false ) {
    talking = true;
    talkTime = 100;
    sss = new TextBox(" sssssss ", 14, true,
    Color.BLACK, Color.WHITE);
    getWorld().addObject(sss, getX()-20, getY()-20);
  }
}

/* ability methods */
protected void sense() {
  // If near, move towards enemy
  lse = getObjectsInRange(INRANGE,Hiker.class);
  pathing = lse.isEmpty();
}

protected void reaction() {
  if( pathing ) {
    speedX = rememberSpeedX;
    speedY = 0;
    if( --pathCounter == 0 ) {
      pathCounter = PATHLENGTH;
      speedX = rememberSpeedX = -speedX;
    }
  } else {
    speedX = lse.get(0).getX() > getX() ? 1 : -1;
    speedY = lse.get(0).getY() > getY() ? 1 : -1;
```

```
        }

    if( talking ) {
      sss.setLocation(getX()-20, getY()-20);
      if( talkTime-- < 0 ) {
        talking = false;
        talkTime = 0;
        getWorld().removeObject(sss);

      }
    }
  }
}
```

Like the implementation of stun() and slow() in the ScrollingEnemy class, we need a delay variable (talkTime) and Boolean (talking) to implement the talk() method. In addition, we need a variable to store—TextBox (sss)—that will contain the sssssss text. The talk() method is structured in the same way as stun() and slow(). However, talk() must also create TextBox and add it to the world.

We can see in reaction() that if the Snake object is in a talking state then the sss TextBox will be displayed offset from the location of the object for a time specified by the talkTime instance variable. Once talkTime expires, it must also remove the sss TextBox variable from the world.

Congratulations! You have finished our new version of MazeWorld. Compile it and try it out. Click the stun, slow, and talk actions in the game. If you have any issues or errors in your game and are having a tough time solving them, compare your version to the completed version at http://www.packtpub.com/support.

The MazeWorld scenario was constructed solely to help demonstrate the concepts covered in *Chapter 7, Artificial Intelligence*, and the current chapter. Therefore, it is not actually great fun to play, but it does have a lot of potential. Using the game design knowledge you acquired in *Chapter 5, Interactive Application Design and Theory*, try making changes to MazeWorld that will enhance its playability.

# Summary

You are now officially a Greenfoot programming ninja. You know how to create Greenfoot games and simulations that contain lively and intelligent actors with various methods that allow user/player interaction. You can implement keyboard/mouse controls, buttons, menus, and customized interfaces.

In the next chapter, we are going to add a gamepad controller support to our Greenfoot scenarios. Gamepads are a great way to capture user inputs, especially for games.

# 9
# Gamepads in Greenfoot

*"Only you can control your future."*

*– Dr. Seuss*

In this chapter, we will cover how to connect and use gamepad controllers in your Greenfoot scenarios. The set of controls you provide to your user really has an impact on their experience. Imagine playing our version of Avoider Game, which we created in the first two chapters of this book, if you had to hit *U* to move up, *D* to move down, *L* to move left, and *R* to move right. In the same way that a bad layout can frustrate a user, a good layout can feel very natural.

Gamepads are designed to heighten the experience of playing games. They provide a natural and expedient way for players to express their decisions to the game without detracting from game play. Early in gaming history, gamepads took the form of simple joysticks with a single button to fire with. Today, typical controllers have over 10 buttons, analog sticks, analog triggers, and a digital D-pad. Many controllers often allow the user to build custom macros as well.

In this chapter, you will learn how to:

- Connect a gamepad to your Greenfoot scenario
- Listen and respond to various gamepad events using the Greenfoot GamePad API
- Connect unsupported gamepads to OS X using controller-mapping software

Adding gamepad support to your scenarios is a great way to add to the playability of the games you create. It also adds a feel of professionalism to your work. After learning about connecting gamepads, we will augment Avoider Game, which we created in *Chapter 1, Let's Dive Right in…*, and *Chapter 2, Animation*, to allow the user to choose between controlling the game with a mouse or a gamepad.

# Gamepad overview

There are many types of gamepads currently on the market for both PCs and Macs. Some resemble game controllers made for popular console gaming systems, such as Xbox, PlayStation, and Nintendo, while others have their own unique design and capabilities. *Figure 1* shows a typical gamepad. These gamepads are designed to put a lot of control options within easy reach.

*Figure 1* identifies several common groupings of gamepad controls. A D-pad is a control often used to allow players to indicate direction (hence, the **D** in the name). It is fairly flat and designed for thumb use. The analog sticks serve as mini joysticks on the controller and allow fast and accurate positional control. For example, some games may use them to allow the player to look around a 3D world or aim a weapon. In a controller designed for an Xbox (and other popular consoles), the analog sticks can also be pushed down, providing two additional action buttons. The action buttons provide the user a way to specify an action in a game (see *Figure 1*). These buttons often control things such as jumping, shooting, ducking, and blocking. Last, we have auxiliary buttons that may be used to do things such as start a game, pause a game, reset a game, or simply provide more action buttons.

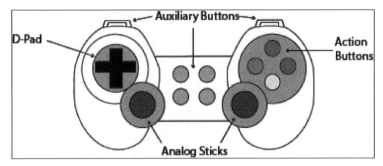

Figure 1: This is a typical layout for a gamepad controller

For many games, a gamepad will provide the best interface (and user experience) for players. In this chapter, we will discuss connecting a controller like the one shown in *Figure 1* to your Greenfoot scenario. You will be able to assign the D-Pad, analog sticks, and action buttons to user-allowed abilities of your choosing.

# Windows setup

There are hundreds of gamepads you can choose from, to purchase for your PC or Mac. In this section, we will cover setting up an *Xbox 360 controller for Windows*. If you have purchased a different controller, make sure to install the associated drivers according to the instructions provided with your gamepad. If you have a Mac and a gamepad officially supported by OS X, then the instructions here should work for you as well. At the end of this chapter, we will look at ways you can still use poorly supported gamepads on your Mac.

# Connecting your controller

Before starting Greenfoot, plug your Xbox 360 controller for Windows into your PC and allow Microsoft Update time to search for, download, and install the required drivers for the gamepad. This should take 5–15 minutes depending on your network connectivity. If you have any problems, try following the instructions given at `http://support.xbox.com/en-US/xbox-on-other-devices/windows/xbox-controller-for-windows-setup`.

# Greenfoot gamepad software

From the Greenfoot website, you can download a template to build Greenfoot scenarios with gamepad support. The template is basically a blank Greenfoot scenario that contains added libraries you can use to access and control gamepads. You can download the gamepad project template at `http://www.greenfoot.org/doc/gamepad`.

When you wish to create a scenario with gamepad support, you need to perform the following steps:

1. Move the `GamePadTemplate.zip` file downloaded from the previous URL, to a directory of your choice.

2. Unzip `GamePadTemplate.zip`.

3. Rename the `GamePadTemplate` folder created in the previous step, to a name you want your new scenario to have.

4. Open the scenario and add your changes.

*Figure 2* shows what your new Greenfoot scenario will look like after completing the preceding steps. As you can see, you will subclass the World and Actor classes as you normally would to add content to your scenario. You are also provided with two additional classes, seen in the **Other classes** section, that you will use to connect to and manage gamepads.

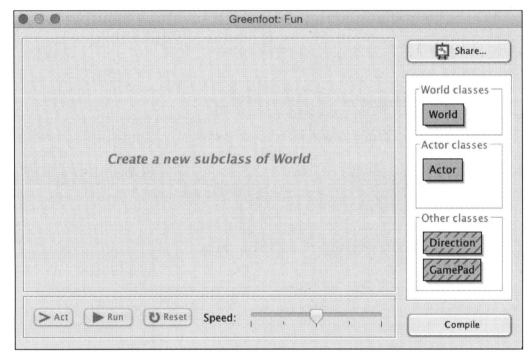

Figure 2: This is a new Greenfoot scenario built from the gamepad template. The scenario pictured was renamed to "Fun"

We will discuss the GamePad and Direction classes in the next section.

# The Greenfoot Gamepad API

The Greenfoot Gamepad API supports all of the controls shown in *Figure 1* except that there are only two auxiliary buttons at the top (colored orange). First, we will discuss the API at a conceptual level and then look at the specific classes that implement the API.

# Overview

In theory, receiving user input from a gamepad is a lot like receiving input from the keyboard. We are going to poll the buttons and analog sticks on the gamepad to see whether they are presently being pressed. The analog sticks are a bit more complicated as they have more states than being pressed or not. For them, you need to know both the direction they are being pushed in and the strength of the push.

With gamepads, you might have multiple gamepads connected to your computer, so the API also provides methods to access all of the gamepads and connect to only the ones you specify.

As we saw in the gamepad template scenario, the Gamepad API is implemented in two classes. The first is the GamePad class and the second is the Direction class.

**The static keyword**

In Java, you have a keyword that you can use to change how variables and methods are accessed and how memory is managed for them. This keyword is known as static. Adding this keyword to the declaration of a class variable or method ensures that this variable or method is stored only once regardless of the number of objects of the class created. So, for example, if you declared a variable named counter and assigned it an initial value of 1, then all objects of the class would see the value of that variable as 1. If one of the objects increments counter, then all objects created would now see the value of this variable as 2.

When used on methods, the methods can be invoked without needing an instance of that class created. For example, many methods contained in the Greenfoot class are static, such as getRandomNumber() and setWorld(). Note that when we call these methods, we do not create an instance of the class. We just add the following code:

```
int randomNumber = Greenfoot.getRandomNumber(10);
```

# The GamePad and Direction classes

The GamePad class is a special type of class known as *singleton*. For a singleton class, the constructor is declared as private; therefore, no code external to the class can create a new instance of the class. All other attempts to create a new object will fail with an error stating that the constructor has private access. It is a singleton class because you want to ensure that only one object represents a gamepad controller.

The methods you will commonly use from this class are `getGamePad()`, `isDown()`, `getAxis()`, and `runConfigurePad()`. The first thing you need to do to use a gamepad in your scenario is call `getGamePad()`. This method will return a `GamePad` object that represents the gamepad controller connected to your computer. Here is an example of its use:

```
GamePad pad = GamePad.getGamePad();
```

Once you have the `GamePad` object for your controller, you can check whether the user is pressing an action button (shown in *Figure 1*) by calling `isDown()`. The `isDown()` method is used exactly like the `isKeyDown()` Greenfoot method we used to detect keyboard input. To detect keyboard input, we supply the name of the key we are interested in. For gamepads, you specify which button you are interested in using the `GamePad.Button` enumeration, which provides the following labels that correspond to gamepad buttons: `ACTION_DOWN`, `ACTION_LEFT`, `ACTION_RIGHT`, `ACTION_UP`, `L1`, `L2`, `L3`, `R1`, `R2`, `R3`, `SELECT`, and `START`. So, to determine whether the user was pressing the blue action button shown in *Figure 1*, you would use the following lines of code:

```
if ( pad.isDown(GamePad.Button.ACTION_UP) ) {
    System.out.println("The ACTION_UP key is being pressed.");
}
```

Getting user input from the analog sticks is a two-step process. First, you get the direction information from the analog stick in the following way:

```
Direction direction = getGamePad().getAxis(GamePad.Axis.LEFT );
```

The `Axis` enumeration provides labels you can use to specify the D-pad, the left analog stick, or the right analog stick. The labels are `DPAD`, `LEFT`, and `RIGHT`, respectively. Secondly, once you have a `Direction` object, you can determine the angle at which the analog stick is being pushed and how far it is being pushed. Here are two lines of code that demonstrate how to extract this information:

```
int angle = direction.getAngle();
float strength = direction.getStrength();
```

The last method you will often use is the `runConfigurePad()` method. This method will present a GUI interface the user can use to specify how the controls on their gamepad should map to the labels provided in the `GamePad.Button` enumeration and the `GamePad.Axis` enumeration. This is needed because not all gamepads have the same layout.

For more information, refer to the official documentation of this class at `http://www.greenfoot.org/files/gamepad/GamePad.html`.

**Singleton classes**

Design patterns are solutions to well-known or common problems. They provide a blueprint that programmers can easily follow. One of the most used design patterns in Java is the singleton pattern. You use this design pattern when you want to ensure that one and only one object of a class is instantiated. Why would this be useful? Well, imagine you wanted to manage and share a resource such as a printer or network connection within your application. It is much simpler and more efficient to only allow the creation of one object that represents that single resource. A class that follows the singleton design pattern enforces this behavior.

# Avoider Game with Gamepad

We went over how to connect a gamepad to your Greenfoot scenario and how to use the Gamepad API. Now, it is time to code. We are going to add gamepad support to our version of Avoider Game, which we finished creating in *Chapter 2, Animation*. You can access a copy of that scenario at http://www.packtpub.com/support.

We have two main changes to make to Avoider Game. First, we need to add a reference to a `GamePad` object associated with our controller and pass that reference between all three worlds in that scenario: `AvoiderGameIntroScreen`, `AvoiderWorld`, and `AvoiderGameOverWorld`. Second, we need to change the `Avatar` class to be controlled by a gamepad, if present. Otherwise, we default to mouse control.

The entire `AvoiderWorld` class is not shown in the following code; only the methods that need changing are shown. Here are the changes for `AvoiderWorld`:

```
private GamePad pad;

public AvoiderWorld(GamePad p) {
  super(600, 400, 1, false);

  bkgMusic = new GreenfootSound("sounds/UFO_T-Balt.mp3");
  // Music Credit: T-Balt at
  // http://www.newgrounds.com/audio/listen/504436
  bkgMusic.playLoop();

  // set gamepad
  pad = p;

  setPaintOrder(Eye.class, Avatar.class,
  Enemy.class, PowerItems.class,
```

```
      Counter.class);
      prepare();
      generateInitialStarField();
  }
```

First, we need an instance variable named pad to hold a reference to our gamepad. Change the constructor function to accept a reference to a GamePad object and then use that value to initialize our pad variable. This value will be passed to us from AvoiderGameIntroScreen. We will also need to pass the value of pad to AvoiderGameOverWorld, so we need to modify the endgame() method as shown in the following code:

```
public void endGame() {
  bkgMusic.stop();
  AvoiderGameOverWorld go = new AvoiderGameOverWorld(pad);
  Greenfoot.setWorld(go);
}
```

The last thing we need to change in AvoiderWorld is pass the pad instance variable to the single Avatar object we create in this game. Thus, we need to change one line of code in the prepare() method, as follows:

```
private void prepare()
{
  Avatar avatar = new Avatar(pad);
  addObject(avatar, 287, 232);
  scoreBoard = new Counter("Score: ");
  addObject(scoreBoard, 70, 20);
}
```

AvoiderGameIntroScreen has the responsibility of detecting and configuring the gamepad. Here are the changes to make that happen:

```
import greenfoot.*;
import java.lang.IllegalArgumentException;

public class AvoiderGameIntroScreen extends World
{
  private GamePad pad;

  public AvoiderGameIntroScreen() {
    super(600, 400, 1);

    try {
      pad = GamePad.getGamePad();
```

```
        pad.runConfigurePad();
    } catch(IllegalArgumentException e) {
        System.out.println( "Exception caught: " + e.getMessage() );
        pad = null;
    }
}

public void act() {
    if( Greenfoot.mouseClicked(this) ) {
        AvoiderWorld world = new AvoiderWorld(pad);
        Greenfoot.setWorld(world);
    }
}
}
```

First, we add an instance variable, pad, to the class and then initialize that variable using the GamePad.getGamePad() method of the Gamepad API. We have to surround the call to GamePad.getGamePad() in a try-catch block because the getGamePad() method will throw an exception if there is no gamepad plugged into the computer. The type of exception thrown is IllegalArgumentException, so that is what we have to catch. You will notice that we added another import statement at the top to define the IllegalArgumentException class. If we do not have a gamepad, then we set pad to null. We also call the runConfigurePad() method in the try block. This will bring up a dialogue box that will prompt the user as to whether they want to redefine the buttons for their controller. Last, we pass pad to AvoiderWorld in the act() method.

**Exceptions**

Java exceptions provide an organized and flexible way to handle runtime errors. They allow you to detangle your code from error detection code, making your code more readable and maintainable. The main keywords associated with exception handling in Java are throw, try, and catch. To learn more about Java exceptions, refer to http://docs.oracle.com/javase/tutorial/essential/exceptions/.

The changes needed to the AvoiderGameOverScreen class are simple. It only needs to pass the reference to the gamepad it got from the prior instance of AvoiderWorld and pass it back to a new instance of AvoiderWorld if the player clicks on the screen to play again. Here are the changes:

```
import greenfoot.*;

public class AvoiderGameOverWorld extends World
{
```

```
    private GamePad pad;

    public AvoiderGameOverWorld(GamePad p) {
      super(600, 400, 1);
      pad = p;
    }

    public void act() {
      if( Greenfoot.mouseClicked(this) ) {
        AvoiderWorld world = new AvoiderWorld(pad);
        Greenfoot.setWorld(world);
      }
    }
  }
```

The class that deals directly with receiving events from the gamepad is the Avatar class. We need to modify this class to use the gamepad to accept user input or default to the mouse if no gamepad is present.

Here are the changes to the Avatar class:

```
import greenfoot.*;

public class Avatar extends Actor {
  private static final float MIN_STRENGTH = 0.5F;
  private int health = 3;
  private int hitDelay = 0;
  private int stunDelay = -1;
  private int lagDelay = -1;
  private int nextImage = 0;
  private Eye leftEye;
  private Eye rightEye;
  private GamePad pad;
  private boolean useGamepad = true;
  private int gpStepX = 3;
  private int gpStepY = 3;
  private int gpLagStepX = 1;
  private int gpLagStepY = 1;

  public Avatar( GamePad p ) {
    pad = p;
    if( pad == null ) {
      useGamepad = false;
    }
  }
```

```
protected void addedToWorld(World w) {
  leftEye = new Eye();
  rightEye = new Eye();
  w.addObject(leftEye, getX()-10, getY()-8);
  w.addObject(rightEye, getX()+10, getY()-8);
}

public void act() {
  userControls();
  checkForCollisions();
}

public void addHealth() {
  if( health < 3 ) {
    health++;
    if( --nextImage == 0 ) {
      setImage("skull.png");
    } else {
      setImage("skull" + nextImage + ".png");
    }
  }
}

public void lagControls() {
  lagDelay = 150;
}

public void stun() {
  stunDelay = 50;
}

private void checkForCollisions() {
  Actor enemy = getOneIntersectingObject(Enemy.class);
  if( hitDelay == 0 && enemy != null ) {
    if( health == 0 ) {
      AvoiderWorld world = (AvoiderWorld) getWorld();
      world.endGame();
    }
    else {
      health--;
      setImage("skull" + ++nextImage + ".png");
      hitDelay = 50;
    }
  }
```

```
    if( hitDelay > 0 ) hitDelay--;
}

private void userControls() {
  if( stunDelay < 0 ) {
    if( lagDelay > 0 ) {
      if( useGamepad ) {
        moveViaGamepad(true);
      } else {
        moveViaMouse(true);
      }
      --lagDelay;
    } else {
      if( useGamepad ) {
        moveViaGamepad(false);
      } else {
        moveViaMouse(false);
      }
    }

    leftEye.setLocation(getX()-10, getY()-8);
    rightEye.setLocation(getX()+10, getY()-8);
  } else {
    stunDelay--;
  }
}

private void moveViaGamepad(boolean lag) {
  int stepX = lag ? gpLagStepX : gpStepX;
  int stepY = lag ? gpLagStepY : gpStepY;

  Direction dir = pad.getAxis( GamePad.Axis.DPAD );
  if ( dir.getStrength() == 0 ) {
    dir = pad.getAxis( GamePad.Axis.LEFT );
  }

  if ( dir.getStrength() > MIN_STRENGTH ) {
    final int angle = dir.getAngle();

    if ( angle > 315 || angle <= 45 ) {
      setLocation(getX()+stepX, getY());
    } else if ( angle > 45 && angle <= 135 ) {
      setLocation(getX(), getY()+stepY);
```

```
      } else if ( angle > 135 && angle <= 225 ) {
        setLocation(getX()-stepX, getY());
      } else {
        setLocation(getX(), getY()-stepY);
      }
    }
  }
}

  private void moveViaMouse(boolean lag) {
    MouseInfo mi = Greenfoot.getMouseInfo();

    if( mi != null ) {
      if( lag ) {
        int stepX = (mi.getX() - getX())/40;
        int stepY = (mi.getY() - getY())/40;
        setLocation(stepX + getX(), stepY + getY());
      } else {
        setLocation(mi.getX(), mi.getY());
      }
    }
  }
}
```

At the beginning of the Avatar class, we define a few additional variables that we will need to allow instances of the class to be controlled by a gamepad. We declare pad to hold a reference to the gamepad and some integers to specify how fast to move the Avatar object. We also declare the Boolean useGamePad variable that we will check later in class methods.

In the constructor, we initialize pad and set useGamePad. You will remember that we set pad to null in AvoiderGameIntroScreen if no gamepad was detected.

We have refactored the userControls() method. Both lag and stun delays work the same, but now we call a method to actually move the object. If useGamePad is true then we call moveViaGamepad(); otherwise, we call moveViaMouse(). The moveViaMouse() method contains the same logic we had previously to move the object. The moveViaGamepad() method is completely new and contains the logic to move the Avatar object by detecting input from the user's gamepad.

In `moveViaGamepad()`, we first set the speed to move. If we are lagging, we will go slower. The implementation of lagging for the gamepad is a little different than the implementation of lagging using the mouse. However, the effect in either case is to slow the user movement. Next, we check to see whether the user is presently pressing the D-pad by checking the strength of the push. If it equals 0, then we assume the user is using the left analog stick. We then detect the angle at which the user is pushing the D-pad (or analog stick) and translate that angle to the direction—up, down, left, or right.

## Try it out

We have added all the code we need to use a gamepad controller with our version of Avoider Game. Compile all the changes you typed in previously, fix any errors you have, and play the game. I really feel that playing the game with a gamepad is more natural and satisfying.

You will notice that we still have a lot of unused buttons on the gamepad. What could you add to the game to take advantage of those?

# OS X setup/workarounds

OS X does not directly support many gamepads. If you have a gamepad that is not directly supported, you can still use that gamepad to control your Greenfoot games.

# Gamepad mapper software

There are several OS X applications available that will map a gamepad controller to keyboard keys and mouse actions. For example, you could map the D-Pad up, down, left, and right actions to the *W*, *S*, *A*, and *D* keys. Typically, these applications have better gamepad support than `JInput`, which is at the heart of gamepad support in Greenfoot and, therefore, will permit a wider variety of controllers to connect to your game. Another advantage is that you can program your scenarios without any thought to gamepad support. You assume standard keyboard and mouse controls, and the gamepad mapping software handles the rest. Here are some popular programs that do this mapping:

- Joystick Mapper: `http://joystickmapper.com`
- Enjoy: `https://yukkurigames.com/enjoyable/`
- ControllerMate for Mac: `http://www.macupdate.com/app/mac/17779/controllermate`

# Exporting games with gamepads

There is one thing you need to keep in mind when you add gamepad support to your Greenfoot scenarios. If you have it, then your game will not be able to be played on the Greenfoot site. This is due to the fact that there is no Java support to connect to a gamepad via a web application. However, you will still be able to export your scenario as a desktop application if you follow the simple steps at `http://www.greenfoot.org/doc/gamepad_export`.

# Summary

The Greenfoot Gamepad API is simple to set up and use and allows you to provide a well-designed control interface to your users. By giving your users the option to use mouse, keyboard, or gamepad controls, you allow them to interact with your Greenfoot creations in a way that is natural and comfortable to them. In previous chapters, you learned how to work with both the keyboard and mouse and, in this chapter, you learned how to use gamepads.

# 10
# What to Dive into Next...

*"The best thing for being sad," replied Merlin, beginning to puff and blow, "is to learn something. That's the only thing that never fails. You may grow old and trembling in your anatomies, you may lie awake at night listening to the disorder of your veins, you may miss your only love, you may see the world about you devastated by evil lunatics, or know your honour trampled in the sewers of baser minds. There is only one thing for it then – to learn. Learn why the world wags and what wags it. That is the only thing which the mind can never exhaust, never alienate, never be tortured by, never fear or distrust, and never dream of regretting. Learning is the only thing for you. Look what a lot of things there are to learn."*

*– T.H. White, The Once and Future King*

Whether you started this book as a novice programmer, experienced programmer, artist, storyteller, or just a highly curious individual, I am sure you have learned a lot along the way. We have covered numerous solutions to common problems encountered in writing and developing interactive programs. Writing interactive programs requires not only technical expertise, but also a clear understanding of how to engage and entertain users. We also covered software design, code organization, debugging, and an accepted process for software development for an object-oriented language. These skills will transfer to future programming projects, even if you end up coding in a different programming language.

In this book, we covered the following topics:

- Animation
- Collision detection
- Projectiles
- Interactive application design and theory
- Scrolling and mapped worlds

- Artificial Intelligence
- User interfaces
- Gamepads

Regardless of your background when you started reading this book, you now have an impressive array of creative skills. *Let's not waste them!* Moving forward, I would like to challenge you to exercise and improve your skills. In this chapter, we will explore courses of action to do just that.

# Build something larger

While we have built programs of some size, we have kept the scope of the work small for pedagogical and practical reasons. However, you have the skills to create large, complex forms of entertainment. Brainstorm a project for yourself that you feel could keep someone engaged, via learning or playing, for over an hour. Spend a considerable amount of time on the design, story, and content of your project. Before coding, create a storyboard that will serve as an outline of your project and as the initial artifact that you can show users (or players) to get some early feedback.

**Storyboards**

Storyboards are an efficient way to explore the design of a movie, play, book, or any form of interactive entertainment. For games, they are especially useful. In simple terms, a storyboard is very similar to creating a comic book of the story you are telling. With storyboards, the individual panes of the comic book are put on separate pieces of paper, making it easy to rearrange their order or insert/delete specific scenes.

Storyboards provide a medium to quickly understand the sequence, content, and flow of a piece of work. As they can be easily pinned on a wall for easy viewing, they also work well in aiding collaborations between writers, programmers, musicians, and artists. Disney was the first company to use them in their process (1930s) to create animated stories.

You need to go back and review *Chapter 5, Interactive Application Design and Theory*, and follow the ideas and processes discussed there to carefully grow your project in a way that will engage users/players. Remember that a project like this requires you to expand the project over time through user/player feedback.

Do you have any artistic skill or know a friend or two good at creating digital art? Enlist their help and really give your project a polished and professional look. Pay attention to all of the details and enhance all aspects of your project to improve the overall experience. Are you a musician or know one? Adding original musical scores and sound effects to your project can really elevate its impact.

# Share your work

Greenfoot provides you with several ways in which you can share your work with others. A music teacher will often arrange recitals for his/her students, giving them true motivation for improvement. In the same way, you should always plan to share your work with a wider audience. Knowing that your work will be on display gives you extra incentive to be thorough and detailed in your work. More importantly, sharing your work provides the opportunity to collect valuable feedback from players, programmers, and game designers. Feedback from this audience is crucial to perfecting your skills.

# Publishing on Greenfoot.org

Greenfoot allows you to easily and immediately share your Greenfoot scenarios online. In the upper-right corner of your scenario window, you will see the **Share…** button. This button will allow you to share your scenario directly on Greenfoot's online gallery. Through the gallery, anyone on the Internet will be able to access, play, download, and make comments on your work. The Greenfoot online community is large and very supportive and can provide you with a wealth of feedback and information. To share your work, perform the following steps:

1. Click on the **Share** button.
2. Click on the **Publish** tab.
3. Fill out the form shown in *Figure 1*.
4. Click on **Submit**.

If everything went well, your project will open up in your web browser. Make sure to check your comments often and be prompt in your replies.

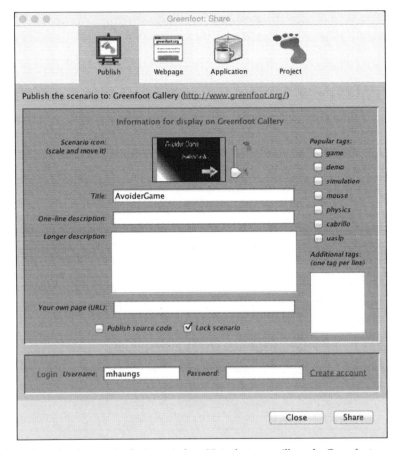

Figure 1: This is Greenfoot's scenario-sharing window. Note that you will need a Greenfoot account to share your work online

# Desktop application

It is even easier to export your Greenfoot scenario as a desktop application. To do this, perform the following steps:

1. Click on the **Share…** button.
2. Click on the **Application** tab.
3. Choose the location where you want your executable created.
4. Click on **Export**.

You can now double-click on the `.jar` file created, and your scenario will run. *Figure 2* shows what your application will look like running in this environment. Note that you don't have the code-editing features of Greenfoot.

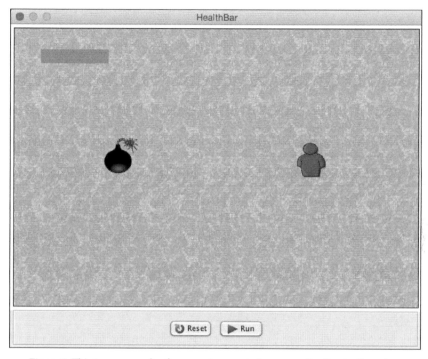

Figure 2: This is an example of a scenario exported as an application in Greenfoot

# Exporting as a web page

Through the same sharing mechanism mentioned earlier, you can export your scenario as a web page. You will only want to use this option if you have your own web space or hosting service that allows you to upload custom web pages.

# Explore other input devices

We spent quite a while in *Chapter 9, Gamepads in Greenfoot,* covering Gamepads and how they can enhance user experience. There are other, very interesting devices you can connect to your Greenfoot scenarios as well. For example, you could connect a Leap Motion or Microsoft Kinect device to provide a very unique and compelling form of user interaction. Also, you can use Greenfoot to control devices such as the Finch robot.

This provides a whole new avenue for you to exercise your creative skills. The following are the resources you can consult to learn more about connecting these devices:

- For **Leap Motion**, refer to `https://developer.leapmotion.com/getting-started`

- For **Microsoft Kinect**, refer to `http://www.greenfoot.org/doc/kinect`

- For **Finch Robot**, refer to `http://www.greenfoot.org/doc/finch`

# Learn more Java

You have learned much about Java. Through the course of this book, you have used variables, methods, classes, objects, inheritance, and polymorphism, but there are some key areas of Java we did not cover, including advanced file I/O, networking, threading, and Swing (a GUI widget toolkit). Java is an industrial-strength language used for everything from programming toasters to providing large, online financial systems. Knowing Java will give you the ability to create games, mobile applications, web applications, and much, much more. To continue your Java education, you should consider reading the following resources:

- **The Java Tutorials**: `http://docs.oracle.com/javase/tutorial/`

- **Coursera**: `https://www.coursera.org`

- **Lynda**: `http://lynda.com`

- **Packt Publishing**: `https://www.packtpub.com`

# Summary

In writing this book, I have tried to imagine your desire to be creative, your troubles, and your successes as you worked your way through this book. I wanted to provide you with a path that challenged you, yet did not overburden you with facts and information tangential to the task at hand. And now, I realize I am going to miss having this discussion with you. I hope you have found some worth in this book and that you are inspired to create. This is the end of our discussion, but just the beginning of your creative journey with Greenfoot.

# Index

## Symbols

**2D scrolling, mapped worlds**
about 182
Hiker class 184-186
HikingWorld2D class 183, 184
ScrollingActor class 186
using 186

## A

**abstract classes**
about 68
URL 68
**achievement badges, Avoider Game**
about 151
Magically Delicious 152
Master Avoider 152
Turkey 152
Unbreakable 152
**actors**
creating, in ZombieInvasionWorld 85, 86
**actors, as tiles**
about 187, 188
Hiker class 191
HikingWorld class 188-191
ScrollingActor class 192
**actors, Cupcake Counter**
bullets 133
launching 125-132
particle effects 132
turrets 133
**A* pathfinding**
about 203, 208
algorithm 209, 210

definitions, in algorithm 210
Mouse class 210-221
overview 209
resources 210
**Artificial Intelligence (AI)**
about 195
intelligently behaving actors 203
MazeWorld scenario 196
**Avatar class**
modifications 74-78
**Avoider Game**
about 81
achievement badges 151-157
gamepad, connecting 263-269
high-score list 148-150
player conditioning 157
playtesting 165
recap 147, 148
revisiting 38
storytelling 158
**AvoiderWorld class**
modifications 78-81

## B

**background music, game**
adding 25
music code, analyzing 26, 27
music code, writing 26
music, stopping 27
**basic game elements**
about 2
game, creating 17
playability, enhancing 28
scenario, creating 2

player conditioning, Avoider Game 157
playtest, Avoider Game
  conducting 165
power-downs 64
power items
  exponential easing 71, 72
  linear easing 68-71
  sinusoidal easing 73
power-ups 64
Press Space To Win (PSTW) 138
project
  brainstorming 274, 275

# R

random actions
  about 58
  blinking 58
removeTouching() method 92
RGBA color model
  URL 45
Rocket class, side-scrolling game 169, 170

# S

scenario, Avoider Game
  about 2
  character, adding 7
  character, creating 6, 7
  enemies, adding 12
  memory management 15, 16
  mouse, using as game controller 7-10
  world, creating for game 3-5
  world, unbounding 14, 15
scoring system
  about 29
  Counter class, adding 29-31
  score, increasing over time 31
ScrollingActor class, actors as tiles
  Lake class 193
  tiles 193
setImage()
  calling, based on Actor location 40-42
  used, for animating enemies 39
  using 39

setLocation()
  star field, creating 43
  using 43
SideScrollingActor class, side-scrolling
    game
  clouds 173, 174
  creating 172, 173
  walls 174
side-scrolling game
  CloudsWorld class, creating 171, 172
  creating 168, 169
  trying 175
  Rocket class, creating 169, 170
  SideScrollingActor class, creating 172, 173
side-scrolling, mapped worlds
  about 176
  creating 176
  Hiker class 179-181
  HikingWorld class 177-179
  trying 182
  ScrollingActor class 181
single-object collisions
  detecting, at offset 97, 98
Singleton design pattern 152
sinusoidal easing 73
Star class 43-46
star field
  blank slate 43
  creating 43
  GreenfootImage class, using 53, 54
  moving field, creating 47
  parallax, using 47-53
  Star class 43-46
storyboards 274
storytelling
  about 141
  fictional worlds 141
  narrative descriptors 142, 143
storytelling, Avoider Game
  about 158
  score, modifying 160-162
  sound effects, adding 162-164
  story screen, adding 158-160
synchronization 54

## Thank you for buying
# Creative Greenfoot

## About Packt Publishing

Packt, pronounced 'packed', published its first book, *Mastering phpMyAdmin for Effective MySQL Management*, in April 2004, and subsequently continued to specialize in publishing highly focused books on specific technologies and solutions.

Our books and publications share the experiences of your fellow IT professionals in adapting and customizing today's systems, applications, and frameworks. Our solution-based books give you the knowledge and power to customize the software and technologies you're using to get the job done. Packt books are more specific and less general than the IT books you have seen in the past. Our unique business model allows us to bring you more focused information, giving you more of what you need to know, and less of what you don't.

Packt is a modern yet unique publishing company that focuses on producing quality, cutting-edge books for communities of developers, administrators, and newbies alike. For more information, please visit our website at www.packtpub.com.

## About Packt Open Source

In 2010, Packt launched two new brands, Packt Open Source and Packt Enterprise, in order to continue its focus on specialization. This book is part of the Packt Open Source brand, home to books published on software built around open source licenses, and offering information to anybody from advanced developers to budding web designers. The Open Source brand also runs Packt's Open Source Royalty Scheme, by which Packt gives a royalty to each open source project about whose software a book is sold.

## Writing for Packt

We welcome all inquiries from people who are interested in authoring. Book proposals should be sent to author@packtpub.com. If your book idea is still at an early stage and you would like to discuss it first before writing a formal book proposal, then please contact us; one of our commissioning editors will get in touch with you.

We're not just looking for published authors; if you have strong technical skills but no writing experience, our experienced editors can help you develop a writing career, or simply get some additional reward for your expertise.

## Scratch 2.0 Game Development HOTSHOT

ISBN: 978-1-84969-756-9          Paperback: 330 pages

10 engaging projects that will teach you how to build exciting games with the easy-to-use Scratch 2.0 environment

1. Discover how to make the most of the new Scratch 2.0 interface.

2. Understand how video games work under the hood.

3. Make your projects come to life, using practical programming principles.

## Scratch 2.0 Beginner's Guide
### Second Edition

ISBN: 978-1-78216-072-4          Paperback: 296 pages

Create digital stories, games, art, and animations through six unique projects

1. Discover how to use the new Scratch Version 2.0 to create games, animations, and digital stories.

2. Six hands-on projects that get you learning by doing with projects for all ages and experience levels.

3. Learn universal computer programming basics with no previous programming knowledge required.

# Learning Libgdx Game Development

ISBN: 978-1-78216-604-7      Paperback: 388 pages

Walk through a complete game development cycle with practical examples and build cross-platform games with Libgdx

1. Create a libGDX multi-platform game from start to finish.

2. Learn about the key features of libGDX that will ease and speed up your development cycles.

3. Write your game code once and run it on a multitude of platforms using libGDX.

# Unity 3D Game Development by Example: LITE Beginner's Guide

ISBN: 978-1-84969-160-4      Paperback: 104 pages

Get up and running as a Unity game developer

1. Fast paced crash course in game design, programming, and Unity.

2. Build your first complete game in Unity.

3. Humorous writing style, serious content.

Please check **www.PacktPub.com** for information on our titles

Made in the USA
San Bernardino, CA
15 September 2017